Recommended

COUNTRY INNS

The Southwest

"Eleanor Morris has captured the flavor and scope of . . . favorite inns. Her brief, accurate descriptions provide all the information a traveler needs in selecting a relaxing spot for a week or a night. . . . [This book] truly establishes Eleanor Morris as one of the top travel writers in this region."
—Frank Lively, former editor, *Texas Highways*

"Unique, highly selective Southwest travel guide."
—*Home & Away*

"This carefully researched and written guide describes . . . unique inns . . . in the three states. . . . Morris vividly notes the inn's specialty, whether architecture, menu, view, history, or atmosphere."
—*Review of Texas Books*

"Home-baked muffins, gourmet meals, flowers in the room, a rocking chair on the front porch so visitors can watch the wildlife or chat with the amiable innkeeper—all these amenities are available when travelers are in-the-know. To locate non-clone travel lodging, this carefully written guide introduces and describes . . . unique inns . . . in vivid and colorful language."
—*Beaumont* (TX) *Enterprise*

"A handy help in planning as well as an inn-side peek at three states' lodging options."
—*Houston Chronicle*

"An absolute necessity for even the most infrequent Southwest traveler."
—*Northside People* (San Antonio, TX)

"Recommended Country Inns" Series

"The guidebooks in this new series of recommended country inns are sure winners. Personal visits have ensured accurate and scene-setting descriptions. These beckon the discriminating traveler to a variety of interesting lodgings."
—Norman Strasma, publisher of *Inn Review* newsletter

The "Recommended Country Inns" series is designed for the discriminating traveler who seeks the best in unique accommodations away from home.

From hundreds of inns personally visited and evaluated by the author, only the finest are described here. The inclusion of an inn is purely a personal decision on the part of the author; no one can pay or be paid to be in a Globe Pequot inn guide.

Organized for easy reference, these guides point you to just the kind of accommodations you are looking for: Comprehensive indexes by category provide listings of inns for romantic getaways, inns for the sports-minded, inns that serve gourmet meals . . . and more. State maps help you pinpoint the location of each inn, and detailed driving directions tell you how to get there.

Use these guidebooks with confidence. Allow each author to share his or her selections with you and then discover for yourself the country inn experience.

Editions available:

Recommended Country Inns
New England • Mid-Atlantic and Chesapeake Region
The South • The Midwest • West Coast
The Southwest • Rocky Mountain Region
also
Recommended Romantic Inns
Recommended Island Inns

Recommended

COUNTRY INNS™
The Southwest

Arizona • New Mexico • Texas

Fourth Edition

by Eleanor S. Morris
illustrated by Bill Taylor, Jr.

A Voyager Book

The Globe Pequot Press

Old Saybrook, Connecticut

Library of Congress Cataloging-in-Publication Data

Morris, Eleanor.
    Recommended country inns. The Southwest : Arizona, New Mexico, Texas / by Eleanor S. Morris; illustrated by Bill Taylor, Jr. —
4th ed.
    p. cm. — ("Recommended country inns" series)
"A Voyager book."
Includes index.
ISBN 1-56440-090-5
    1. Hotels, taverns, etc.—Arizona—Guidebooks. 2. Hotels, taverns, etc.—New Mexico—Guidebooks. 3. Hotels, taverns, etc.--Texas—Guidebooks. I. Title II. Series
TX907.3.A6M67 1992
647.947901—dc20   92-25077
                                                         CIP

Manufactured in the United States of America
Fourth Edition/First Printing

Contents

Indexes

A Few Words about Visiting Southwestern Inns

Webster's Dictionary says that an inn is a hotel, usually a small one. *Thorndike Barnhart* says that an inn is a public house for lodging and caring for travelers. In my travels in the Southwest, I have found that an inn, or at least what we understand down here as a country inn, is much more. It is a place where, away from home, you feel at home, not necessarily because of the physical attributes of a place (although that's important, too), but more likely because of the people you find there, both the innkeepers and the guests.

Many of my innkeepers say, "Our guests are a special breed." I maintain the reason for that is because country innkeepers themselves are a special breed. As in a family, sharing your home with strangers makes for companionship along with sensitivity to another's moods, a concern with well-being, comfort, and need. Almost without exception my innkeepers really like other people, they are *interested* in them, and they want to *interact* with them. (Those that find they do not soon drop out of this fast-growing industry.) And since like attracts like, innkeepers attract as guests people who are open, adventurous, and who are interested in other people, too.

I think this people-interest, this interaction, is why the inn movement is growing so rapidly, at least in my section of the country where just a short time ago such a thing as a country inn was almost impossible to find. Even when people travel on business, they're learning what it means to come "home" at the end of the day to someone's home, to someone who greets them with genuine interest on a personal basis. The world is becoming so hectic, so rushed, that we often feel it's passing us by; we'd better hurry just to catch up. Along the way how nice to stop for a breather, stay with people who are interested in us and whom we can be interested in, too. It's as simple as that.

Inns of the Southwest range from romantic Victorian cottages to sprawling haciendas secluded behind high adobe walls, from grand old-time mansions to rustic country cottages, from small historical hotels with "ghosts" to lively dude ranches, and their number is growing. Although some lodgings may disappoint you, innkeepers seldom will. Their guests become their extended family, many returning again and again. The inn movement in the Southwest is definitely "in."

About This Inn Guide

Without exception, every innkeeper in this book to whom I posed the question "Why are you doing this?" answered, "The people. We love the people."

"The people" is you, the traveler, and here are some pointers that will smooth your path to better and more beautiful inn experiences:

Inns are arranged by states in the following sections: Arizona, New Mexico, and Texas. Because it is so large, Texas is divided into five geographical areas: North Texas, East Texas, Central Texas, Gulf Coast/Border Texas, and West Texas.

At the beginning of each section is a map and an index to the inns in that section, listed alphabetically by town. At the back of the guide is a complete index to all the inns in the book, listed alphabetically by name. Additional indexes list inns by special categories.

Abbreviations:

AP: American Plan. Room with meals.

EP: European Plan. Room without meals.

MAP: Modified American Plan. Room with breakfast and dinner.

EPB: European Plan with Breakfast. Room with full breakfast. Where room rate includes continental breakfast only, this is mentioned in text.

There is no charge of any kind to an inn to be mentioned in this guide. The inclusion is a personal decision on the part of the author, who visited each inn, as well as many others that were not included. Please address any questions or comments to Eleanor S. Morris, The Globe Pequot Press, P.O. Box 833, Old Saybrook, CT 06475.

Rates: I have listed the range from low to high, double occupancy (single where applicable), at the time I visited, realizing that it's up to you to decide how many in your party and what level of accommodation you wish. Rates change without notice, however, sometimes overnight, so I cannot promise that there will be no surprises. Always check beforehand. The rates given do not include taxes.

Reservations/Deposits: These are uniformly required, and if you do not show up and the room is not rented otherwise, you will most likely be charged. Expect to pay a deposit or use a credit card.

Minimum Stay: I have noted this wherever necessary, but most inns in this guide have no such restrictions. Check when you make your reservation, though, because policies change. Often during slow times minimum stay can be negotiable. And special rates are often available for an extended stay.

Personal Checks: All the inns in this book accept personal checks.

Credit Cards: Most inns accept the major credit cards. The few that do not are so noted in the text and listed in an index at the back.

Children: Many inns' descriptions give children's rates or mention special facilities or attractions for children. Inns that expressly welcome children are also listed in an index at the back of the guide. If you're not sure whether a specific inn will be a happy setting for young children, however, always check with the innkeeper(s).

Pets: A number of inns are prepared to deal with pets, with some restrictions, and I have listed them in an index at the back of the guide as well as in the text.

Food: I have noted which inns serve food, whether food is included in the rates as in a bed and breakfast inn, or whether there is restaurant service on the premises. Where there is food service for meals other than breakfast, the "Facilities and activities" item for the inn explains this. Where there is not, most of your innkeepers will have an assortment of menus on hand for your perusal and are happy to make recommendations.

BYOB: It is usually perfectly all right to bring your own bottle, especially to an inn that has no bar or lounge facilities. Often the innkeeper will provide setups (ice and mixes), and many serve wine where licensing laws permit.

Smoking: Many inns, particularly in Texas, have restrictions as to where, when, and if their guests may smoke. This information appears in the text. An index at the back of the guide lists inns that do permit some smoking.

King, Queen, Double, or Twin: If you have a preference, always ask when you make your reservation.

Television and Telephones: I have listed where these are available, although I imagine that, like me, you may want to get away from it all when you go inning. Many inns have both television and phone located in the common rooms.

Air Conditioning/Heating: I have not listed these amenities, because almost without exception they are taken for granted in the Southwest if climate warrants. I have noted if climate does not.

Wheelchair Access: A number of inns have wheelchair accessible rooms. Look for this information in the "Rooms" item for the inn.

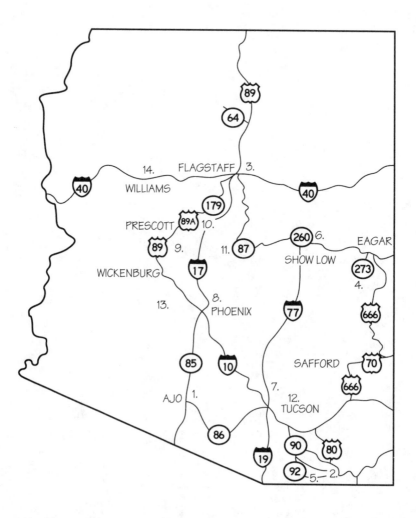

Arizona

The Guest House Inn
Ajo, Arizona
85321

Innkeepers: Norma Walker, Michael and Chris Walker
Address/Telephone: 3 Guest House Road; (602) 387–6133
Rooms: 4; all with private bath. No smoking inn.
Rates: $49 to $59, double, EPB.
Open: All year.
Facilities and activities: Patio with picnic table. Nearby: restaurants and shops in Ajo, museum, open pit copper mine, golf, scenic drives, Organ Pipe Cactus National Monument, Cabeza Prieta Game Refuge, bird watching.

This is an unusual house, with the four guest rooms square in the middle. Each room has French doors opening onto the light, bright glassed-in porch that makes a U-shape around the center rooms. The inn was designed in 1925 as a guest house for visiting officials of the Phelps Dodge Corporation, whose copper mines were the town's main industry. Now the mining is over, and Norma Walker has sort of "inherited" the lovely house.

"I was the housekeeper; I was in charge of this place until the mine closed down in 1985," she says. "The Dodges were so nice, they needed someone and my boys were in school. I was my own boss here, and I wanted the house when the mine closed down. When we found out it was for sale, my boys said, 'Mom, do you still want it?'"

Norma is a born hostess, coming from a home where, she says, hospitality was the rule. She can't get over how guests write letters of thanks for her hospitality. "I don't know why they thank me; they are paying, after all," she says in wonder. I could tell immediately why. Norma is one of nature's nurturing people, warm and giving, and she enjoys it one hundred percent. On ironing bed linens, for instance. "They are supposed to be wrinkle free, but I won't have guests sleep on them. I figure if we are going to have a nice place, we are going to do it right!"

On afternoon tea: "I give people a choice; you never know what people want. Everything is homemade; I always want to have something to offer when people arrive unexpectedly." That's how I arrived, and I was plied with warm-from-the-oven chocolate chip cookies, vegetable soup, and didn't I want some fresh vegetables as well? "If people reserve ahead, I bake them a cake, or grasshopper pie. If they are repeat guests, I bake them a different cake." Norma's repertoire includes chocolate cake, tequila cake, piña colada, "many kinds."

Breakfast on the long table in the bright dining room at the back of the house varies from pecan waffles to *huevos rancheros* with choriza (sausage). Always fresh muffins with homemade jams and, for late risers, perhaps quiche. "Too heavy for early risers," says Norma.

Both sons helped decorate, and guest rooms are large and uncluttered, with lamps on nightstands for bedtime reading and dressers and chairs to put things on. Each room is furnished individually, from Victorian marble-topped antiques to handcrafted Southwestern pieces.

Bird-watchers are in for a real treat here in the Sonoran Desert, where Gambel's quail and the cactus wren are plentiful. And there's always a chance you might spot a wild javelina trotting along—just don't get in the way!

How to get there: From Phoenix, take I–10 west to Highway 85 and 85 south to Ajo. From Tuscon, take Highway 86 west to Highway 85 and 85 north to Ajo. In Ajo turn south at La Mina Avenue (the only traffic light in town) to Guest Hill Road. Turn right, and the inn will be facing you at the end of the road. There is a sign.

The Mine Manager's House Inn
Ajo, Arizona
85321

Innkeepers: Jean and Micheline Fournier
Address/Telephone: One Greenway Drive; (602) 387–6508
Rooms: 5, including 2 suites; all with private bath; wheelchair accessible.
Smoking in Catalina Suite only.
Rates: $65 to $99, double, EPB.
Open: All year.
Facilities and activities: Jacuzzi and covered patio with refrigerator, coin laundry facilities, VCR, gift shop. Nearby: restaurants, and shops in Ajo; pet care, museum, open pit copper mine, golf, scenic drives, Organ Pipe Cactus National Monument, Cabeza Prieta Game Refuge.

Ajo was the birthplace of Arizona's mining industry, and the small town was a railroad and airline stop back then. Now you pretty much have to drive, either from Tucson or Phoenix.

The Mine Manager's House was exactly that, the home of the manager of the New Cornelia Company copper mine in 1919. Eventually part of the Phelps Dodge Corporation, the mine closed in 1985.

The inn is situated on the top of a hill with a view of the southwestern Arizona desert and the huge open pit mine, giving a lesson in how miners dug copper ore from the earth. The inn's enclosed front porch is a small shop full of local crafts. "Indian crafts, and those made by local ladies," Jean explains. The back porch, also enclosed, is the reading room. In between, the New Cornelia Suite, the Greenway Suite, the Early American Suite, and the Nautical Room offer different motifs, with a harmonious mix of antiques and contemporary furniture, old photographs, and comfortable space. The Early American Suite overlooks the town and a lovely jacaranda tree; from the Honeymoon Suite there's a view of the mountains toward Organ Pipe Cactus National Monument. The Nautical Room is accessible for wheelchair, and the Catalina Suite is detached, off the patio, and accessible to smokers.

For breakfast, it's Jean who does the cooking: eggs Benedict or low-cholesterol Belgian waffles served with strawberries and yogurt; orange juice, fruit cup, blueberry muffins.

On major holidays, when Ajo restaurants are closed, guests can reserve a place at the family table. "They become part of the family; they're included," Jean says.

One hundred miles south of Ajo takes you to the Gulf of California, famous for fabulous deep-sea fishing in its brilliant blue waters.

How to get there: From Phoenix, take I–10 west to Highway 85 and 85 south to Ajo. From Tuscon, take Highway 86 west to Highway 85 and 85 north to Ajo. In Ajo, turn south at La Mina Avenue (the only traffic light in town) to Greenway Drive and follow the road up to the top of the hill. There is parking in front of the inn.

The Bisbee Inn
Bisbee, Arizona
85603

Innkeepers: Joy and John Timbers
Address/Telephone: 45 OK Street (mailing address: P.O. Box 1855); (602) 432–5131
Rooms: 18, all with washbasin, share 5 shower rooms and 7 rest rooms. Pets permitted. No smoking inn.
Rates: $29, single; $34 to $39, double; EPB.
Open: All year.
Facilities and activities: TV room, laundry facilities. Nearby: Brewery Gulch, Copper Queen Mine Tour, Lavender Pit Mine Tour, Bisbee Mining Museum.

This historic inn first opened its doors in 1917 as the LaMore Hotel, overlooking Brewery Gulch, then a wild boomtown street. Owners Joy and John Timbers kept the mining hotel's spartan but comfortable Victorian atmosphere when they undertook the certified historic restoration. I like the spare but clean look that solid light oak, lace curtains, and brass bedsteads can give. It's real, all right—the brass-painted beds (innkeepers point out that they're not really brass) and oak furniture are the original hotel pieces, in excellent condition. In the closets I found flowered and plain flannel robes hanging for guest use, a thoughtful touch.

Both lounge and dining rooms are homey. Three rooms form the dining area, the center one a small atrium. Look up, and you'll see a set of stairs and a wrought-iron balcony under the skylight. Lace cloths are on the tables, with places marked by pretty ruffled mats. Furnishings are carefully restored original oak pieces.

Breakfast, made in quantity and of quality, consists of "all you can eat": two kinds of juice, fruit salad, whole wheat bread made by Joy, scrambled or fried eggs, bacon, pancakes, potatoes, waffles, and French toast made with homemade bread.

"We're in there hosting," says John, an enthusiastic innkeeper. "I like the type of person that inns attract—adventuresome people who like to try something and who enjoy it, too."

The entire crew gets into the innkeeping act. When there's a full house, Joy (who teaches) comes up after school. She and John take part, help cook breakfast—everybody works together. It's the kind of place where guests often help serve evening refreshments to other guests.

The social hour can take place wherever you like—in the dining room, in the television room, out on the porch, or even in your room if by chance you want to be alone.

The inn is cooled in summer by evaporative coolers and is centrally heated during the winter. To add to guests' comfort, there are new custom-made quilts on the beds. "A local lady hand-quilts them for us," says Joy.

All the crew will recommend good Bisbee eateries, and the Timbers also own the Plaza, a restaurant in the Warren area of Bisbee. (The town is really three small towns strung out along the copper mountains. Get a map, brochures, and a walking-tour map from the Chamber of Commerce on Commerce Street.) At the Plaza, be sure to try the homemade cream-of-mushroom-and-broccoli soup and the pineapple-pecan cake with almond cream cheese frosting. I promise you won't regret it!

How to get there: From Highway 80 take the business exit into the heart of Old Bisbee and go straight up the hill, which is OK Street. The inn is 200 yards up the steep and narrow street, and there's parking to the right just beyond the inn building.

Copper Queen Hotel
Bisbee, Arizona
85603

Innkeepers: Karen and Mark Carrera and Fran and Howard Schonwit
Address/Telephone: 11 Howell Avenue (mailing address: P.O. Drawer CQ);
  (602) 432–2216
Rooms: 43; all with private bath, phone, and TV; wheelchair accessible.
Rates: $63 to $80, double; $5 extra person; EP.
Open: All year.
Facilities and activities: Restaurant, lounge, outdoor cafe, swimming pool.
  Nearby: Copper Queen Mine Tour, shops, Coronada Trail, hiking, and
  rock hunting.

Copper fortunes built the beautiful old Copper Queen, and
Karen and Mark feel fortunate to be in charge of this historical treasure. "She's an old love, a gracious old lady," everyone says of the
hotel, which was built shortly after the turn of the century.

Antiques furnish many of the rooms, and both dining room
and saloon are restored to their original Western Mining Town
ambience.

"It's a funky old bar, and people have a lot of fun here," Karen
reports. "This bar is like some of the locals' living room—they come
every evening to have a glass of beer or wine." Local musicians
come to play the piano or bring their own instruments on nights
the saloon doesn't offer entertainment.

I loved the huge oil painting in the bar; it shows Lily Langtry and Eros reclining on a chaise longue with a Cavalier on horseback in the background. When Langtry came to Bisbee she sang at the Opera House, causing quite a sensation. When the hotel was built, Bisbee was the largest copper-mining town in the world. You can tour the Copper Queen Mine (no longer in operation) and take wonderful photos of the hills, a blazing rust-orange color from the ore.

The hotel's past also includes Teddy Roosevelt and "Black Jack" Pershing, who was sent to comb the nearby hills for Pancho Villa. (He didn't find him.) Other guests of note include John Wayne and Lee Marvin, and you might run into some more current ones—"Film people frequent the hotel," says Karen.

In the lobby is a gift shop with silver and turquoise jewelry crafted by local silversmiths.

Food is served outside on the veranda as well as in the restaurant. As the innkeepers say, "Our weather here is super." I especially enjoyed the breakfast special "Queen's Favorite," a savory mix of scrambled eggs, sautéed spinach, ground beef, and Parmesan cheese.

Gourmet dinner specials include roast duck a l'orange and prime rib, in addition to other specialty items. Bisbee may be a mining ghost town, but the Copper Queen Hotel is right up to the minute!

How to get there: From I–10 drive into Bisbee taking Howell (not Tombstone Canyon Road), and you'll see the hotel; you can't miss it. Streets are narrow, winding, and one-way, so drive by the hotel and on up to the parking lot at the YWCA at the end of the street.

Birch Tree Inn
Flagstaff, Arizona
86001

Innkeepers: Sandy and Ed Znetko, Donna and Rodger Pettinger
Address/Telephone: 824 Birch Avenue; (602) 774–1042
Rooms: 5; 3 with private bath; no air conditioning (elevation 7,000 feet). No
   smoking inn.
Rates: $55 to $70, single; $60 to $80, double; military and seniors, 10 per-
cent discount; EPB.
Open: All year.
Facilities and activities: Bicycles, tennis rackets (tennis courts nearby), pool
   table, game room, piano. Nearby: restaurants and Downtown Histori-
   cal District, cross-country skiing, Grand Canyon.

How do two women decorate one house? Good friends for
years, Sandy and Donna hit on a perfect plan when they decided to
go into the inn business together. "I have an idea," one of them
said. "You take two rooms and I do the same, and no questions
asked!"

The results are a lovely inn that everyone is happy with. The
house was built in 1917 by a Chicago contractor who moved to
Flagstaff with a large family. "It was never considered a mansion, so
we decided to decorate in comfortable country," Sandy says. All
four innkeepers are from Southern California, and the ties go back
since Donna and Ed knew each other in the fifth grade! "We go
back more than thirty-five years," she says.

They work together well, with Sandy doing the cooking and Donna taking care of the artistic touches. "She does the flowers, folds the napkins, decorates real pretty," Sandy says. Sandy's specialty is a Farmer's Breakfast, with skillet potatoes and a healthy frittata of eggs, cheese, broccoli, carrots, and green beans, served with fresh fruit and muffins. "Depends upon the mood I'm in, maybe they'll be banana-apple with nuts and orange." Sometimes there will be German pancakes with apples and syrup or strawberries and whipped cream.

"We like to serve afternoon refreshments in the parlor," both Donna and Sandy say. "It gives up a chance to know our guests."

Pella's Room has Dutch lace curtains and a handmade quilt. In Carol's Room they let a daughter pick out the wallpaper. The antique armoire was hauled all the way from California. The pale lemon-painted Wagner/Znetko Room, named after Ed's grandparents, has a basin in the room and a private bath attached.

The Wicker Room speaks for itself, in blue and white and a queen-sized bed. The aqua Southwest Suite has a king bed, corner windows, and a huge bath with the house's original fixtures on a black and white tile floor. Downstairs, the soft rose and blue color scheme is restful—and so is the swing, out on the veranda. A wheelbarrow in the front yard is filled with bright flowers.

The innkeepers keep a book of restaurant menus handy for guest information; but in desperate situations, "like being snowbound," Sandy says with a laugh, they've served guests soup and fresh bread. "Donna is a good tour guide," she adds, which is a handy thing to know if you want to see some of the many attractions of the area, like the Museum of Northern Arizona, the Coconino Center for the Arts, Lowell Observatory, the Pioneer Museum, and the campus of Northern Arizona University.

How to get there: At the intersection of I–17 and I–40, take exit 195B (which becomes Milton Road). Follow it around to Highway 180 (which becomes Humphry's Street) and go left 2 blocks to Birch Avenue. Turn left to the inn at 824.

Dierker House
Flagstaff, Arizona
86001

Innkeeper: Dottie Dierker
Address/Telephone: 423 West Cherry Avenue; (602) 774–3249
Rooms: 3 share 1 bath; no air conditioning (elevation 7,000 feet). No smoking inn.
Rates: $35, single; $43.50, double; EPB. No credit cards.
Open: All year.
Facilities and activities: Lightly equipped kitchen, microwave. Nearby: tennis courts, Downtown Historic District, museums, Indian ruins, skiing, white-water rafting on Colorado River, Grand Canyon.

"All my boys were boatmen on the Colorado River," Dottie Dierker says as she points out the joys of the nearby white-water rafting. "Of course," she says, "you have to plan way ahead."

She plans way ahead for her guests, too, providing baskets in her guest rooms for toothbrushes and other commodities that people use regularly. Her rule is that nobody leaves anything in the bathroom. Even towels, used once, go in the hamper, so "Nobody need touch a towel or a washcloth twice."

Dottie was a nurse before she retired. She also raised six children. "I kind of like taking care of people," she says. "I've been in bed and breakfasts in other parts of the world. All over, in Budapest, all over Greece . . . mostly Europe and the Mediterranean. Of course," says this well-traveled innkeeper, "everyone does it in England and Germany." Wherever her guests may have been, they certainly enjoy Dierker House and keep coming back.

Dottie lives downstairs in her house, and guests have the run of the upstairs, which is really a three-bedroom suite. It's so cozy that guests sit around in the kitchen and raid the cookie jar or the refrigerator for refreshments. "They get together and exchange addresses," Dottie says with satisfaction. The single bath is large, with a skylight, plants, a scale, and a stocked medicine chest. "It's the nurse in me, I guess," Dottie confesses.

The three guest rooms, cozy under the eaves with down comforters and antiques and filled with green plants, are a travelogue in themselves. Would you rather sleep in France, Germany, or Greece? Posters and other mementos will take you there in your dreams.

For breakfast in the dining room, Dottie will serve one of four menus ("If you stay longer, you get a repeat," she warns): bran muffins, blueberry muffins, a meat dish, or an egg dish, all served at 8:00 a.m. "That's the only time I cook." But not to worry if you're early or late. "There's the option of a big continental breakfast in the guest kitchen," she adds.

Dottie is pretty much settled into her house. "I've only lived here forty years!" she told me. She raises orchids and she quilts, comfortable with her three Shih Tzu dogs and her canaries, Peachie and Julio, who live in cages in the long garden room behind the dining room.

Skylights light the pool table standing on the Mexican tile floor. A wall of windows opens onto a small bright garden. There's an old Wurlitzer jukebox that lights up like a Christmas tree and plays all those old tunes. Guests occasionally indulge in a game of pool after breakfast. "Fun!" says Dottie.

How to get there: At the intersection of I–17 and I–40, take exit 195B (which becomes Milton Road). Follow it around to Highway 180 (which becomes Humphry's Street) and go left 3 blocks to Cherry Avenue.

Greer Lodge
Greer, Arizona
85927

Innkeepers: Barb and Rich Allen
Address/Telephone: P.O. Box 244; (602) 735–7515
Rooms: 11; 7 with 7 baths in Main Lodge, 4 with 3 baths and kitchen in Little Lodge; no air conditioning (elevation 8,500 feet); wheelchair accessible. Smoking permitted except in dining room.
Rates: Main Lodge: $85, single; $55, per person, double; $20 extra person; EPB. Little *Lodge:* $30 per person, minimum eight persons; $15 extra person, fourteen-person maximum. EP; two-night minimum stay on weekends, three nights on holidays.
Open: All year.
Facilities and activities: Restaurant serving breakfast, lunch (May to September), and dinner; picnic lunches, cocktail bar, stocked trout pond, hiking, horseback riding, skiing, bobsledding, bird watching, canoeing.

Here's another great place for communing with nature. On the inn grounds you might spot a blue heron or two, or perhaps an owl zooming down and buzzing the pond, catching his dinner. If he doesn't get a fish he'll get a duck; owls have been seen pulling a full-sized duck out of the water. Such is the view from Greer Lodge's magnificent two-story greenhouse lounge at the back of the inn, all glass with an indoor stream and waterfall and plants everywhere. The room overlooks the pond and away to the pine-covered mountains in the distance, where you can strike out for a hike or horseback ride into the National Forest.

The inn's spacious, comfortable rooms also have windows with views. The color scheme is rust and white: rust carpets, rust curtains and coverlets with little white flowers sprinkled all over, fresh comforters, linens and towels—"the whole atmosphere is bright," say the Allens, who pride themselves on the way the inn sparkles, bright and shiny.

Everything served in the restaurant is homemade, from the biscuits and gravy to the cinnamon rolls. Breakfast is ordered off the menu, and you can have homemade croissants with your "eggs any way," or waffles, or pancakes. (Breakfast is not included in the rate for Little Lodge.) Lunches are available, packed for picnic, hiking, or fishing trips.

Homemade soups are wonderful here, soups like clam chowder, or my favorite cream of cauliflower or broccoli soup. Fresh homemade Kaiser rolls or whole wheat bread make the thick roast beef, turkey, or ham sandwiches special.

After lunch (or maybe early in the morning?), sit on the back porch and just throw your line in the stream feeding the pond, which is stocked with two-pound rainbow and German brown trout, and Canloupes fresh from the Canadian lake of the same name. Flyfishing schools have become popular at the lodge, taught both on the pond and on the Little Colorado River nearby. Sitting out on the sun deck facing the pond, I see fish jumping out of the water, just waiting for Greer Lodge guests to catch them. Horses graze in the meadows in the distance. Elk and deer graze in the sunny alpine meadows. The hurly-burly of the city is far, far away. "This is Arizona's most beautiful setting," cheerful assistant Bob Pollack says, bragging that "even the governor thinks so!"

How to get there: Greer is at the end of Highway 373, a short road that runs south from Highway 260 between Eager and Indian Pine. The inn is at the end of the road on the left.

Molly Butler Lodge
Greer, Arizona
85927

Innkeepers: Sue and Jake Jacobs
Address/Telephone: Box 134; (602) 735–7226
Rooms: 11, plus 6 cabins; all with private bath; wheelchair accessible; no air
    conditioning (elevation 8,500 feet). Pets permitted (with deposit).
Rates: $30 to $65, double; $5 extra person; EP. Two-night minimum stay
    weekends, three nights on holidays.
Open: All year except first two weeks in December.
Facilities and activities: Restaurant serves dinner. Hunting, fishing, horseback
    riding, hiking, skiing.

    Molly Butler is Arizona's oldest guest lodge, serving fabulous
food since 1910, when Butler's Lodge put out a sign advertising
"regular meals." Rooms number 5 to 12 in the Long House have
plaques on their doors commemorating early settlers. The one on
number 6 marks the Ellen Greer Room, "A Pioneer of the Valley,
1884." Rooms are rustic, as befits the ambience of this rugged little
mountain village.

    I loved being in a log house, which is what the lodge is. There
are cozy fireplaces everywhere—it gets chilly in these mountains. I
sank into one of the two curved sofas around the sunken fireplace
in the lounge, under the large elk rack and the mounted javelina
(wild pig), mule deer, and antelope heads. A huge elk head hangs
on the Indian Room wall—this place is a hunter's paradise.

Two of the three dining rooms have fireplaces, too. The piano in the lounge is "for anyone who wants to play," Jake says, and the bar has a pool table and a television set. The bar serves coffee as well as stronger stuff, and it's a popular hangout for some of the local Greer characters as well as the guests. There's always a friendly bunch gathered there no matter when I come by. Once while I was there a salesman of cheeses came by, and nothing would do but that we all taste his samples to help Sue make up her mind what to order.

The restaurant serves delicious food, and assistant Beverley Burk brags on cook Steve Cooksley's soups. "People drive up from Phoenix just for his special soups," she says. "Whenever he can get hold of asparagus . . . or his cream of broccoli . . . or his chicken Florentine soup." I especially enjoyed the trout amandine sautéed in butter and sherry and the grilled salmon, which Steve, who's been there forever, promises, "It won't be dry, that I can guarantee." The mud pie of coffee ice cream in a chocolate cookie crust, covered with fudge topping and mountains of whipped cream, offered no hardship either.

Neither does the beautiful country hereabouts, not to mention the rainbow and German brown trout fishing, the hummingbird, the elk, deer, antelope, and turkey watching.

How to get there: Greer is at the end of Highway 373, which runs south from Highway 260 between Eager and Indian Pine. The inn will be on your right as you enter the village. There is a sign.

17

White Mountain Lodge
Greer, Arizona
85927

Innkeepers: Sophie and Russ Majesky
Address/Telephone: P.O. Box 139; (602) 735–7568
Rooms: 9; 2 with private bath, 2 with connecting bath; wheelchair accessible; no air conditioning (elevation 8,500 feet). Pets permitted.
Rates: $35 to $65, single or double; $5 extra person; EPB. No credit cards.
Open: All year.
Facilities and activities: Nearby: fishing, hunting, and downhill and cross-country skiing at Sunrise Ski Area 13 miles away.

I loved Russ's answer when I asked why he liked being an innkeeper after supervising in Tucson's main post office. Not only did he say that both he and Sophie like caring for people and that, although a lot of work, it is enjoyable; he added energetically, "and—I gotta have something to do!"

White Mountain Lodge, the oldest building in Greer, began as a farmhouse, built in 1892 by one of the first Mormon families to settle in Greer. The Majeskys have preserved a wonderful landmark in a cozy and comfortable way. Russ, who likes working with wood, did much of the reconstruction, and Sophie decorated the rooms with talent she is just beginning to realize. With a master's degree in nursing, she is now "doing art," as Russ puts it. As often as she can she's off to Show Low, a town almost 50 miles away, for a three-hour 8:30 a.m. painting class.

The enclosed front porch and the main lodge room are comfortably furnished, and the word *cozy* keeps returning to my mind. The feeling is of warmth and interest in guests—genuine hospitality.

"We've never charged a single cent for a cup of coffee in the nine years we've been in business," Russ says. And the pot is on as early as 5:30 in the morning. This is the place for people who wake up early just dying for a cup of coffee.

The full breakfast is served in the family dining room, and in addition to orange juice, coffee, and toast and jam, you'll have fresh fruit, a hot main entree, and homemade breads and rolls. "Homemade foods are our specialty," Sophie says, "and I'm thinking about going back to making homemade donuts." It was a popular attraction, she says, and I can believe it.

Breakfasting together with other guests, the Majeskys believe, "provides spontaneity in talk and in striking up friendships while at the lodge." And in their experience they find that such friendships often are ongoing.

Sophie sometimes cooks for groups, but otherwise sends guests to the Molly Butler Lodge or Greer Lodge, or to the new Green Mountain Shadows Restaurant and Bar for steaks and fried chicken. She and Russ like to drive 17 miles to Springerville to the Safire Restaurant or the Piñon Tree for prime rib or special fried chicken.

Behind the lodge, the farm's original log cattle barn is still standing, and energetic Russ has restored it as an art gallery and craft shop. Artist and sculptor Jim Beavers has recently become part of White Mountain Lodge, and his workshop is open to visitors. Jim specializes in southwest pottery in the styles of the lost Hokokam, Salado, Wimbres, and Anasazi Native American cultures, and his work is for sale.

"We have been blessed with seeing more elk, deer, and antelope grazing in the surrounding meadows," Sophie says, "and of course the beaver continue to play in the ponds created by the Little Colorado River."

How to get there: Greer is at the end of Highway 373, south off Highway 260 between Eager and Indian Pine. The inn will be on your left as you enter the village.

Ramsey Canyon Inn
Hereford, Arizona
85615

Innkeeper: Shirlene Milligan
Address/Telephone: 31 Ramsey Canyon Road; (602) 378–3010
Rooms: 6; 4 with private bath; 3 one-bedroom housekeeping cottages; no air conditioning (elevation 5,400 feet). No smoking inn.
Rates: Rooms: $65 to $85, double, EPB. Cottages: $85 to $105, $10 extra person, EP. No credit cards.
Open: All year.
Facilities and activities: Picnic area. Nearby: Ramsey Canyon Preserves, bird watching, hiking trails in Huachuca Mountains.

Ramsey Canyon Inn sits under tall pine trees at the very entrance to the Ramsey Canyon Preserves Nature Conservancy. Innkeeper Shirlene is a member of the conservancy and of the National Audubon Society, and she says the main reason people come to Ramsey Canyon is that more species of hummingbird have been recorded here than anywhere else in the United States. "Plus two hundred other species!" she adds. "This is a bird-watcher's paradise, made for people who love nature and hiking."

Shirlene also loves to bake pies, and she modestly owns up to winning more than two hundred ribbons for her pastry. A native of the Ramsey Canyon area, she migrated to Alaska for a while and took pie honors at the Kenai Peninsula Fair, only to come home and take sweepstakes honors at the Cochise County Fair. What is her favorite pie? "I like them all!" is her laughing answer. The blackberry slice I had was rich and thick and tasted too much like more! Fruit for the pies comes fresh from her own orchard.

Oh, it's quiet in Ramsey Canyon, birds notwithstanding. "Most of my guests tell me they haven't had a night's sleep like this in years," Shirlene says. From the windows of Room 7 you might catch a glimpse of a pair of golden eagles that nest up in the cliffs every spring and stay all summer. All the rooms are comfortable and cool, furnished with antiques, refinished by Shirlene, who is both artistic and handy. She has stenciled decorations along the walls of each room with designs she painted to match comforters, pillow shams, and bed ruffles. "I like things to match," she says with a laugh. Shirlene also bakes birthday and anniversary cakes and presents flowers to birthday guests, flowers that she has cultivated in spite of the voracious forest creatures that surround her. "The javelina and the deer eat everything I plant but snapdragons!" Along with the birds, the deer, and the javelina, you may see raccoons, coatimundi, ring-tailed cats, mountain lions, fox, and small black bear in Ramsey Canyon.

Shirlene serves a full gourmet breakfast. Individual puffed Dutch pancakes with sliced strawberries and whipped cream, cooked apples, peaches, and blueberries, sausage, and cranberry-pecan or banana muffins will fuel a lot of hours of bird watching. And you can do it lounging on the covered porch or under the tall black walnut, chokecherry, oak, maple, and sycamore trees of the picnic area if you wish, because Shirlene brings the show to her door. "I go through fifty pounds of sugar a week, feeding literally hundreds of hummingbirds," she says.

How to get there: From I–10 take Highway 90 south, turning onto Highway 92 south through Hereford 6.2 miles to Ramsey Canyon Road. Turn right and follow the trail 3.5 miles to the inn, on the right just before you enter Ramsey Canyon Preserves.

Bartram's White Mountain Inn

Lakeside, Arizona
85929

Innkeepers: Petie and Ray Bartram
Address/Telephone: Route 1, Box 1014; (602) 367–1408
Rooms: 3; all with private bath and patio; no air conditioning (elevation 7,000 feet); electric blankets. No smoking inn.
Rates: $55, single; $65, double; $75 for 3; $85 for 4; EPB.
Open: All year.
Facilities and activities: Lunch and dinner by reservation, infant equipment, ski storage, volleyball, badminton, horseshoes. Nearby: restaurants, Woodland Lake Park, Apache Indian Reservation, fishing, hiking, biking, tennis, horseback riding, skiing, golf, and antiques shops.

"We never hear traffic noises," Petie Bartram says happily. "Instead we hear birds and see wild horses, elk, eagles, and bears." The inn overlooks the Apache Indian Reservation, and the other day a herd of wild horses were grazing in the field shared by the inn and the reservation." Petie, having decided that if she kept on the way she was going, she'd be dead, gave up a well-paid job for life here in the woods. "I'm going to be dead a long time when I die," she says, "and this is what I want to be doing now."

Ray is a long-distance truck driver, but with the inn Petie never gets a chance to be lonely. "My guests are fun," she says. "It's such fun when you have people who are willing to be fun back!"

"But Petie," her guests protest, "it's you that's fun." And indeed, Petie works hard to make the inn special; she wants it to be an affordable escape for people who can't manage an expensive getaway resort. She and Ray do things like make homemade ice cream in the summer. "We do whatever fits into someone's lifestyle," she says.

In winter, guests like to curl up with an afghan on the sofa in front of the petrified-wood fireplace and take a cozy nap. The fireplace heats the entire house. On the wall above, there's a collection of Apache snowshoes that guests who want to trek in the snow can borrow.

There are notions in the bathrooms, and hand-decorated towels. Rooms were decorated with great enthusiasm by Petie, and it's a hard choice between the Blue Room, the Peach Suite, and the Satin Room.

Petie is proud of her seven-course breakfast—a whopper. We had: (1) juice, coffee, tea, and hot chocolate; (2) "cheesey eggs" with mushrooms, scallions, cream, and cheese sauce; (3) hashed brown potatoes with paprika and parmesan cheese; (4) two kinds of muffins (banana sour cream with walnuts, and bran raisin sticky buns; (5) bacon (sometimes smoked turkey, ham, or Italian sausage); (6) a fruit platter with cream sauce; and (7) (time to holler enough!) stuffed French toast.

The inn has delightful pets, most unusual ones like Farnsworth, the house-trained pig, and Nugget, the parrot, who lives in a cage in the back room. "Nugget can walk right out here now; he's housebroken," Petie says. "All of our animals are strays. Ray was making a delivery in back of a store at 3:00 a.m. and there was this big green parrot sitting out there. Ray held out his hand and the bird jumped on. They fell madly in love. We advertised, but no one came to claim him." There are also four outside cats and three dogs, the poodle, Shammy, a new collie named Samantha, and the collie, Yum-yum. "But we call him Yummy," say the two animal lovers.

How to get there: From Highway 260 in Lakeside, turn right at the only traffic light, onto Woodland Lake Road; go to the stop sign and turn right. The inn's on the right at the end of the road.

Villa Cardinale
Oracle, Arizona
85623

Innkeepers: Judy and Ron Schritt
Address/Telephone: 1315 West Oracle Road (mailing address: P.O. Box 649);
(602) 896–2516
Rooms: 4; all with private bath, 2 with TV; wheelchair accessible. Pets permitted. One smoking room.
Rates: $40, single; $50, double; EPB. No credit cards.
Open: All year.
Facilities and activities: Lunch and dinner by reservation, patio. Nearby: hiking trails in Oracle State Park, horseback riding, Biosphere 2.

You won't need to ask why this inn is named for cardinals—they're all over, both the real thing and artistic representations of them. Bird plates, bird pictures, even bird place mats, a collection from the innkeepers' travels abroad.

"Ron is particularly fond of cardinals," Judy says, "and we were lucky enough to settle near a breeding pair that return every year. They bring their young to see us. See," she says, "they're out at the feeder." They were,too.

You'll see lots of other wildlife near this small inn where the temperature is always twenty degrees cooler than in Tucson. You're back to nature, and the only pets the inn has, says Judy, are the wild ones. Besides the many small birds there are quail all around, turkeys, javelinas, chipmunks, even a resident bobcat who lives down on the rocks below the inn. "People who get up early get to see them—but anyone with a gun doesn't get to see my bobcats!" she says vehemently.

The Schritts settled here from the Midwest when Judy wanted to combine her antiques business with an inn. "I enjoy doing things with and for people." The common room is also a shop where folks can either relax or buy. There are all sorts of interesting things, especially clocks. Ron's hobby is repairing old clocks, and Judy says he can do "a lot of wondrous things." A cherished piece is a rare wooden clock made before brass works were incorporated into timepieces.

There's a new patio with a firepit, perfect for a bonfire "to cuddle near," Judy says, under the starry skies.

The Hummingbird Room is dainty with blue and white lace; Road Runner has a queen bed and Mexican leather table and chairs; Cactus Wren has a four-poster bed and Ethan Allen chairs; Quail Room has a view of all the live quails out the window. All four rooms open off a shady entrance patio; you can come and go via your own entrance if you want. The small refrigerator out there is for ice and soft drinks, and Judy puts out coffee first thing in the morning. Soft music plays on the stereo, there for guests to use. There's a small fountain in the patio, too, to keep things even cooler. The arched entrance to the patio has a wrought-iron gate with an old locomotive bell overhead. Window boxes brighten each window, and the brick is lovely used adobe from Mexico. "I hauled all this stuff up here from Tucson myself in my little truck," Judy brags. Breakfast is hearty and usually healthy. Judy says she tries to do "fruity things" rather than eggs. Apple crepes with yogurt are a specialty; only one egg dish a stay is her goal.

Ron also enjoys being a part-time prospector. "There's gold in them thar hills; we've had geologists visiting, and they tell us so," he says with a twinkle in his eye.

How to get there: Take Highway 89 north from Tucson to Oracle Junction, then Highway 77 to Oracle. Don't take business route; go on to Rockcliff Boulevard. Turn left; first right is Oracle Ranch Road. The inn is 500 yards on the right.

Maricopa Manor
Phoenix, Arizona
85011

Innkeepers: Mary Ellen and Paul Kelley
Address/Telephone: 15 West Pasadena Avenue; (602) 274–6302
Rooms: 5; all with private bath, phones, and TV; wheelchair accessible.
    Smoking in designated areas.
Rates: $49 to $99, double, continental-plus breakfast.
Open: All year.
Facilities and activities: Hot tub. Nearby: Camelback Road with restaurants
    and shops; museums, state capitol and park, botanical and Japanese
    gardens, golf, tennis, festivals.

Life wasn't busy enough for Mary Ellen and Paul, raising
twelve children; now they've opened their lovely Spanish-style
home as a very luxurious inn. The house is a combination of surprises: Off the spacious entry hall is a very formal living room with
some beautiful French antiques. In fact, two of the fragile-looking
end tables are 1937 reproductions of tables that Marie Antoinette
had, probably at Versailles. Two satin love seats face each other in
front of the fireplace, which has a screen made of Dutch lace.

"But we move it in the winter, when we want a fire," Mary
Ellen assures me. There's a harp, and guests make themselves at
home both here and in the large, modern Gathering Room, with a
cathedral ceiling and The Pit, a sunken corner that's the television
area. Amusing and entertaining is an antique slot machine that still

works. "Some guests are in high heaven with that," Paul says with a twinkle. "If it's your nickel, you keep your winnings; if it's our nickel, we keep."

The dining room is large, and according to Mary Ellen, "It's seen many a family celebration dinner." Three of the children they raised were their own, the others were foster boys, as well as a Salvadoran exchange student who never went home! Married now, he and his family are part of the family.

Mary Ellen serves breakfast—fresh fruit, homemade bread and jams, and gourmet coffee—in a basket and delivers it to each suite. "We've had people take it to Sedona and even the Grand Canyon!" she says. "I change the china, and every morning there's a surprise." This morning it was a delicious quiche.

The inn's five unique and luxurious suites are a delight. The Library Suite has several hundred leather-bound books to read. Well, not all at once, but "that's what they're there for," Paul says. "People should enjoy them."

The Palo Verde Suite, named for the state tree, has an original Franklin stove amid green and pink Laura Ashley fabrics; the Victorian Suite is done up in satins and lace with a mirrored armoire.

Reflections Past has antique mirrors and a canopied bed; Reflections Present, adjoining, is a study in black, gold, and white modernity reflected in a collection of mirrors. "Our son said, 'Let's get out of the antiques for a change'—and it just seemed like a wonderfully crazy idea," Mary Ellen says with a laugh. She's enjoyed the change, even adding her own artistic touch, painting a lacy black tree silhouette on two of the walls and adding the perfect touch of a red, red rose in a vase.

Both the large, beautiful home, with its luxurious space and lovely grounds, and the gracious innkeepers make this a wonderful place to stay. "It's our home," Mary Ellen says simply, "and we now share it with anyone who chooses to come. People," she adds, "are so interesting. They [inn guests] are a special breed."

How to get there: From I–17 take Camelback Road east on Third; then go north on Third to Pasadena Avenue. The inn is one house west of the intersection of Pasadena and Central.

The Marks House Inn
Prescott, Arizona
86303

Innkeepers: Dottie and Harold Viehweg
Address/Telephone: 203 East Union Street; (602) 778–4632
Rooms: 4 suites; all with private bath; no air conditioning (elevation 5,300 feet). No smoking inn.
Rates: $70 to $105, single; $75 to $110, double; $130, for 4; EPB.
Open: All year.
Facilities and activities: Nearby: Historic Prescott Courthouse Square, restaurants, shops, and museums; golf, boating, hiking, tennis, and swimming at area lakes Lynx, Walker, Goldwater, and Watson.

High on a hill overlooking Courthouse Square and Whiskey Row, the historic Marks House stands in regal splendor, a fine old dowager of a mansion built in 1894 by an early Arizonan who was reputed to be the wealthiest man in the area at the time he built the home for his bride, Josephine. Jake Marks, trader, mine owner, and general merchandizer, evidently was quite an adventurer, joining General Crook in fighting the Pitt River Indian Wars. When he wasn't off fighting Indians, he also was involved in both the liquor business and the politics of the time. "He and General Crook were great friends, and the general stayed at the house when he was in town," says Dottie as she serves hors d'oeuvres in the late afternoon on the veranda.

Gorgeous sunsets are on view from the veranda and the

curved windows in the circular corner turret of both the parlor and the Queen Anne Suite above. The old house is on the National Register of Historic Places, and it took seven years to restore it. The spacious mansion certainly bears witness to wealth, with polished hardwood floors and beautiful wood moldings and doors. The dining-room floor is inlaid with a pattern of walnut, oak, and mahogany, and there is a fireplace back to back with the parlor one. The original wood floors creak even when lightly trod upon, and there seem to be several resident ghosts. One is a man "who apparently is a prankster," says Dottie. "He opens doors, turns on lights, and generally misplaces things." The other, according to old tales, is a lady who is looking for her child. "But she lives at the back of the house," Dottie says reassuringly, "and doesn't seem to bother anyone. And the creakings, thumps, and bumps that generally come with an old house add to the mystery.

What was wonderful, if not mysterious, to me was the surprise at finding such lovely features in a house built so shortly after the first settlers arrived in Prescott. Barely thirty years later, here was this two-story Queen Anne Victorian with sunburst window designs, a turret, and my favorite detail, the ornately decorated front porch that wraps around the turret.

The two bedrooms of the Ivy Suite on the main floor are decorated in soft greens, which complement the Victorian antiques; the Princess Victoria Room has an 1890s copper tub from a bathhouse in Syracuse, New York. The Tea Rose Room has a queen-sized bath and is close to the hall bathroom.

Mornings, Dottie serves a main dish of some sort of breakfast casserole, along with fresh or cooked fruit, homemade muffins, coffee, tea, cocoa, and juice, and a side dish of breakfast meat if there's none in the casserole. "My Overnight French Toast Casserole is what most guests seem to like best," Dottie said, generously giving me the recipe. Hint: It's so rich because there's cream cheese in it, too.

How to get there: From Courthouse Square go east up the hill of Union Street to Marina. The inn will be at the corner of Marina on the right.

Victorian Inn
Prescott, Arizona
86303

Innkeepers: Tamia Thunstedt and Judy Koppes
Address/Telephone: 246 South Cortez Street; (602) 778–2642
Rooms: 4, including 1 suite; suite with private bath; no air conditioning (elevation 5,300 feet). No smoking inn.
Rates: $90 to $125, double, EPB.
Open: All year.
Facilities and activities: Gift shop. Nearby: restaurants, antiques shopping, Courthouse Square, historic homes, museum, horseback riding, hiking trails up Thumb Butte, fishing in Goldwater and Lynx Creek Lake, many festivals.

It's a pleasure to see how these two sisters enjoy each other, working together to make this beautiful old house a successful inn. Tamia is a registered nurse and Judy works in her husband's commercial photography studio, but this does not mean that guests are neglected. Judy, who is artistic, loves to set a beautiful table.

"When we walk into the dining room, the mood is set," Tamia says with a fond laugh. "Judy wants us to think 'this is elegance.'" Which we do, and very fitting it is, too, in this elegant Victorian mansion built in the 1890s. Painted blue with white trim and a peaked-roof turret and enclosed in a formal wrought-iron fence, the house is a showplace on the corner of the street.

Judy also sews, upholsters, refinishes furniture, and re-canes chairs; she has done a wonderful job with her twenty-year collection of antiques, which now have come to furnish the inn.

Tamia, who was named after the woman crowned Miss Sweden the year she was born, has a wonderful doll collection, and she feels the same happy proprietary interest in the inn. "I really enjoy sharing it with people, because I am so proud of it," she says.

Guest rooms are large and airy, with wallpapers that are exact reproductions of 1890s Victorian wallpaper. The canopy queen bed in Eve's Garden Room is draped with soft creamy chiffon, and an armoire and rockers in fresh white wicker add to the ambience. The Teddy Bear Room contains a four-poster that was a family piece, and yes, of course, a teddy bear. The Rose Room is bright and soothing; the bathroom has a footed tub and a hand shower of brass.

The settee in the Victorian Suite is a conversation piece. "It's a lovers' seat," Tamia says with a bubbly laugh. "For a man and a woman. One sits, the other lies down—and gets their feet rubbed!"

Breakfast at the table elegantly set by Judy is more than a feast for the eyes. Fresh fruit, Canadian bacon, and a repertoire of hot cross or cashew-coconut buns, main-dish strata, Linzer Torte, vanilla yogurt soufflé, Swedish pancakes, it's all delicious (but of course you don't have it all at once!). The whole family may get into the act one way or another, with Granny Myrtle Thunstedt's muffins or Swedish pancakes—"Mom's recipe," says Tamia. "Mom also made these Victorian outfits we wear to serve breakfast."

After such a feast at breakfast, all I wanted to do was to sit on the front porch swing and relax. Just for a while, though. Because I could see Courthouse Square and its attractions just a block away, beckoning to me over the housetops. . . .

There is a small gift shop in the entrance of the inn, with hand-painted porcelain objects, dried flower arrangements, and mementos of the inn.

How to get there: One block south of Courthouse Square and 1 block east of Montezuma (Highway 89).

Cathedral Rock Lodge
Sedona, Arizona
86336

Innkeepers: Carol and Samyo Shannon
Address/Telephone: Star Route 2, Box 856; (602) 282–7608
Rooms: 3, including 1 suite; all with private bath, suite with kitchen and TV. No smoking inn.
Rates: $65 to $90, double; $5 extra person; EPB. Two-night minimum weekends; special rates for longer stays.
Open: All year.
Facilities and activities: Picnic equipment, library of local history and video tapes of movies filmed in red rock country. Nearby: Sedona with restaurants and arts and crafts, shopping at Tlaquepaque; new 300-acre Red Rock State Park for environmental education; hiking, horseback riding, Indian ruins.

Carol and her son Samyo had no problem deciding what to name their inn—wait until you see Cathedral Rock! From almost every window of the inn, you can see this glorious hunk of the beautiful red rock that the Sedona area is famous for. This is the scenery you oohed and aahed at during all those western movies where the bad guys chased the good guys among gigantic formations of red rock.

Carol, who is from Tempe, near Phoenix, camped here with her children for several years before she acquired the inn. "I wanted to live in this gorgeous country," she says, and she gave up her work as volunteer coordinator between the city's museums, libraries, and senior citizens. Now she earns a living where she once only dreamed of living.

"Since so many people are on cholesterol-free diets, my biggest challenge is finding eggless dishes," she says with a laugh. One specialty is sour cream Belgian waffles with pecans along with ham, fresh fruit, and fresh-ground coffee. A Mexican breakfast is a guest favorite, too, a Mexican soufflé with green chilies, not too spicy unless you want it that way. "You make Mexican food piquanté (hot) with the sauce," Carol reminds me. "And Mexican food stays with you," she promises—in case you're worried about going hungry! Afternoons, she sets lemonade, iced tea, and homemade cookies out in the lounge.

The lounge has a wall of windows, and that huge Cathedral Rock outside, red red rock against deep blue Arizona sky, looks too good to be real. "Viewing Cathedral Rock, that's our most popular local activity," Carol announced one afternoon as she served lemonade to two contented Easterners sitting at the picnic table under the huge old shade trees. "We fell in love with these monster elms; there's nothing like it in Sedona, they must have been planted when the house was built in the forties."

Both guest rooms in the main house are furnished with family antiques, and the beds sport handmade quilts. Connected in back are the Garden Room, with its own wildflower quilt and photographs of Carol's mother and sister, and the Homestead Room, with lace curtains and room for three. The Amigo Suite overhead, with a private deck, has a king bed, a double-bed couch, and a kitchen. When I visited, a pair of grandparents were happily ensconced up there with a small grandchild.

The guest addition in the back connects with back stairs to the kitchen of the main house. "In cold weather, guests just come down in their robes," Carol says. Informality and comfort are the rule here. The common room is packed with books and magazines, children's films for the VCR, and information on hiking, historical sites, and Indian ruins to visit—once you decide to quit loafing at this happy inn.

How to get there: Go south on Highway 89A through Sedona and West Sedona to traffic light at Y in road. Go 4.1 miles farther to Upper Red Rock Loop Road. Turn left for 2.7 miles, some of it unpaved, passing Disney Lane on the left. Cathedral Rock is the next lane on the left.

Garland's Oak Creek Lodge
Sedona, Arizona
86336

Innkeepers: Mary and Gary Garland
Address/Telephone: P.O. Box 152; (602) 282–3343
Rooms: 15 cabins; all with private bath; no air conditioning (high elevation).
  No smoking in dining room.
Rates: $138 to $158, double, MAP.
Open: March 30 to November 18.
Facilities and activities: Tennis court, private creek for swimming and fishing.
  Nearby: golf, tennis, hiking, horseback riding, bicycling; shopping at
  Tlaquepaque in Sedona.

To reach Garland's I had to turn onto a small unpaved road down a hill and over a stream. The stream was Oak Creek, one of the prettiest spots in Arizona, a state full of pretty spots. Thick greenery above and all around enveloped me, insulating me from the rushing highway sounds.

"We feel we're in a very nice place," Gary Garland says modestly, "and we want to share it with our guests. It's an escape for us and we hope it's an escape for them."

Located as it is, on the far side of the creek in utter privacy, Garland's combines the beauty of wilderness with all the comfort and familiarity of back home. Vegetables grow in the garden; fruits come from the orchards. Wild blackberries are plentiful, in season, and everybody, even inn guests, joins in the fun of picking them.

Everybody eats the jam, too, on the inn's delicious homemade bread and rolls. New is a large greenhouse to help supply the fresh produce that makes Garland's Oak Creek Lodge such a healthy and delicious place to dine.

Meals are served in the cathedral-ceilinged, rock-walled dining room. Breakfast of *huevos rancheros* came with not only fresh-squeezed orange juice but apple juice pressed from fruit grown in the apple orchard. New for breakfast are the breakfast enchiladas: grilled tortillas wrapped around and absolutely stuffed with scrambled eggs, black beans, and cheese and flavored with chilies and fresh tomatillo.

Dinner of smoky squash soup, chili cheese bread, orange tarragon salad, and Cornish game hen Southwest style, served with a mélange of carrots, cauliflower, and zucchini, was complemented by an excellent Riesling wine. Another specialty in this garden of culinary Eden is rack of lamb with a chutney or peanut-butter sauce, served with a salad of mixed greens in parsley vinaigrette, corn rye bread, broccoli, and carrots, and topped with devil's food cake. But my most favorite dessert is Garland's Apple Tart, caramel-like, crunchy, superb, unlike any apple tart I've ever tasted.

You can see why I was not surprised—although I was impressed—to see Mary Garland's collection of ribbons from the Coconino County Fair hanging in the entry.

Complimentary tea is offered in the afternoon at 4 p.m. "Not exactly 'high tea,'" Mary says with a laugh, "but always a sweet and a savory snack to tide guests over until dinner is served." Gives guests a chance to relax and visit, too.

Most of the cozy cabins have fireplaces. Number 4 has a porch practically hanging over the creek; you can imagine the spectacular view. Flower-patterned Austrian shades at the windows are the kind of touches that make this rustic retreat special. "We're professional but not formal, that's what people like about our place," say the Garlands.

The home-grown, homemade food is no deterrent, either!

How to get there: The lodge is 8 miles north of Sedona off Highway 89A.

Graham's Bed &
Breakfast Inn
Sedona, Arizona
86336

Innkeepers: Marni and Bill Graham
Address/Telephone: 150 Circle Canyon Drive (mailing address: P.O. Box 912);
(602) 284–1425
Rooms: 5; all with private bath. No smoking inn.
Rates: $80 to $125, single; $95 to $140, double; EPB.
Open: All year except January.
Facilities and activities: Pool and spa. Nearby: restaurants, tennis, golf, racquetball, shopping at Tlaquepaque, horseback riding, jeep rides, hiking, Indian ruins.

Graham's lovely inn is located in the heart of Arizona's red rock country, surrounded by jagged strata of bright orange rock jutting dramatically against the blue, blue sky. The inn, smooth and square and white, makes a cool contrast to its surroundings.

Innkeepers Marni and Bill say they can't say enough about the beauty of the countryside, and I agree with them. It is extraordinary.

"I wouldn't trade places with anyone in the world," Marni says, adding, "as long as Bill and I are doing this together." She and Bill recruited the talents of a California-trained designer, and their inn is outstanding. Each room has a name with a theme to match.

The Heritage Room is red, white, and blue; the San Francisco Suite is all peach and pale gray; the Garden Room, green with green and red geranium-flowered wallpaper, has white wicker furniture. The Southwest Suite . . . well, I could go on and on.

Bill was sales manager of a food company, Marni a legal secretary, and with three daughters grown, they decided they were in a position to make a dramatic change. They also wanted to work together. "We both like the openness of the countryside," Bill says. "But meeting people is the high point. Bed and breakfast people are gregarious. Innkeeping restores your faith in human nature—people are really pretty nice!"

Late afternoons Marni puts out sodas, fruit juices, nibbles like salted almonds, cheese and crackers, cream cheese with chutney, and often—a Pennsylvania custom—pretzels dipped in horseradish mustard. "People sit around, get to know each other."

A breakfast specialty is cheese strata, perhaps inspired by the scenery. Meat, cheese, cubed bread soaked in milk and mustard is baked slowly and eaten up in a hurry! With it are fruit juices, fruit bowl with yogurt, and plenty of good hot coffee or tea. Or else a fresh fruit bowl, homemade bread, and either *huevos rancheros*, breakfast quiche, or Red Rock Pancake, a real specialty, dedicated to the scenery. Then you're really fortified for the outdoors. Bill stands ready with National Forest Service maps of hiking trails so you can enjoy the beautiful red rock country.

Bill and Marni say they are still awestruck by their surroundings: "The ever-changing drama of sun and clouds playing on majestic red rock turret formations; the striations of soft tan, paprika, and rich cinnamon brown against the backdrop of the azure skies, the dark green juniper and pine. . . ." Sedona is one of nature's wonderlands, a happy combination of fabulous scenery and fantastic weather.

How to get there: Canyon Circle Drive circles off Bellrock Boulevard, which is in the south Sedona suburb of the Village of Oak Creek. From Highway 179 turn west at the intersection that has a convenience store and a service store on the right—that will be Bellrock Boulevard. Canyon Circle Drive and the inn will be on your right about a block down the road.

Lantern Light Inn
Sedona, Arizona
86336

Innkeepers: Kris and Ed Valjean
Address/Telephone: 3085 West Highway 89A; (602) 282–3419
Rooms: 3; all with private bath. No smoking inn.
Rates: $65 to $85, double, EPB.
Open: All year.
Facilities and activities: Nearby: restaurants, shops, hiking, horseback riding.

Kris and Ed have named their inn for Kris's collection of lanterns, which are an interesting sight, especially if you arrive after dark and you see the entrance one all lit up. Two posts at the entrance make the inn easy to find: On one post there's the inn sign, and on the opposite post is, of course, a lantern, and a huge one at that.

This small cozy inn is also fresh with green plants and bright flowers. The curved drive of small, earth-colored stones leads to an open breezeway, also full of plants and hung with lanterns. "I've collected them from everywhere," Kris says. "I even have eighteen more, in the garage, waiting for a place!"

She and Ed are from Los Angeles, where Ed was involved in the Premier Market, his family's gourmet food market for fifty years. "We thought we'd probably open a food store," Kris says, "but I'm really pleased with the inn." She was a department store buyer, and in furnishing the inn her merchandising experience came in handy. "I love furniture," she says, as she beams at the antiques that fill the room. "Being in merchandising for so many years, I know how to shop," she adds when she's complimented on the inn's rich red, blue, and green color scheme. Right now she's excited about the new oriental rug in the long hall, all lovely reds and blues.

The inn has a unique arrangement in that the guests get the downstairs and the Valjeans have the upstairs. The well-furnished common area is a long room that's for both sitting and dining, with books and brochures, as well as a television/VCR corner, and up the stairs are the innkeepers' living quarters and the kitchen.

Two guest rooms are off the long hall in the main building: The Queen's Room, mauve and pink, opens onto a lovely back garden with a sun deck; the King's Room next door is done in blue with oriental rugs. The Ryan Room across the breezeway is large, with a sofa bed and a kitchen as well as an entrance all its own.

Kris is the cook, although she gives Ed credit for helping. But she says he's better at charting out trips for guests. "He really sits down with them and plans outings," she says. "He's much better geographically than I am."

She comes into her own at breakfast, with fulsome meals that include fresh-squeezed orange juice, mixed fruit salads with lemon yogurt sauce, and hashed brown or home-fried potatoes with a Southwest casserole of chilies, egg, and three cheeses. Other specialties are Belgian waffles or thin blueberry hotcakes, with sausage. "No pork; all sausage, bacon and ham is really turkey. Kris is health-conscious," says her sister, Mary Sica, who helps out now and then. "She's an angel," Kris says, and I certainly found her to be a very pleasant addition to Lantern Inn.

"We've always had guests in our home, people coming and going," Kris says. "We're not thrown by having people around. We give guests the freedom of the downstairs and we have ours upstairs. We find it's perfect, if that's the way they prefer it."

How to get there: Take Highway 89A west. The inn will be on the left.

Saddle Rock Ranch
Sedona, Arizona
86336

Innkeepers: Fran and Dan Bruno
Address/Telephone: 255 Rock Ridge Drive; (602) 282–7640
Rooms: 3; all with private bath. No smoking inn.
Rates: $95 to $125, double, EPB.
Open: All year.
Facilities and activities: Swimming pool and spa, Sedona airport transportation. Nearby: restaurants, shops, hiking, fishing, horseback riding.

This luxurious home is not what you would expect from a place that calls itself a ranch. Today the historic homestead, built in 1926, is on the edge of a residential area. But it sits on three acres of hillside overlooking Sedona, and it has starred in many Old West films.

"I just saw a late-night 'thirties movie, *Angel and the Bad Man*," Dan says, "and there was our whole house! It was a dude ranch back then, and the wife of the owner always played an Indian princess in the films," he adds with a laugh.

Fran and Dan, who met while both were employed at a prestigious California hotel, are experts in providing special attention to guests. What you'll get is the same VIP treatment that they gave to many of the "rich and famous." And before that, Dan had a rather adventurous career: You might recognize his name because he played football for the Pittsburgh Steelers.

"He's lived every man's fantasy," Fran says. "He also raced with Mario Andretti on the Indy circuit." They moved to Sedona for the climate, and now Dan and Fran are having an adventurous time innkeeping. "Our guests are wonderful, outstanding, and we want them to have the same total experience throughout their visit. It's a point of pride to us that our guests get not only the best of what we have to offer, but what Sedona has to offer as well," Dan says, so you can expect full concierge service with restaurant reservations at Sedona's finest—concerts, theater, tours, and anything else you, or they, can think of.

Guest rooms are elegantly comfortable, as is the living room. Large Saddle Rock Suite has a country French canopied bed and a rock fireplace; furniture in the Rose Garden Room was Dan's great-great-grandfather's, and the room has its own private walled rose garden; The Cottage in back, with wood-paneled walls, is surrounded by panoramic vistas. Robes, nightly turndown, chocolates, bottled water, afternoon snacks, guest refrigerator and microwave oven—just make yourself at home in this just-about-perfect inn.

There are cuddly teddy bears everywhere, and it's Dan who collects them! "I was born at home, and the doctor brought a bear when he delivered me—I still have it," he says. It lives in retirement with other teddy bears on a daybed that belonged to his great-great-grandfather.

Breakfast is served in the large and sunny dining room, and specialties are heart-shaped peach waffles and individual Dutch babies (pancakes) filled with apples and vanilla ice cream or yogurt. "I like to use our local Sedona apples, peaches, and pears," Fran says. Orange juice is always fresh-squeezed, and if you prefer tea to coffee, there are sixteen different ones to choose from.

At the rear of the property, a national forest shelters wildlife; deer come to the salt lick, and quail abound. The inn has tamer specimens in Diane and Fergie, miniature schnauzers. "But guest quarter are off-limits to them," Fran says, "unless you particularly request some puppy love!"

How to get there: Take Highway 89A (Airport Drive) to Valley View; go south 1 block to Rock Ridge Drive, left to Forest Circle, and right to Rock Ridge Circle; continue beyond Rock Ridge Drive and take gravel road on left up the hill to Saddle Rock.

Sipapu Lodge
Sedona, Arizona
86336

Innkeepers: Lea Pace and Vincent Mollan
Address/Telephone: 65 Piki Drive (mailing address: P.O. Box 552); (602)
  282–2833
Rooms: 5; 3 with private bath. Pets permitted. No smoking inn.
Rates: $68 to $98, double; $7 extra person; EPB. No credit cards.
Open: All year.
Facilities and activities: Nearby: Sedona with restaurants and arts and crafts,
  shopping at Tlaquepaque; hiking, horseback riding, Indian ruins.

Sipapu is a Hopi Indian word for the opening in a kiva, an Indian adobe oven. The name is unusual, and unusual also is the building made of Sedona red rock. "That's rare here, I don't know why,"
Lea says of the old house she bought and adapted to a Southwest
ranch-style lodge. A native Arizonan, Lea taught for years in California—but innkeeping is what she always planned to do.

"I always planned on coming back home but didn't plan on
doing it so soon," she says with a laugh. "But I found this property
that said 'buy me,' so I did!" Son Vincent joined her and works with
her. "I could not do this by myself; his pottery, the arrangement of
things, that's all Vince."

Family things are everywhere. "Our family history—of three
generations living in the same place—and the history of Arizona are
in this house," Lea explains. Grandfather Fanning was an archaeol-

ogist in the 1920s and '30s, and Lea and Vince enjoy sharing the fine collection of Indian artifacts with inn guests.

The long picnic table in the dining-kitchen area is a cozy place for guests to sit, play cards, visit. Breakfast here is of great Southwestern cuisine, dishes like Sipapu Strata (an egg dish with chilies and garlic), herbed potatoes (herbs from Lea's herb garden), blue corn chips, sweet breads and rolls, three or four fresh fruits from nearby orchards, two kinds of juice, tea and coffee.

The Kopavi Room is named for a classic Hopi figure, a sort of hump-backed flute player. The cool blue and white room contains a mask of a young warrior. The Nishoni Room is named for a goat!— and the name means "I am beautiful." Not to worry, the goat is not alive. "She's a good girl," Lea says of the silky small decorative figure.

The Pueblo Room is full of family relics, work by Vince, and collectibles amassed by Lea, who likes to look around for old things. Vince made the Hopi ceremonial objects in this room, as well as planting pennies and dimes in the bathroom floor when he installed the tile. The dates on the coins are the year Lea was born. "I told Vince he could do what he wanted in this room, and this is what he did." I think she's pretty pleased by his whimsy. The Wrangler Room is newly remodeled with old Western cowboy relics and memorabilia from Lea's Arizona roots. "Vince's artistic decor is obvious throughout this 'real West' guest room, too," Lea reports with delight.

The Kachina Room, named for a painting of the little gods, has its own private sun deck. The huge living room downstairs has a wonderful rock fireplace, cozy sofas, and a museum display case of artifacts. "Anything here 150 years old or younger was bought by Vince," Lea explains. "Anything older is what Grandad got." The room opens onto a deck facing a pleasant wooded area.

How to get there: From Highway 89A west of town, turn north onto Dry Creek Road; turn right about 1 long city block to Kachina, turn left and drive about .4 mile to white arrow on tree saying PIKI. Turn left onto Piki; the second house on the left is Sipapu Lodge.

A Touch of Sedona
Sedona, Arizona
86336

Innkeepers: Doris and Dick Stevenson
Address/Telephone: 595 Jordan Road; (602) 282–6462
Rooms: 4; all with private bath. No smoking inn.
Rates: $85 to $95, double, EPB.
Open: All year.
Facilities and activities: Exercise room with treadmill, Arctic track, exercycle.
    Nearby: downtown shops and restaurants 6 blocks away.

Doris Stevenson has taken advantage of the Sedona art scene and decorated the inn with the work of other artists as well as her own. "I've joined a 'dumb bunny' art class," she says, by which I think she means one for amateurs. She calls herself an oil-painting novice, but she has been sculpting and doing stained glass for years.

While Doris is artistic, Dick is musical. The Stevensons have been Sedona residents for several years, and Dick plays with the Rim Country Band. The pair are also avid motorcyclists and have traveled the roads of the United States and Canada on their wheels.

The Stevensons are from Florida; they retired early, and after traveling all over, they decided they would like to try innkeeping. With breakfast, Doris says, they bend over backwards, never repeating the menu for five days. Variations include German pancakes, Hawaiian bananas, blue corn pancakes, frittata with cheese, and blintz soufflé. These are served with baked pineapple and granola, raisin bread, or apple-wheat muffins. The Stevensons grind their own flour.

There is a television in the common room, and kaleidoscopes to play with. A small kitchen adjoining is available for travelers to heat take-out food in the microwave oven. There are dishes, but no pots and pans: "We discourage cooking," Doris says.

The inn's Contemporary Eagle Room earned its name because of the purple eagle painted on the wall. The Kachina Room has paintings of Indian figures. The Roadrunner Room sports curtains that Doris painted to match the rest of the decor. The Hummingbird Room also has art, and the entire inn is decorated with stained glass lamps and antiques mixed with contemporary furnishings. Colors are Southwestern in feeling: sand tones, beiges, aqua. Scents are of pine and lavender.

It's just a few blocks to fine restaurants and to Tlaquepaque, some forty shops specializing in art, fine jewelry, and other treasures. Sedona is fabulous red rock country, and the scenery is magnificent.

How to get there: Driving west into Sedona on Highway 89A, just past the Midgley Bridge turn north (right) at the third street, which is Jordan. Go north to 595.

Strawberry Lodge
Strawberry, Arizona
85544

Innkeeper: Jean Turner

Address/Telephone: HCR 1, Box 331; (602) 476–3333

Rooms: 12; all with private bath; wheelchair accessible; no air conditioning (elevation 6,000 feet). Pets permitted.

Rates: $40, double, ground floor; $48 to $50, upstairs with fireplaces; EP. No credit cards.

Open: All year.

Facilities and activities: Restaurant, barbecue patio. Nearby: gateway to the Mongollon Ridge with fishing, hunting, horseback riding, hiking, scenic attractions.

I knew this was a happy place the minute I walked in the door. If it hadn't been the vibrations telling me so, it would have been the happy voices in the crowded restaurant, which is where everybody enters the lodge, although there's a perfectly good entrance to the inn lounge.

The restaurant is packed all the time. "This is the best meal I've had since I left home," customers constantly tell Jean. The "coffee klatch table" next to the fire is filled with regulars, and their wives join them at 3:00 p.m. They're always sold out of the Saturday night prime rib and apple pie. "We have never compromised on quality," Jean says firmly.

Many wonderful things have been added to the menu, "most

of them 'healthy,'" Jean says. "Lower fat—broiled, vegetarian dish-es—we are trying to cater to our health-conscious customers!" But don't worry, she is still making her super homemade pies and still serving great prime rib on Saturday nights; also specialties like Mex-ican food on Monday and barbecued ribs on Wednesday, and if you're interested, you had better make a reservation. Otherwise, lots of other people will get there before you!

Back when Jean's children were small and her husband, Richard, was alive, the family drove through Strawberry on a holiday.

"Oh," she said with her wonderful enthusiasm, "Wouldn't this be a heavenly place to live!" It seemed like fate when later on they saw "a little two-line squib about a hunting lodge for sale" in that very place. Richard was a Zane Grey fan (Grey wrote about the Mongollon Rim area) and that cinched it: They became innkeepers. Now Jean runs the inn herself, and she is doing a grand job of it.

The lodge was so neglected it was a big challenge. "My hus-band, who had never built a thing in his life, built all the fireplaces and did all the woodwork." Each of the newer guest rooms has a real wood-burning one, and each is different. Richard used all native materials in remodeling the inn, learning how to do it him-self. Rooms are rustic but warm and comfortable, with wood-pan-eled walls and nice touches like coordinated print wallpaper in the bathrooms.

The entire family pitched in to make the inn the great place that it is. As a Christmas present for her folks one year, daughter Cindy made a set of hand-carved tiles for each shower.

For her part, Jean learned how to cook for crowds. "I was known for my piecrusts, but not in such quantity!" she says with a laugh. "Some people go through life with talents they never devel-op. I'd never cooked for anyone but my family, so it was a traumat-ic thing for me." Now the lodge is famous for her pies as well as all the other good food.

I was dying to know how the town got its name. "The original settlers found this whole valley a mass of wild strawberries—at least that's the story," Jean says. Now the only strawberries are at happy Strawberry Lodge.

How to get there: Strawberry is on Highway 87, and the inn will be on your left just as you drive into the town from the south.

El Presidio Inn
Tucson, Arizona
85701

Innkeepers: Patty and Jerry Toci
Address/Telephone: 297 North Main Avenue; (602) 623–6151
Rooms: 4; all with private bath, phone, and TV. No smoking inn.
Rates: $55 to $90, single; $65 to $105, double; EPB. Weekly and monthly rates available. No credit cards.
Open: All year.
Facilities and activities: Courtyard garden. Nearby: restaurants, historic district, Sonora Desert Museum, Old Town Artisans handicrafts.

Patty is strongly dedicated to two things. The first is the landmark historic district that surrounds the El Presidio Inn. The second, in my opinion, is the marvelous food she serves her guests.

The Tocis have won several awards for their restoration of the old property. "My focus," Patty says, "is this landmark historical property and the entire district. This is where Tucson began, at El Presidio, when Tucson was a walled city to protect the settlers from Apache Indians."

The delightful Territorial Victorian adobe building looks deceptively small. Built on a corner, it hides a large back courtyard—the pride of Patty and Jerry's gardening talents, centered with a fountain Jerry found in Mexico and shaded with a huge magnolia that provides greens for Christmas celebrations.

"I'm a good old Southern girl," Patty says. "We always had

magnolia greens back home for Christmas, and when old friends visit us here, they can't believe our big magnolia, growing right here in Tucson, Arizona!"

Breakfasts on the glassed-in sun porch are leisurely feasts, so don't be in a hurry. Patty says she has so many repeat guests that she makes notes on what she fed them last. The long table is beautifully appointed. On my visit we began with fresh orange juice, then progressed to a magnificent fruit cup of kiwi, strawberry, orange, pineapple, and cantaloupe. Next came two kinds of French toast, one made of cinnamony raisin bread, the other stuffed with homemade peanut butter and bananas. Canadian bacon came with this, and yet I really could not resist having two of the lemon nut muffins topped with streusel. Like every good cook, Patty was pleased as punch to see me stuff myself!

"The recipe for the lemon muffins isn't original with me," she says. "But the streusel topping is." She puts her happy touch on everything. Guest rooms are provided with fruit, juice, coffee, teas, and snacks. There are bathrobes to wrap up in. The Victorian Suite, with a huge sitting room furnished in cool white wicker, has a photograph of Patty's grandmother setting the period mood. The Carriage Suite combines an Eastlake lady's desk with a collection of Southwest antiques, including a trunk that held a pioneer's goods. The Gatehouse Suite has Bar Harbor–style wicker furniture. The Zaugan Room, the lovely common room, has a tile fireplace, wreaths of fragrant dried flowers, books to read, and current magazines providing information on the best of Tucson. "We've been living here long enough to know the best things to do," the Tocis say. "The Mexican and craft festivals here in our neighborhood during spring, summer, and fall have become grand affairs."

How to get there: From I-10 take the St. Mary's exit and go right 4 blocks to Granada. Turn south, and after you cross the railroad tracks Granada changes to Main Avenue. Go 1 block past the traffic light and turn right into West Franklin. The inn is on the corner of Main and West Franklin. Curbside parking is permitted if you get a permit from Patty to put on your windshield.

La Posada del Valle
Tucson, Arizona
85719

Innkeepers: Debbi and Charles Bryant
Address/Telephone: 1640 Campbell Avenue; (602) 795–3840
Rooms: 5; all with private bath, 2 with phone. No smoking inn.
Rates: $87.50 to $110, double, EPB.
Open: All year.
Facilities and activities: Lunch and dinner catered by reservation, bicycles, patio. Nearby: restaurants, Sonora Desert Museum, art and photography museums, Old Town Artisans handicrafts.

La Posada del Valle occupies a lovely villa designed in 1929 by a renowned Tucson architect, Josias T. Joesler. Built of adobe and stucco, the inn is a perfect example of early Santa Fe–style architecture moving westward.

"We love to stay in bed and breakfast places ourselves," Debbi says, "and after we took a trip to California several years ago, we just fell in love with the idea. Tucson had none, and it took us two and a half years to open the inn, but by George, we did it!"

The patio is lovely, with a fountain and ornamental orange trees. The trees were planted by nuns from a nearby church who lived in the house a while back. But I doubt the nuns would recognize it now, divided as it is into Pola's Room, Isadora's Room, Claudette's Room, Sophie's Room, and Zelda's Room. All have private entrances.

"We picked out names of women who were popular back when the house was built, carrying out the twenties and thirties theme." Each room has black-and-white still photographs of the actresses and the dancers. Fresh flowers from the gardens make each room fragrant, and Debbi and Charles provide personal touches such as turned-down beds, freshened rooms, and candy and mints. There's a menu basket in the living room; the innkeepers make a point of helping with guests' plans and reservations for dinner.

It's delightful to sit out under the orange trees and breathe in their fragrance. The oranges there are not for eating, alas, but grapefruit and lemons from inn trees are served. Breakfast might be cream cheese blintzes with raspberries, and there are always home-baked bread, muffins, and coffee cakes.

Debbi has a helper, Pattie Bell, whom she claims as her "right arm." But, she adds, "We make Charles fix breakfast on Saturday mornings." Not to worry: he fixes Eggs a la Charles, "something he made up, and it's delicious!"

Afternoon tea, with the beverage either hot or cold, is served with cookies, fancy bread, and butter scones in a living room appointed with fine art deco furnishings from the 1920s and '30s. "At teatime we either mingle with the guests or leave them alone," Pattie says, sensitive to the prevailing mood.

Charles is a hospital administrator and Debbi was a homemaker. "But I never knew what I *really* wanted to do until I fell into this. Then I found my calling!"

How to get there: From I–10 take Speedway Boulevard exit and go east on Speedway to Campbell Avenue. Take Campbell north to Elm Street. The inn is on the corner of Campbell and Elm; the inn entrance is on Campbell, but there is guest parking at the side of the inn on Elm.

The Suncatcher
Tucson, Arizona
85748

Innkeeper: David Williams
Address/Telephone: 105 North Avenida Javelina; (602) 885–0883 or (800) 835–8012
Rooms: 4; all with private bath, phone, TV, and VCR; wheelchair accessible. No smoking inn.
Rates: $110 to $130, double; $25 extra person; EPB.
Open: All year.
Facilities and activities: Heated pool and spa, bicycle. Nearby: restaurants, tennis and health club, hiking, horseback riding, Saguaro National Monument.

"I've tried to take all the qualities of a first-class hotel and put in the charm of a bed and breakfast," Dave says of his luxurious inn. A sure clue is each guest-room name: There's the Connaught, the Four Seasons, the Regent, and the Oriental. With the hotels as his inspiration, Dave gave up his law practice to become an innkeeper.

"I was traveling a lot and I was ready for a change," he says. "I began thinking about other things I could do." Now Dave likes to open the door wide and call, "Welcome to The Suncatcher!" He was pleased with my delighted reaction, which was just what he has learned to expect.

"I see the guests' eyes open," he says, "and it's such a pleasure.

As for the name, The Suncatcher, why do people come to Tucson?" he asks. "The sun, the dry heat, the desert," he answers himself. "And I thought, what do I want my place to be? A retreat, a get-away—so I invented the name." Dave also created the inn emblem, little terra-cotta faces that are on the walls and elsewhere.

The huge common area (70 x 70 feet) with its soaring ceiling has several focal points. In one corner there's a large copper-hooded fireplace; in another, a mirrored mesquite bar. A centerpiece is the grand piano that Dave's parents bought for him when he was fifteen. "I play a little," he says modestly; he'd rather encourage guests to entertain. Display cases contain many personal treasures he collected on his travels.

The room is done so well I assumed it was decorated by a professional—it would make a beautiful spread in a fashionable home-decorating magazine. "But," says Dave, "I did it all myself, and I'm pretty proud of that." The entire area—sitting, dining, kitchen—is open, and you can watch the chef prepare breakfast, beginning with grapefruit halves, juices and coffee, on to cold cereals, egg strata, bagels, and honey-date muffins. "I always ask the night before what time you'd like breakfast," he tells me, which I think is pretty accommodating. Any time is fine, and late in the day there are complimentary hors d'oeuvres. "My pleasure is sitting down and speaking with my guests," Dave says.

One guest room opens off the huge airy and spacious common area, two have French doors opening off the pool, and the fourth is around the corner with its own entrance.

The Connaught (London) is furnished with Chippendale-styled furniture in gleaming dark mahogany; the Four Seasons with a formal canopied bed; the Regent (Hong Kong) has lovely original oriental scrolls, and the Oriental (Bangkok), the largest, has among its other splendors its own Jacuzzi. All have at least one comfortable chair, writing desks, original artwork, and fresh flowers.

How to get there: The inn is on the edge of Saguaro National Monument. From I-10 and downtown Tucson, take Broadway east, crossing as a last landmark Houghton. Continue on to Avenida Javelina, bearing in mind that Avenida Javelina is beyond the DEAD-END sign on Broadway. Turn north on Javelina, and the inn will be on the left in the middle of the block.

Key Bar El Ranch
Wickenburg, Arizona
85358

Innkeeper: Jane Nash
Address/Telephone: Box 2480; (602) 684–7593
Rooms: 10; all with private bath; no air conditioning (elevation 2,093 feet).
Rates: $95, single; $175, double; children 2 through 6 $30, 7 through 12 $45; AP. Weekly and monthly rates available; two-day minimum stay, four-day minimum holidays.
Open: Mid-October to May 1.
Facilities and activities: Swimming pool, horseback riding, and yard games. Nearby: hiking, bird watching, tennis, golf, museums, art galleries, Western and jewelry stores in nearby Wickenburg; local festivals.

"We don't have sophisticated pursuits—this is a dude ranch," Jane says. "About the most excitement we generate in the evenings is a hot game of Trivial Pursuit. This is not a big nightlife place, and that's the way we like it!" The fireplace blazes almost every night in the lounge—or the "Great Hall" as one guest calls it—and everybody relaxes with books, magazines, television, or the piano in the huge but homey room.

Sometimes there are dances and cookouts. Mostly, though, there's horseback riding, swimming, loafing—and eating. "We're known for our food," Jane says. Chef Jackie Brown has been written up in *Gourmet* magazine. "We have only one seating for each meal, and when we ring the bell they better show up—and believe me, they do!"

Dinner the day I was there was mouth-watering: chicken breasts with cream wine sauce and artichokes, mixed wild and white rice, and famous Kay Bar El pie, a citrus chiffon confection. Hardly the stuff of chuckwagons fare! When the inn has just a small group of guests, they like to eat in the staff dining room, watching the birds outside and smelling the good cooking smells.

"We've tried to get everybody to sleep late on Sunday mornings," Jane confesses, "but they're here at seven, their noses pressed against the door!"

The ranch's adobe buildings cluster in a little valley along the Hassayampa River. Low hills lead to scenic trails under cloudless cerulean sky. The ranch is the second-oldest dude ranch in the state, the oldest in the neighborhood; it has been here more than eighty years. It's a family operation, down to the Western motifs appliqued on all the towels, done by Jane's sister Jan Martin. Even the linens are printed with a Western scene, and furniture is original Western furniture from Monterey, California, circa 1920.

"Periodically we have guest 'rodeos' we call 'dudeos,'" Jane says. "We get together with other ranchers in town for these and other special events,"—things like the Gold Rush Days in February, the Bluegrass Festival in November, the Cowboy Poetry Gathering in December—"A good time is had by all," says Jane.

There's a huge salt cedar tree out on the grounds, and the largest saguaro cactus I've ever seen. Jane says it's three hundred years old. Often there are golden dogs on the grounds, too. "We raise golden retrievers and periodically we have puppies. Kittens, too." You'll even see a pet cow, given to a staff member by an inn guest. "It depends what kind of mood she's in," Jane says, "whether or not she'll come up and talk to guests."

How to get there: Turn right off Highway 60 to Highway 89/93 at the only stoplight in Wickenburg. The ranch will be on your right 2 miles north. There's a sign that leads down the unpaved road to the entrance.

Canyon Country Inn
Williams, Arizona
86046

Innkeepers: Sue and John Einolander
Address/Telephone: 442 West Bill Williams Avenue; (602) 635–2349
Rooms: 9, plus 1 cottage; all with private bath, phone, and TV; cottage with
 wheelchair access. No smoking inn.
Rates: $25 to $65, double, winter; $35 to $75, double, summer; continental
 breakfast.
Open: All year.
Facilities and activities: Nearby: small town with walking map of shops and
 restaurants; Grand Canyon, Grand Canyon Railway, Grand Canyon
 Helicopter tours, 9-hole golf course, hiking, hunting, fishing, skiing.

If it's an inn you want, the Canyon Country Inn is the closest
place to the Grand Canyon you can find. Don't be put off by the
large motel sign on the end of the building; there's a reason for
that.

"We wanted a country inn, not a motel," Sue says of the building they constructed to replace a defunct motel, and they built a
Colonial-style frame house right in the center of Williams. "But as
soon as we opened, all the motels in town tacked 'inn' onto their
names, so we had to add 'motel' in self-defense." (She's pleased,
however, that they've earned a prestigious "motel" rating.)

Although the entry is small, coffee and tea are waiting for the traveler, and the innkeepers greet you warmly. Up the stairs on the right is a cozy sitting room, and the guest rooms off the sitting room are almost master-suite size. The many windows under the eaves make for nice, bright space, and rooms have flowered carpet and spreads or pale rose carpets and patchwork spreads; all are different. Sue has worked hard to create what she hopes is a "romantic, charming, and elegant country inn." She and John are from California, where they remodeled houses *and* inns, so she had definite ideas about what she wanted to do.

Two things are in particular abundance; teddy bears and intriguing lamps. "I like teddy bears," she confesses, as though it weren't apparent! "I used to make them myself, before I got so busy," she adds with a laugh. "But now I get homemade ones from a lady in town." She also collects antique lamps. One in particular, in a small upstairs sitting area, caught my eye: It was a cherub half covered with a gold silk lampshade dripping with long, black fringe.

While the upstairs rooms have the most ambience, the smaller downstairs ones, with outside entrances along the long porches running the building's length both front and back, reveal careful attention, too. Beds are comfortable pine copies of antiques, and the rooms, mostly with a color scheme of soft rose and blue, have decorator touches such as decorative wallpaper moldings along the ceilings. A great deal of thought has gone into the decorative wallpapers, towels and linens, comforters and spreads, satin clothes hangers, ceiling fans, and lace curtains that make Canyon Country Inn a cozy hideaway in this rural area of northern Arizona.

Breakfast, what Sue likes to call "a beary special continental," is brought to your door. Coffee, tea, fresh juice, and warm homemade muffins can be eaten in your room or in the small common room at the head of the stairs.

How to get there: From I–40 take Highway 64 south to Bill Williams Avenue, which is one-way running east. If you're coming from the east (Flagstaff), you'll have to turn right and go west on Railroad Avenue instead, turning south at 5th Street. The inn is on the corner of West Bill Williams and 5th.

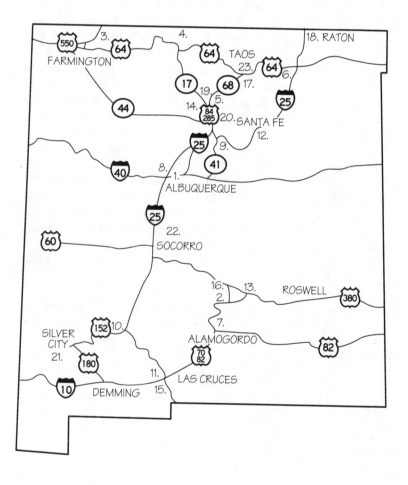

ARIZONA NEW MEXICO

TEXAS

550
3. 64
FARMINGTON

4.

64 TAOS
23. 64
6.

18. RATON

17 19 68 17.
14. 5.
84 20. SANTA FE
285
12.

44

25 9.
40 8. 41
1.
ALBUQUERQUE

25

22.
60 SOCORRO

16. 13. ROSWELL
2. 380
7.

152 10.
SILVER
CITY
21. 180

ALAMOGORDO
70 82
82

11. LAS CRUCES
10 DEMMING 15.

New Mexico

Numbers on map refer to towns numbered below.

Adobe and Roses
Albuquerque, New Mexico
87114

Innkeeper: Dorothy Morse

Address/Telephone: 1011 Ortega NW; (505) 898–0654

Rooms: 3, including 1 suite; all with private bath, kitchen, fireplace, private entrance, phone, and TV. Pets at discretion of innkeeper. No smoking inn.

Rates: $50 to $65, double; $75, suite (1 to 2 guests, $5 each additional person); EPB. $10 surcharge for single-night stay, discount for six or more days. No credit cards.

Open: All year.

Facilities and activities: Laundry facilities, tennis court, handball court, barbecue grill. Nearby: tennis courts and handball, Indian Pueblo Cultural Center, Albuquerque Old Town.

Adobe and Roses is tucked away in a corner of Albuquerque you could never find without directions. That's because Dorothy is a horse person and she wants to be out where there's a lot of room, which makes the inn peaceful and private. She boards horses, and although you can't ride them, you can enjoy watching them.

"People from an urban area, especially, really like seeing the horses out the window," she says. "I used to ride seriously; I tried out for the Olympic team in the sixties. Didn't make it," she adds with a laugh. Now she's a fan of contemporary crafts as well as a booster of local cultural affairs with strong connections with the Albuquerque Symphony. She has musical evenings, which guests as a matter of course are invited to join.

Innkeeping, says Dorothy, suits her personality. "I always have liked having guests—interesting, adventurous people who are fun to talk to." Even before she went in for innkeeping, she had the suite built for house guests "so they wouldn't feel in the way." She goes all out, especially for honeymooners in the suite. "I get out my Limoges, I use table linens, crystal, when people have a really big do."

Busy, energetic, Dorothy is a whirlwind at improving the property she has lived in for more than thirty years. In addition to gardening (her brother is a horticulturist, and her garden reflects his expert advice), she laid the adobes and tile for the two guest rooms housed in a separate building, built the small ponds with water lilies and goldfish, and created the rock garden. She planned it, she says, "so that from every room you will look at something wonderful." At sunset the Sandia Mountains in the distance turn to pink; closer in, the lily ponds reflect the sinking sun and the towering cottonwood trees.

"I want people to feel comfortable, to be at home. I don't know," Dorothy says with a laugh, "maybe I get a lot of ego satisfaction from it."

Rooms have fresh flowers; a bowl of fruit and a plate of homemade cookies waits; in the suite a dart board hangs on the wall and there's a piano. Since nights at 5,000 feet are chilly, down comforters and pillows are on the beds.

Breakfast, served in the main house family room or out on the portal of the guest house, might be Dutch baby, a giant popover with powdered sugar and lemon juice (my mother used to call it a German pancake) along with strawberries and bananas in whipped cream, a heavenly delight.

How to get there: Take Rio Grande exit off I–40 west; go north on Rio Grande 6 miles to Ortega Road; turn right on Ortega for approximately .4 mile until you see a blue mailbox on the right side of the road with 1011 on it. The inn is to the left. Dorothy likes to keep a low profile, so there is no sign.

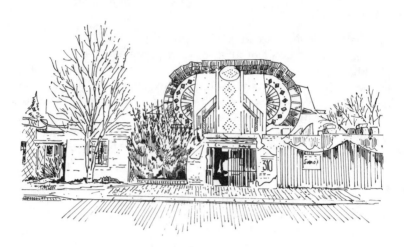

Casas de Sueños
Albuquerque, New Mexico
87104

Innkeepers: Robert Hanna and Mari Penshurst-Gersten
Address/Telephone: 310 Rio Grande SW; (505) 247–4560 or (800) 242–8987
Rooms: 12 casitas; all with private bath, phone, and TV; 1 with wheelchair access. No smoking inn.
Rates: $66 to $225, double, seasonal; $15 extra person; EPB.
Open: All year.
Facilities and activities: Dinner by reservation. Nearby: Old Town Plaza with restaurants, shops, and galleries; health club, museums, zoo, festivals, golf, swimming, horseback riding, longest aerial tram in North America.

Be prepared for a wild surprise when you drive up to this adobe inn. Above the entrance gates looms a most unusual structure, added to the inn in 1976 by Albuquerque's famous artist Bart Prince. "I tried to call it the Nautilus, but our neighbors call it 'the snail,'" Robert says. "People become different in that space." Robert, who sold his law practice to become a full-time innkeeper, adds: "When you're in it, there's no contention, no divorces. People let go of their preconceptions."

Nautilus or snail, whatever you call it, it's a fascinating structure, and I wasn't surprised to hear that people come knocking on the door to ask, "What *is* that thing?" Just as fantastic inside as it is out, it's entered by a spiral staircase, and it serves as a lounge, as well as a television and meeting room. The view of nearby mountains is impressive from any of the amazing structure's three levels.

You'd think it would be hard for the rest of the inn to live up to such an introduction, but not so. These "houses of dreams" (Casas de Sueños) were built in the 1930s by artist J. R. Willis, growing into a cluster of small casitas around a huge old elm in the courtyard. "To support his painting, Willis kept building these casitas to rent to friends," Robert says. Today the innkeepers have turned them into a delightful collection of suites, each one unique.

Guest rooms are furnished with antiques, heirlooms, art, oriental and Indian rugs, goosedown comforters, bath amenities, and luxurious towels; some have kitchens, and most have fireplaces as well as adjoining sitting rooms and outdoor garden areas. Cascada even has its own waterfall. The Cupid Suite has a skylight; the Georgia O'Keeffe Suite features reproductions of her work; the Rose Room blends the romance of yesteryear with the comfort of today; Route 66 Suite is so named because it's just 1 block off the famous highway. (That's why the rate remains $66, too! even though other room rates may increase in time.) But I won't tell everything; I'll let you make discoveries for yourself.

The dining room was the artist's studio, and the large northern wall of windows faces the gardens. There's always coffee, tea, and cake on hand, and breakfast is a buffet of gourmet coffee and tea, fresh fruit, cereal, yogurt, and a specialty such as decadent French toast with fresh fruit sauce, or perhaps a Southwest dish. "You can stay a week and never have a repeat, and we always accommodate special dietary requests," helper Shay Tindall says, as she serves late-afternoon guests moist poppyseed cake crunchy with Brazil nuts, along with their coffee.

The inn often hosts public receptions for visitors to the local university, and since inn guests are welcome to attend, it's a real treat to stay here. "Lots of buildings need to be held up," Robert says. "This is the first that needs to be held down!"

How to get there: From I–40 west take Rio Grande exit south toward Old Town. Cross Mountain Road and Central Avenue and go 2 more blocks. The inn will be on the left, facing the Albuquerque Country Club Golf Course.

Casita Chamisa
Albuquerque, New Mexico
87107

Innkeepers: Kit and Arnold Sargeant
Address/Telephone: 850 Chamisal Road NW; (505) 897–4644
Rooms: 3; 1 in main house with private bath, 2 in guest house with shared
  bath (rented to one party at a time). Pets permitted. No smoking inn.
Rates: $60 to $100, per room, EPB.
Open: All year except November.
Facilities and activities: Indoor swimming pool, hot tub, archaeological site
  under and around the inn. Nearby: Old Town Plaza, Albuquerque
  Museum, and Indian Cultural Center 15-minute drive away.

Two things are particularly fascinating about Casita Chamisa.
One is the fact that Kit is an archaeologist and has been in charge of
Indian digs right on the inn property, sponsored by the Maxwell
Museum of Anthropology of the University of New Mexico. The
other is that Arnold makes sourdough bread from a starter that's
more than one hundred years old! Kit will take you on a tour of the
site and tell about the "ancient ones" who lived here more than
seven hundred years ago, and Arnold will serve you his delicious
bread.

Toasted for breakfast, the bread is a treat, or perhaps you'll
have sourdough crepes filled with apricots and almonds. Served
with lots of fresh fruit—melon, grapes, strawberries, depending
upon what's in season—the sourdough starts the day out right, just

as it did for a Basque shepherd in Idaho long ago.

If you arrive in the early afternoon, you'll be offered iced or hot tea; if in the evening, possibly a glass of wine. "It depends upon whether people are rushing off or not," Kit said. The Sargeants spend a lot of time enjoying their guests; they make dinner reservations for them and "sort of steer them around making sure they are happy," Kit said. "I've had people call from New York and say, 'I'm coming for ten days. What shall I do while I'm there?'" For one thing, in the Albuquerque Museum in Old Town, you'll see arms and armor used during the Spanish conquest, and in the New Mexico Museum of Natural History there's a journey through the life and death of dinosaurs. She often recommends nearby restaurants for dinner: "Four good restaurants serving Mexican food are only a few minutes away," Kit says. "We like Casa Benevidas, which is small and has strolling guitarists. Casa Vieja serves northern Italian and French cuisine in a lovely old Spanish house, and the Maria Teresa is located in another handsome nineteenth-century house."

The large guest room in the main house, a nineteenth-century adobe casa, has a private entry, a Mexican tile floor, a viga ceiling, and a corner fireplace. The guest house is also complete with fireplace and has a kitchenette. Most unusual is the plant-filled greenhouse porch opening off one of the two bedrooms.

How to get there: From south, east, or west, take Rio Grande Boulevard exit off I-40. Go 5 miles north to Chamisal Road. Turn right on Chamisal Road, and the inn will be on your right shortly—there's a small blue sign, so keep a sharp lookout.

The W. E. Mauger Estate
Albuquerque, New Mexico
87102

Innkeepers: Chuck Silver and Brian Miller
Address/Telephone: 701 Roma Avenue, NW; (505) 242–8755
Rooms: 6; all with private bath. Pets permitted.
Rates: $55 to $75, single; $69 to $89, double; EPB.
Open: All year.
Facilities and activities: Nearby: historic old town, Indian Pueblo Museum, Rio Grande Zoo, museums, restaurants, shopping, Sandia Peak Tramway to Sandia Peak and the ski area.

The Mauger (pronounced "Major") Residence has been on the National Register of Historic Places since 1985. The inn, once an old boardinghouse, won a blue ribbon for elegant restoration from the local board of Realtors. Now the new owners are carrying on the inn's aim of "offering comfortable Victorian accommodations for sixteen souls in a style reminiscent of an era when graciousness, thoughtfulness, and elegance were a way of life."

The Queen Anne house was built in 1897, for the whopping sum of $1,600, by the daughter of a local tavern owner. An unhappy marriage sent her into the arms of a New Yorker, and she left the house to be sold to William and Brittania Mauger, who were in the wool business. The Wool Room, on the second floor, was the business office.

There are three other guest rooms on the second floor. The

66

Brittania, the original master bedroom, has three windows overlooking downtown and the beautiful Sandia Mountains. The Boston Sleeper was a screened sleeping porch for summer dog days—now it's all glassed in with an additional room for use as a suite. The Tuers Room was a bedroom/sewing room, and it too has a fine mountain view, as well as morning sun.

Upstairs on the third floor, the Graystone is a spacious two-bedroom attic suite, presenting an interesting and surprising contrast to the nostalgic Victoriana below. The two rooms are furnished in an almost art deco style, with color schemes of pink and gray and pink and black and wild print linens to match.

The inn is cozy, with lace curtains in the windows, and there are green plants in the breakfast room. Chuck does wonderful soufflés, crab or spinach being specialties. Also delicious is an omelet with cilantro, green chilies, and tomato. Add fresh home-baked scones, a fruit dish such as fruit of the season served with yogurt and granola, orange juice, and coffee, and you're more than set for the day!

Chelsea, a blond cocker spaniel, lives primarily in the back of the inn with her owners, but if you want her, she's delighted to be friendly.

How to get there: From I-25 take the Grand Street exit west to 7th Street. Turn right on 7th 1 block to Roma, and the inn is on the northwest corner.

Sierra Mesa Lodge
Alto, New Mexico
88312

Innkeepers: Lila and Larry Goodman
Address/Telephone: Fort Stanton Road (mailing address: P.O. Box 463); (505)
  336–4515
Rooms: 5; all with private bath; no air conditioning (elevation 7,000 feet).
  No smoking inn.
Rates: $75, single; $85, double; EPB and high tea.
Open: All year.
Facilities and activities: Indoor spa, games, murder mystery weekend. Nearby:
  skiing, horseback riding, fishing in Alto Lake, Ruidoso Downs race
  track and golf, hiking trails in Lincoln National Forest, restaurants in
  Ruidoso.

   "We'd been planning this for thirteen years," Lila says of the
bright blue-and-white inn high above the Sierra Blanca range of
New Mexico, just north of Ruidoso. "Larry took early retirement,
and we thought of emigrating to New Zealand; we checked out the
Caribbean; we went all over the world." When they saw this area,
they were hooked. Larry wanted to build a small hotel, but Lila
argued that "meeting people is what an inn is all about."
   She enjoys her guests; she says it's like having family in the
home. "We play cards, dominoes with our guests; we're good
friends by the time they leave." If the guests want television,
they're banished upstairs to the television room, where there's a

telescope, too. "We want them to visit, we don't want the television turned on; that's the end of the conversation," she says with a laugh.

Lila has two hobbies: cooking—and making delicate porcelain dolls. Each guest room has an occupant, a china doll that she created from scratch. "I walked into a paint store for some paint and a woman was demonstrating doll making. Just like that I was lost!"

Guest rooms are individually decorated with flair. The mirrored black enamel queen bed in the Oriental Room is an eye-catcher, and the other authentic oriental pieces are outstanding, too. A magnificently embroidered oriental marriage robe hangs on the wall.

Each room has a window seat, but otherwise variety reigns. There are the Victorian, French Country, Country Western, and Queen Anne rooms, each ruled over by one of Lila's dolls. Comforters, goose down pillows, kimonos, rockers, and chaise longues may spoil you rotten.

So will the food, Lila's and Larry's other area of expertise. For breakfast you are at the mercy of the cook, but not to worry—you'll manage to live through waffles, quiches, poppyseed bread, fruit parfait with honey and sour cream, perhaps Lila's blintz soufflé. Lila will even pamper you with breakfast in bed.

Afternoon tea means a special chocolate bread with cream cheese, peanut-butter cream pie, chocolate streusel. Evenings guests gather around the cheery fire for wine and cheese and good conversation. If you don't object, Magnum, the big black and friendly mix of a dog, will join you.

The lodge is now offering exciting Murder Mystery weekends if you get five friendly couples together for two evenings of fun and fine food: breakfast, afternoon tea, dinner, and late-night wine and cheese.

How to get there: Take Highway 48 north from Ruidoso approximately 6 miles to Fort Stanton Road on your right. Keep to the left at the fork in the road and you'll find the inn on your left about 2 miles down the road. There is a sign.

The Aztec Residence Hotel
Aztec, New Mexico
87410

Innkeepers: Vicki and Rick Clark
Address/Telephone: 300 South Main Street; (505) 334–3452
Rooms: 9; all with private bath and TV, 5 with kitchenette.
Rates: $65 to $85, double, EP. No credit cards.
Open: All year.
Facilities and activities: Nearby: restaurants, festivals, Aztec and other ruins,
   Aztec Museum, fishing, boating on Navajo Lake 20 miles away, skiing.

This quaint little hotel sits on the main street of Aztec. There are thirty-eight Aztec buildings on the state Register of Historic Places; the town received a Main Street project grant in 1986.

The hotel's front door is an eye-catcher with stained glass panels, and the pine paneling in the reception hall is a nice touch. Each bedroom has a period brass bed or beds. There's a small lounge area upstairs, with books and magazines for guests to read.

Interesting to see are the photographs on the hall wall, showing the hotel during different eras. First, there is a surrey in front of the entrance; next, an early automobile. The inn's Abstract of Title is dated 1878, and the inn was built from 1905 to 1907.

Vicki and Rick came to this small town from Denver and Montana. "I needed more sunshine," Vicki says. "I like a small town." Aztec counts 5,006 residents and Vicki says that the six tacked on at the end are "old soreheads." The whole town turns out to bury Mr.

Gloom once a year; they drive him down Main Street, take him out to the fields, "and we've helped bury him," Vicki says delightfully. "This is a cute little town—we have parades all the time." The whole town turns out for Veterans Day and Founders Day, and you can sit on the front porch and watch the parades go by.

The Aztec Ruins, a national monument just minutes away, are a mystery. About A.D. 1106, Indians built one of the largest pre-Spanish pueblos, a massive 500-room apartment complex. No one knows why it was abandoned (about 1300), and fear of the ghosts of the "Old People" kept Navajos and Apaches away.

The inn does not serve any meals, but if you want to dine out (as opposed to cooking in your kitchenette), Vicki and Rick warmly recommend an international assortment of nearby restaurants. "There's the Chinese restaurant, the Mexican restaurant, and at the end of Main, the Aztec is a general restaurant and very popular."

Aztec's climate is beautiful all year round, with just two or three little snows. "It's all up in the mountains," the innkeepers assured me, which delights the skiers.

Two very happy fishermen were staying at the hotel when I was there. They come regularly for the fishing and were pleased to show me quite a catch, which they kept fresh for dinner in their kitchenette refrigerators.

How to get there: Highway 44 North becomes Main Street in Aztec. The inn will be on your right when you reach the 300 block.

Oso Ranch and Lodge
Chama, New Mexico
87520

Innkeepers: Martha and Bruce Peck
Address/Telephone: P.O. Box 808; (505) 756–2954
Rooms: 6; all with private bath and TV; wheelchair accessible; no air conditioning (high elevation).
Rates: Summer and fall: $50 single, $65 double, EP; $70 single, $85 double, EPB; $100 single, $150 double, AP. Winter: single or double, $45 EP, $65 EPB; $300 AP.
Open: All year.
Facilities and activities: Outdoor Jacuzzi, hunting, fishing, horseback riding, hiking, sailing, cross-country skiing, snowmobiling, overnight pack trips. Nearby: Cumbres & Toltec Scenic Railroad.

Ah, wilderness. Where the deer come down and feed at night. Where coyotes and eagles can be sighted. Where the mountain air is crisp and clear, the sky an incredible blue. Where snow-capped peaks and momentous sunsets are the norm.

"Right here you have the feeling of being isolated," say Martha and Bruce, "but we're only five minutes from town." Oso Ranch, 2 miles south of the small town of Chama, is a perfect place for sportsmen and nature lovers. The log lodge has a huge activities room with hunting trophies not only over the mantel but hanging from the rafters. The biggest trophies personify the inn's name. Oso means "bear" in Spanish, and there are several big stuffed ones in the room.

You'll find Western and Indian art, too, and a Western history library, as well as a piano, game and pool tables, and a wide-screen television. Some folks just like to relax around the big fireplace, and I don't blame them, particularly if they're waiting for a meal to begin. Served at tables at one end of the room is good wholesome food like rich pecan rolls with fried potatoes and ham and eggs for breakfast; homemade chili for lunch (or a packed lunch if you'll be out enjoying nature); and maybe roast beef, potato salad, carrots and corn, homemade bread, and banana pudding for a hearty dinner. Especially delicious is Martha's pull-apart Cinnamon Delight.

Six guest rooms are down a hall off the big room. Each door is completely covered with a scene made from colored leather, very unusual and very individual, making it easy to find which room is yours. Your room will be large and comfortable too, with twin or king beds and a mountain view from the window.

No license is required to fish in the ranch lakes, personally stocked with rainbow trout by the innkeepers. For a small fee you can have a lesson in fly fishing, if, like me, you've never done it before. Or you can fish for trout in the nearby Chama River. If you're lucky enough to catch something, Martha will fry it for your breakfast or dinner, whichever you'd like. Hunting? There's bear, cougar, elk, deer in the hills. Then it's back home to the warmth and welcome of Oso Lodge.

The village of Chama offers distinctive gift-shopping opportunities. Nearby Tierra Wools raise their own sheep and shear, dye, and spin the wool; and you can watch the weaver at work making unique woolen items. Adventure of a different kind happens on the Cumbres & Toltec Scenic Railroad, a spectacular steam-powered train that makes a round trip to Osier, Colorado, from mid-June through October.

How to get there: From Highway 84 turn west on Seco Drive (about 2 miles south of Chama). Drive ½ mile to the end, over the river, and up to the lodge.

Hacienda Rancho de Chimayo
Chimayo, New Mexico
87522

Innkeepers: Florence and Laura Jaramillo
Address/Telephone: P.O. Box 11; (505) 351–2222
Rooms: 7; all with private bath.
Rates: $54 to $81, double, continental breakfast.
Open: All year except January.
Facilities and activities: Restaurant (closed in January). Nearby: 1850s Church
 of Santuario, the "Lourdes of the U.S."; weavers' shops famous for
 rugs, jackets, cushions.

Chimayo is a very small town with an interesting history
bound up in Hacienda Rancho de Chimayo and in the Restaurante
Rancho de Chimayo, which serves native New Mexican cuisine just
across the road from the inn. Both establishments belong to a family that has lived in Chimayo since the 1700s and traces its roots to
the first Spanish settlers.

In the 1880s two brothers, Hermenegildo and Epifanio
Jaramillo, built family homes facing each other across the road.
Their descendants restored the homes, creating in 1965 the Restau-
rante Rancho de Chimayo in Hermenegildo's home and in 1984 the
Hacienda Rancho de Chimayo in the house that once belonged to
Epifanio and his wife, Adelaida. I found the sense of history here
intriguing.

The inn's rooms open off a walled courtyard with a sparkling fountain and bright flowers. The view is toward the mountains, and my room had the same view. French doors opened onto a little balcony, and that's where I had my simple continental breakfast, although I was tempted to join other guests in the courtyard. The restaurant is justly famous: Lunch was a small sopapilla (puffed slightly sweet Mexican roll) stuffed with chili and cheese, served with guacamole. For dinner I had *carne adovada* (pork marinated in chili), another specialty of the house. The inn now has a cookbook available if you want to try these delicious dishes yourself.

All guest rooms have fireplaces, and my very large room had twin mahogany beds forming a king-sized bed. At the foot was a taupe velvet sofa, a coffee table, and two wing chairs; every room has a similar area.

I appreciated such details as the pink linens, rose lace shower curtain, and old prints on the walls. It seemed just like home—or like home ought to be!

"We've traveled a lot in the States, and we always like to sit for a while in our room, perhaps have some wine and cheese and relax, before we go out to dinner," says Florence Jaramillo. There's wine in the kitchen of the office/lobby for whoever wants it, and a bottle of wine is placed in your room if you notify ahead of a special occasion.

Other evidences of thoughtfulness were the small cans of fruit juice I found in my room. Each room is practically a suite, there's so much space, and the antique furniture is well selected. I particularly admired my room's mahogany dressing table and the antique blanket stand holding a white woven afghan in case I got chilly. I asked Florence how they were lucky enough to have so many lovely pieces.

"We searched all of San Antonio, Austin, and Denver for our antiques!" Florence says. She and Laura have done a wonderful job, recreating the distinctive charm of the colonial New Mexico of their ancestors.

How to get there: From Highway 285 north of Santa Fe, take Highway 503 east 8 miles to Highway 520 north; continue for 3 miles to Chimayo. The highway runs right between the inn and the restaurant.

Casa del Gavilan
Cimarron, New Mexico
87714

Innkeepers: Harriet Faudree; Vern and Darren Sanchez
Address/Telephone: P.O. Box 518; (505) 376–2246 or (800) 445–5251
Rooms: 6; all with private bath, fan; air conditioning not needed (high elevation). No smoking inn.
Rates: $65 to $100, double; $20 extra person; EPB.
Open: All year.
Facilities and activities: Nearby: restaurants in Cimarron, historic and scenic drives, hiking, wildlife watching and hunting (turkey, elk, and brown bear), fishing, Kit Carson home in Rayado.

What a wonderful setting for this huge, rambling white house—the blue skies of New Mexico and a backdrop of scenic mountain splendor. Located on one of New Mexico's deserted highways, with nothing but nature all around, Casa del Gavilan seems like a mirage. "It was just sitting here, the family place," says owner Harriet Faudree, "and I decided to use it. I'm a widow, and I was just sitting here by myself; I decided to share it." The home was built in the early 1900s and has been in the Faudree family since 1970. All the wonderful furnishings are a result of Harriet's collecting. "A long time," she says with a laugh.

Gavilan means sparrow-hawk, but there are lots more wildlife around here than that. To my question about inn pets, the answer was "No—just our wild animals." There are deer, turkey, even brown bears; I wondered if they were the reason for all the ornamental bars on the windows. Chef Vera, who helps Harriet make guests welcome, laughs. "You feel pretty safe with the bars," she says. "Although if a bear came, I would probably faint." But of course she's joking.

But no, it's not the bears, it's the deer that might be called a problem—they eat all the flowers! When you come up the long curved drive to the porte cochere, you may be impressed by bright flowers crowding in pots and in the old wagon alongside the house; but sad to say, they aren't for real. Soon as the real things are planted, the deer come for a feast, so Harriet has given up and put in artificial. Who could blame her?

Guest rooms, whether off the long breezeway or along the grassy courtyard, are spacious and pleasantly appointed. White adobe walls, viga ceilings, interesting Southwest antiques, all bring back days of the Santa Fe Trail, when Cimarron was a cutoff along the way. Zane Grey, in fact, used Casa del Gavilan as the setting for his novel *Knights of the Range.*

Wide open spaces, the majestic peak of "The Tooth of Time" rising up behind the inn, the wild animals—all make this an incomparable inn experience. And the food—breakfasts of country sausage and biscuits smothered in country gravy; Bavarian waffles with strawberries; "hors d'oeuvres and wine in the evening when guests settle in," says Vera. But no lunches or dinners, when Cimarron offers the St. James Hotel, the Kit Carson Inn, and Heck's Family Restaurant, good for Italian and Mexican food.

The television room has a telephone for guest use if needed; there are games and cards, books and magazines. The office is also a gift shop with lots of intriguing things to look at and buy. The huge living room and dining room are cozily furnished and inviting.

How to get there: From Highway 64 through Cimmaron, take Highway 21 south for approximately 6 miles. The inn will be on your right after the Philmont Scout Ranch.

St. James Hotel
Cimarron, New Mexico
87714

Innkeepers: Ed and Sandy Sitzberger
Address/Telephone: Route 1, Box 2; (505) 376–2664
Rooms: 25 share 21 baths; 12 with phone, 12 with TV; wheelchair accessible; no air conditioning (high elevation). Pets permitted.
Rates: $35 to $65, single; $37 to $80, double; continental breakfast.
Open: All year except Christmas Day.
Facilities and activities: Coffee shop, dining room, lounge, gift shop, pool, game room, meeting rooms. Nearby: hunting, fishing, skiing.

Cimarron means "untamed" in old Spanish, and that's what the St. James was in its heyday. Which is strange, because Henry Lambert, who built the hotel in 1875, came from a country considered the quintessence of civilization: France. Chef Lambert cooked for Napoléon III and, later, for both Abraham Lincoln and Ulysses S. Grant. What was he doing in wild Cimarron? Looking for gold— and he must have found it, because the St. James is an unexpectedly elegant find in this mountain town of approximately 900 souls.

The handsome building is as full of antiques as it is of history. Frederic Remington painted in the hotel. Lew Wallace was a guest; Zane Grey wrote one of his Western sagas here. Buffalo Bill Cody, Annie Oakley, and Blackjack Ketchum stayed here too.

The inn is supposed to have a ghost, or, at the very least, an unsolved mystery. I'll let Ed tell you about it.

But some of the guests may not have been welcome. Jesse James and Wyatt Earp, well, perhaps, but certainly not Clay Allison, the desperado who danced on the bar, killed fifteen men, and left the famous bullet holes in the walls and ceiling of what is now the dining room.

"Everyone wants to see the bullet holes," says the innkeeper, and I was no exception. But I also wanted to see the main-floor rooms that are kept as a museum, full of beautiful antique furniture. (Upstairs and annex guest rooms are modernized and comfortable.) The lobby, too, is reminiscent of gracious and spacious living. A huge painting of one Don Diego de Vargas hangs alongside that of Spanish priest Fra Junípero Serra. Ornate wire cages contain tropical birds; Japanese *koi* (carp) swim in a small pool. The furniture is the hotel's original.

But that's as far as the formality goes; the St. James is a people place. This is Ed's home—he was born and raised across the street from the hotel and grew up playing here. Sandy's grandfather owned the nearby ranch that today is the Philmont Boy Scout Ranch.

The restaurant menu is surprisingly sophisticated, from escargots to broiled swordfish steak. I had pasta with white clam sauce— a delicious medley of clams and pasta blended with fresh vegetables, herb butter, and white wine.

How to get there: From Highway 64 into town, follow the signs south across the railroad tracks to 17th and Collinson. The hotel is on the corner.

The Lodge
Cloudcroft, New Mexico
88317

Innkeepers: Carole and Jerry Sanders

Address/Telephone: P.O. Box 497; (505) 682–2566 or (800) 395–6343

Rooms: 47 in main lodge, 11 in Bed and Breakfast Pavilion, including 2 suites; all with private bath; no air conditioning (elevation 9,200 feet).

Rates: $65 to $165, single or double, seasonal; $10 extra person; $7.50 roll away; crib no charge; EP.

Open: All year.

Facilities and activities: Restaurant, lounge, saloon on weekends, swimming pool, Jacuzzi, sauna. Nearby: village with shops and restaurants, 9-hole golf course, skiing, Sacramento Peak Observatory at Sunspot.

Set like an eagle's aerie 9,000 feet high in the clouds, overlooking the San Andres Mountains, the Black Range, and White Sands National Monument, The Lodge looks like the mansion of a prospector who finally struck gold.

The fanciful facade, unchanged by numerous interior renovations, graces a hostelry that was built in 1899, was burned and rebuilt in 1911, and has never closed its doors since. Glassed-in verandas, sprawling wings, gabled windows, and a five-story copper-clad tower, all in a mixture of styles no one can quite put a name to, make the inn's appearance as colorful as its history. A porte cochere adds an air of stately elegance.

Stars such as Judy Garland and Clark Gable have stayed here;

so have presidents and astronauts. Even Pancho Villa was a guest when he was an escapee from Mexico in 1911.

The two-story lobby is surprisingly cozy, like a larger-than-life but wonderfully comfortable living room. I was taken by surprise by the huge stuffed bear guarding the great high fireplace, which takes off the mountain chill present even in summer.

Hallways and stairways branch off the lobby like a rabbit warren, but an elegant one. Rooms, furnished with antiques, are all sizes and shapes and offer different views. Maybe you'll get a pine-studded mountain, maybe the golf course (highest and most scenic in the country), or even the glistening White Sands National Monument miles away.

The Honeymoon Suite is a sight for Victorian eyes, all red velvet and gold, with a red-satin-covered four-poster topped by a gold and mirrored crown. Complimentary champagne and breakfast comes with all this!

Innkeepers Carole and Jerry have capitalized on the myth of the beautiful Rebecca, flame-haired ghost of a redheaded maid who disappeared when her lumberjack lover found her in the arms of another. They've named their haute cuisine restaurant after her.

"She's a friendly spirit," says Carole. "She roams the corridors in search of a new lover, in particular haunting Room 101, the Governor's Suite." Carole hastens to assure us that they have accomplished an expensive renovation of The Lodge without disturbing the friendly ghost, who evidently knows a good home when she sees it. She hasn't yet made an appearance, however, at the Bed & Breakfast Pavilion ¹/₄ mile down the road, which serves a continental breakfast of juice, coffee and tea, muffins, and Danish. It's also possible that Rebecca is not alone. Another ghost may haunt The Lodge: The long, polished wooden bar in the lounge once belonged to notorious Prohibition gangster Al Capone.

The Lodge wins cuisine awards for taste, composition, preparation, presentation, and difficulty at New Mexico Culinary Arts Shows, and the quality of the restaurant food reflects this.

How to get there: Cloudcroft is approximately 8 miles east of Alamogordo on Highway 82. Signs point to The Lodge.

Corrales Inn
Corrales, New Mexico
87048

Innkeepers: Laura Warren and Mary Briault
Address/Telephone: 58 Perea Road (mailing address: P.O. Box 1361); (505)
    897–4422
Rooms: 6; all with private bath and wheelchair access, TV upon request. Pets
    welcome. Smoking in designated areas.
Rates: $50, per room, EP; $55, per room, EPB.
Open: All year.
Facilities and activities: Hot tub in courtyard. Nearby: Rio Grande irrigation
    ditch, a 9-mile trail along irrigation system; the *bosque* (woods), with
    muskrat, beaver, ducks; horseback riding on Sandia Indian Reserva-
    tion trails.

Laura and Mary spent many years in Europe and learned what
an inn should really be like. The sophisticated continental atmosphere in this spacious, almost luxurious, inn, makes for a wonderfully relaxing stay. "We are often told this inn is one of the best in
the country," they say with pride. Both women are originally from
Chicago and taught there before setting out in the world. Mary
taught French; Laura taught drama and performed in New York
and Europe. They both lived in Europe at the same time but didn't
know each other then. It was a lucky day when they met up; they
are a perfect combination.

"Mary is gifted—she's the chef. I'm the people person," Laura
says. The gifted chef learned from a French mother-in-law; it was

like having "your own Cordon Bleu." Mary specializes in country French and continental cuisine, and people practically beat down the door to the inn as well as plead with them to repopen the restaurant they used to have in front of the inn.

"We have people who return just for the breakfast," Laura says with a laugh. "We have people who will do anything, even beg. We're known for our food. We used to offer a public brunch, and people keep hoping we'll return to it." They long for the stuffed croissants, the New Mexican green chili and mushroom omelets, the blue corn pancakes, the country fried potatoes, homemade applesauce—need I go on?

But there's food for the soul, too. The stars at night are just marvelous, and a walk through the *bosque* (woods) is like being carried back to France or Italy, two centuries ago—timeless. Laura is busy with a reclamation project, claiming the land around the inn for native grasses and wild flowers to attract birds, "for people to get an idea of what the land was like before cattle and people made it into a desert," she says.

Sherry and port evenings in the Great Room are part of the ambience. The room is surrounded with bookshelves, classical music plays softly (Laura is a violinist), and the walls are hung with interesting collections—old iron keys, masks, the first yoke that ever was used to plow Indiana's soil.

Rooms are spacious and bright. I especially liked the Balloon Room, decorated with balloon bedspread and posters in honor of nearby Albuquerque's hot-air balloon festival. "The prevailing winds bring the balloons up here, and we're filled up from one year to the next for the occasion," Laura says.

The American Indian Room, the Victorian Room, the Southwest Room, the Kiva Room, the Oriental Room—each one is imaginatively decorated. Two rooms have twin beds, two have queens, and two have king-sized beds.

How to get there: From I–25 north of Albuquerque, take Alameda exit 233 west approximately 4.6 miles to traffic light at Corrales Road. Turn right (north) and go approximately 2.7 miles until you see a restaurant in small Plaza San Ysidro on your left. (You'll pass a school on the right.) Turn left onto dirt road just edging the south wall of the restaurant. The inn is immediately behind the restaurant.

The Galisteo Inn
Galisteo, New Mexico
87540

Innkeepers: Joanna Kaufman and Wayne Aarniokoski
Address/Telephone: Box 4; (505) 982–1506
Rooms: 12; 8 with private bath; no air conditioning (elevation 6,300 feet);
  wheelchair accessible. No smoking inn.
Rates: $55 to $165, double, EPB.
Open: All year except last three weeks in January and first week in December.
Facilities and activities: Box lunches, dinner by reservation Wednesday
  through Sunday, horseboarding, swimming pool, hot tub, sauna, trail
  bicycles, hiking, horseback riding, skiing the Turquoise Trail and the
  Santa Fe Ski Basin. Nearby: old pueblo, old church, old Spanish grave-
  yard, museum, petroglyphs (Indian rock paintings) 8 miles south of
  town, Old Turquoise Trail mines.

New owners came to this more-than-250-year-old classic
Spanish adobe inn, and now, Joanna says, "It looks even better
than ever." Wayne is a landscape contractor, and they have beauti-
fied the inn even further to please their artistic eyes. But they have
no quarrel with the pink and blue mountains that surround them.

"We fell in love with New Mexico," Wayne says. "The clean
air, the serenity. . . ." So these two fugitives from California gathered up young daughter Paige and headed for these hills.

Centuries ago The Galisteo Inn was the hub of a Spanish trading post, a fourteen-room hacienda owned by the Ortiz y Pino fami-

ly. All remodeling was done carefully so that the inn continued to fit in with its surroundings, which include some of the oldest colonial buildings in America. (Remember that the Spanish were here long before the Pilgrims landed in the Northeast.)

The inn is situated on eight acres of land under huge old cottonwood trees. It's a long, low adobe building hidden behind a long, low stone wall and I almost missed it. Galisteo is not much more than a mark on the map; I don't advise looking for it in the dark!

But what a wonderful place to discover, no matter if I had a little difficulty finding it. Staying here is like going on a retreat. The simple rooms have whitewashed walls with wood vigas above. Handmade furniture and handwoven rugs are the decor; some rooms are angled, some have adobe fireplaces, all are clean, simple, and uncluttered.

Breakfast is a refreshing eye-opener with fruit smoothies (a kind of fruit milk shake), a fruit platter, and may include waffles, breakfast breads, or quiche. "We use seasonal and local foods whenever possible," Joanna says.

Dinners are superb, a heavenly feast in the wilderness (the inn is 23 miles south of Santa Fe). The food is a delicious combination of Southwest and nouvelle cuisine. Spinach-and-chorizo (sausage)-stuffed duck, and blue corn polenta are specialties. The innkeepers tend their own garden—they use fresh lettuce, peppers, squash, and herbs, as well as fruit from their orchards—and a vegetarian meal can be requested. "We have a lot of health-conscious people who come here," Joanna says.

They come for what I was delighted to find, a beautifully decorated Southwestern retreat, quiet and low-key. Two cozy cats, Rudy and Murphy, are still on the premises, legacies from the previous owners. Smart animals: They know The Galisteo Inn is too good a place to leave!

How to get there: From Albuquerque, take I–40 east to Moriarty, 41 north toward Santa Fe through Galisteo. Or from Santa Fe, take I–25 north to 285 south toward Lamy, 41 south to Galisteo.

The Enchanted Villa
Hillsboro, New Mexico
88042

Innkeeper: Maree Westland

Address/Telephone: Highway 152 (mailing address: P.O. Box 456); (505) 895–5686

Rooms: 5; 1 with private bath; wheelchair accessible; no air conditioning (elevation 5,280 feet). Pets permitted in kennel. Smoking permitted in public rooms.

Rates: $35, single; $50, double; EPB.

Open: All year.

Facilities and activities: Lunch and dinner by reservation. Nearby: bird watching, hiking, rock hounding; tours of silver, gold, and copper mines.

This is an exciting area, where you can go panning for gold up in the hills surrounding this very small village.

"People come into the area not knowing what they're going to find," Maree says. "They're fascinated with what they do find. I've always worked with people, and here I see a big difference; they're here to relax and enjoy." Maree enjoys it because it's like coming home for her: Her family vacationed here when she was a child in California, and the house is bound up in family memories. A great-aunt of hers from Beverly Hills designed and decorated this rustic retreat for a British magnate, Sir Victor Sassoon (whose great-great-grandfather was also that of the hairdressing Sassoon), in 1941. I was curious: What brought a British titled gentleman to this tiny town in the middle of New Mexico? (Hillsboro is so small, at present there isn't even a gas station!) Maree said that while he was in India he met a Hillsboro attorney, and he began to visit the attorney so frequently that he decided to build the house, although he never lived here. He called it El Refugio (the Refuge), and that's what this enchanted corner of New Mexico is for those who have discovered it.

There's a nice feeling of space throughout the rustic inn, which is uncluttered and simply furnished, mostly with old pieces that were either original to the house or were given to Maree by friends and her mother, who now lives across the street. "It's a collection," she says delightedly. The large living room has the sort of comfortable sofas and chairs that invite lounging in front of the fire, and both the large dining room and kitchen invite companionship. "Everybody always ends up in the kitchen anyway, don't they?" Maree asks. "So it ought to be large."

Sir Victor's room is the grandest, large and decorated in pink, white, and aqua and bright with windows, and it has a private bath. The other rooms share—two in the main part of the house share a bath, and two, back behind the kitchen in what were the servants' quarters, share a second bath.

Maree serves a hearty breakfast, and she's very flexible. "I always ask, in case people are on special diets, but I love to cook," she says. "Mexican, New Mexican, Italian, soufflés, quiches . . . chili goes on everything except cold cereal," she says with a laugh, but I imagine you don't have to have it on your soufflé if you don't want to!

The cats, Peaches and Buckets, like to sit out on the front wall and "talk" to people when they're loading or unloading their vehicles. "Men, more than women, sit outside with coffee and play with the cats," Maree says after making a study of the phenomenon.

How to get there: From I–25 take Highway 152 to Hillsboro (50 miles north of Las Cruces) and go west. Hillsboro is 15 miles west of I–25 and 49 miles east of Silver City. As you turn onto Highway 152, there's a sign that says NO GAS FOR THE NEXT 49 MILES, but by then it's too late if you're on empty, so be sure to fill your tank *before* you turn off I–25 (or leave Silver City).

Inn of the Arts
Las Cruces, New Mexico
88005

Innkeepers: Linda and Gerald Lundeen
Address/Telephone: 618 South Alameda Boulevard; (505) 526–3327
Rooms: 15; all with private bath, 2 with kitchenette, 3 with phone and TV; wheelchair accessible. Pets permitted. Limited smoking permitted.
Rates: $50 to $90, per room, continental breakfast.
Open: All year.
Facilities and activities: Kitchen open for guest use, bicycles, Elderhostel program. Nearby: Old Mesilla, Herschel Zohn Theater, Rio Grande River, hiking in Gila Mountain Wilderness and Bosque del Apache Bird Refuge.

Walking in one front door of the Inn of the Arts, you'll find yourself in an art gallery first and foremost, with wonderful paintings by such New Mexico artists as Keb Barrick, who studied with Grant Wood. A side entrance, located off the quiet, tree-shaded patio, leads directly into the Merienda Room, two stories high with enormous arched windows. This common room, also filled with art, was designed by Gerald to connect the two historic Llewellyn Houses that make up the inn.

Gerald is an architect, Linda has the gallery, and both are wide-awake, vital, energetic people who make guests feel part of the electricity in the air. Both are actively involved with the arts in Las Cruces; they print a newsletter that keeps guests informed.

"Our guests are part of the family immediately—we treat them like that," says Linda. "We have a man from Bogotá, Colombia, a regular guest, who needs a phone, so we put a jack in his room." The inn has all sorts of international guests, and you're bound to meet very interesting people, perhaps even in the kitchen! I liked having the freedom of the modern, attractively tiled kitchen, where a guest from Portugal was poaching his own eggs, an actor fixing his health breakfast, and a vegetarian woman preparing her own special brought-along food.

The *Merienda*, an afternoon social hour from 5:00 to 7:00 p.m., is complete with wine and Southwestern hors d'oeuvres: *chili con queso*, guacamole, perhaps shrimp soufflé. If it's an off day, there will be a basket of fruit in your room instead.

Downstairs guest rooms lead right and left off the two-story Merienda Room. A circular stairway leads up to a balcony overlooking the large room and into the upstairs guest rooms.

Each room is named for an artist famous in the Southwest—names like Georgia O'Keeffe, Fritz Scholder, Olaf Weighorst. The Weighorst room has headboards cunningly made from antique gas-grate hoods padded with decorator fabric matching the bedspreads. I loved the bathroom's footed tub, painted bright red.

Two weeks of every month are devoted to the Elderhostel program, with the knowledgeable Lundeens holding forth on "Ancient Art and Architecture" and "Historic New Mexico Art and Architecture." Gerald has built a *horno*, an Indian oven, at the end of the garden; guests helped make the adobe bricks. Now every third morning or so, the Lundeens bake thirty-six loaves of fresh bread! While watching the oven work, you can play croquet or toss horseshoes or perhaps watch a filming. The inn was used by a film studio last year to make a movie, which gives you an idea of the vibrant atmosphere and architecture here.

"We all interact," says Linda, and it's easy to see how, at the Inn of the Arts.

How to get there: The inn is on Alameda Boulevard next to the First National Bank Tower, the only high rise on the street.

Carriage House Inn
Las Vegas, New Mexico
87701

Innkeepers: Kera Anderson Cozens and Richard Cozens
Address/Telephone: 925 6th Street; (505) 454–1784
Rooms: 5 share 2 baths; no air conditioning (high elevation). Pets permitted.
Rates: $34, single; $39, double; $5 extra person; EPB.
Open: All year.
Facilities and activities: Kitchen available to guests. Nearby: walking tour of historic district, water skiing on Storrie Lake, Sipipu Ski Area, fishing in Santa Fe and Kit Carson national parks.

It's always fun to find something different at an inn, and this inn is also an antiques shop. As I walked in the front door and down the wide hall, I could see treasures in the large rooms on each side. There are treasures in all the rooms, too, and if you take a fancy to any of them, Kera will be happy to sell them to you.

"If you like your bed or dresser," Kera says, "we'll be happy to wrap it up for you!"

This way, the rooms are always changing, and you never know what you'll find. "I bought up an entire estate last month," Kera tells me. "Such great stuff!" She thinks the inn looks better than ever, but it always looks great to me. It sure is snazzy, however, with its new coat of paint: apricot with dark orange, turquoise, and white trim. Carriage House is one of Las Vegas's lovely Victorian houses, a relic of the gracious days of long ago. Rooms are large, ceilings are high, the air is friendly.

The common room has television and games. There's a night manager on duty: The Cozenses live in the carriage house in the rear that gives the inn its name.

The bay window in the dining room lets lots of light shine on the buffet, which turns out to be a bar from an old Texas saloon. Carriage House Inn is full of such surprises.

The wide upstairs hall leads to rooms that are color-coded. My favorite is number 3, the Peach Room, with an antique four-poster covered with a crocheted spread.

Baths are large, with claw-foot tubs. Kera rebuilt the entire inside of the house, and each room's fresh sprigged flowered curtains and bedspreads set off bright painted walls.

The third-floor suite, with its own kitchen, can be used as three singles or as a three-bedroom suite. Summertimes, guests can sit on the upstairs porch amid its lovely plants.

Kera's breakfasts are gourmet, with such tasty treats as shrimp-and-bacon quiche, eggs Benedict, or ham-and-swiss omelets accompanied by country-fried potatoes. Homemade doughnuts and chocolate chip or honey bran muffins, too, appear on the antique tables in the dining room. Kera also always serves a fruit and yogurt dish as well as orange juice, coffee, and tea. The newest thing in her repertoire is cottage fries with a secret ingredient. No, I'm not going to give it away!

How to get there: Take University exit off I–25 to 6th Street and turn right to number 925.

Plaza Hotel
Las Vegas, New Mexico
87701

Innkeeper: Wid Slick

Address/Telephone: 230 Old Town Plaza; (505) 425–3591

Rooms: 38, including 4 suites; all with private bath, phone, and TV; wheelchair accessible. Pets permitted with $25 deposit.

Rates: $50 to $90, single; $55 to $95, double; $5 extra person; children under 12 free; EP.

Open: All year.

Facilities and activities: Restaurant, lounge, use of fitness center. Nearby: 18-hole golf course, Armand Hammer's United World College, Fort Union National Monument; Montezuma Castle, Rough Riders Museum, National Wildlife Refuge, Plaza Bridge Street art galleries, Douglas Street shopping district.

This century-old hotel was remodeled in 1982, but the renovation didn't vanquish the resident ghost, an old man in a top hat and old-fashioned clothes, reported to be Byron T. Mills, a past owner of the hotel. According to the staff, he does little pranks. "Guests see him, and then he vanishes."

But I wouldn't blame him for wanting to hang around this charming hotel, situated right on Las Vegas's tree-shaded old plaza. The large lobby has fresh wicker furniture and an old upright piano that guests actually play. Grand double stairways lead to the wide halls of the three-story structure.

The large rooms are furnished in antique style, and I particularly liked my big dressing room. I was pleased to learn that every room offered such roomy luxury. They really knew how to build spaciously in the good old days, which is why it's always a pleasure to stay at one of the past's remodeled "grandes dames." I liked the ambience, too, of this small hotel.

"A lot of our guests tell us they feel at home, not at a hotel," says Wid. "But then, we treat them like family. We try to make people feel that they're extra special."

You'll feel like a lumberjack after you fill up on the hotel's Lumberjack Breakfast of eggs, bacon, and hotcakes. The "Tom Mix" at lunch is a great mix too, a giant sandwich of turkey, ham, bacon, lettuce, tomato, cheese, and avocado.

For dinner, the hotel is known for its Mexican food. Especially tasty are Piñon Chicken and the chicken *fajitas*. If it's possible that you could still be hungry, the hotel makes its own desserts, rich and satisfying. Or have an after-dinner drink in Byron T's, the hotel lounge, which is named after the ghostly owner "just in case he needs a place for a little interaction," says Wid. While you're there you may catch a glimpse of that funny old man in the top hat and the old-fashioned clothes.

The hotel was built in the Italianate bracketed style in 1882, the first major hotel constructed after the railroad arrived in Las Vegas. It earned the name of "the Belle of the Southwest" and hosted Tom Mix during silent film days. The hotel has starred in films itself: *Easy Rider* and *Red Dawn*. Unfortunately, in the 1950s the Plaza fell prey to modernization: The original tin ceilings were covered, windows were bricked in, and the elegant twin staircases were closed off. It cost around $2 million to undo the damage in 1982! The hotel is listed on the New Mexico Register of Cultural Properties and the National Register of Historic Places. The Plaza is a real treat, and Las Vegas has 918 buildings listed on the National Register of Historic Places—the highest count in the state. The hotel's a good place to pick up copies of a self-guided walking tour if you're feeling ambitious.

How to get there: From I–25 go north on Grand Avenue. Follow the signs to Old Town Plaza and the hotel.

Casa de Patron
Lincoln, New Mexico
88338

Innkeepers: Cleis and Jeremy Jordan
Address/Telephone: P.O. Box 27; (505) 653–4676
Rooms: 3, plus 2 2-room casitas; 3 rooms with private bath, casitas with private bath, hide-a-bed, and kitchen; no air conditioning (elevation 5,700 feet). No smoking inn.
Rates: $59 to $69, casa; $82 to $90, casita; EPB and afternoon drinks and snacks.
Open: All year.
Facilities and activities: Dinner by advance reservation. VCR, special entertainment such as German Evenings and musical Salon Evenings. Nearby: Billy the Kid country with state monuments and Heritage Trust museums, Lincoln National Forest, hiking, skiing, horse races at Ruidoso Downs, soap-making and quilting workshops.

Innkeepers Cleis (pronounced Cliss) and Jeremy used to camp in nearby Lincoln National Forest, and she fell in love with the little town of Lincoln.

"I told Jerry I *had* to live here," Cleis says with a laugh. "He thought I was bananas; this house was a wreck. But it had great charm, and after it was fixed, we decided to share it."

The historic nineteenth-century house was the home of Juan Patron, born in 1855. The Jordans decided to name the inn after his family, who lived in the house and kept a store there during the mid-1800s. Young Juan lost his father in an 1873 raid on Lincoln, forerunner of the Lincoln County Wars. Billy the Kid, Sheriff Pat Garrett, murders, and rival mercantile establishments—these are the ingredients of the bloody Lincoln County Wars. I'll leave it to you to visit the museums and flesh out the story, but it was pretty wild in Lincoln back then.

Today there's peace and tranquillity in the beautiful forested country, the calm broken only by the many festivals and pageants in the tiny town and in nearby Capitan (home of Smokey the Bear) and Ruidoso.

Each guest room in the spanking white adobe-and-viga house is decorated with collectibles and antiques like the 1800s spinning wheel from Jerry's family back in Deerfield, Illinois. The number 1 Southwestern Room has twin beds and a full bath; number 2 Southwestern Room has a queen bed and washbasin and private bath around the corner; the Old Store has a queen bed, private bath, and outside entry to a patio. The casitas are completely private, and the Jordans are understandably proud of the fact that they built them from scratch. Casa Bonita has a cathedral ceiling in the living area and a spiral staircase winding up to the loft bedroom.

Breakfast might be Cleis's baked egg soufflé, strawberry-walnut muffins, home-fried potatoes, and fresh fruit—in the clear mountain air, appetites are hearty. The huge kitchen has a wonderful collection of washboards, those old-fashioned thingamajigs for scrubbing clothes. Hot or cold drinks in the evening are enhanced by music, with Cleis at the baby grand in the parlor or at the real live pipe organ in the dining room. You can be sure the music is professional—Cleis has a master's degree in organ music.

As for dinner, you can drive to La Lorraine in Ruidoso, Chango in Capitan, or Tinnie's Silver Dollar in Tinnie; but, says Cleis with a laugh, "that's one of the reasons why we went into the dinner business (by prior arrangement only): People said, 'What, you mean we have to get in the car and drive 12 miles?'"

A Salon Evening might be a night of ragtime and American cuisine, or German specialties accompanied by suitable music. "But it's the people, that's the fun part," says Jerry.

How to get there: Casa de Patron is located at the east end of Lincoln on the south side of Highway 380, which runs between Roswell and I–25. The highway is the main and only road through the tiny town.

Orange Street Inn
Los Alamos, New Mexico
87544

Innkeepers: Susanne and Michael Paisley
Address/Telephone: 3496 Orange Street; (505) 662–2651
Rooms: 5; all with private bath; no air conditioning (elevation 7,500 feet).
No smoking inn.
Rates: $35 to $45, single; $45, double; $5 extra person; EPB.
Open: All year.
Facilities and activities: Group lunch and dinner by reservation; bicycles, golf
clubs, tennis racquets, and skis and assorted boots available. Nearby:
restaurants, Aquatic Center, golf, tennis, hiking, skiing, canoeing, raft-
ing, Indian pueblos and prehistoric ruins, shops.

You have to wind your way up the mountain to reach this
homey inn on a mountaintop. And there's only one way down,
too. But you'll be glad you made the climb when you meet
innkeepers Susanne and Michael.

"We feel we're a nice change from Santa Fe, and people use
Los Alamos as a hub," Michael says. "They'll go down to Santa Fe,
to Taos, and then come back. We're an excellent location for hitting
the high spots." They're also an excellent location for meeting international scientists—people from Scandinavia, Austria, or Germany,
for example, who come for a time to work at Los Alamos—if, says
Susanne, "we can keep them from talking too much shop!"

Shop or not, and scientists or not, people linger over the table at Orange Street breakfasts. In addition to fresh fruit and juices, there will be Susanne's homemade pot cheese to spread on homemade granola breads and muffins, and perhaps chicken soufflé, or maybe delicious Southwestern specialties like breakfast quesadillas or sopapillas. "We certainly emphasize our good food," Susanne says, especially since Michael has added oven puff pancakes, Italian frittata, oatmeal soufflé, French breakfast sandwiches, and *huevos los Alamos* with corn crepes to the menu.

I could emphasize their other objectives: to provide nicely decorated rooms (not large but comfortable, in country or New Mexican motifs) as well as unusually good food—"and cleanliness is important to us." Michael adds that being sensitive hosts is important; they try to ask guests what they want and like. "If someone picks up the newspaper, we leave them alone. Otherwise, we'll talk."

Guests can make themselves at home in the kitchen, make popcorn, use the microwave or the dishwasher, check the refrigerator for beverages, frozen yogurt, and other good snacks. "People can bring food in if they want," Michael says. There's also access to a copier (some of their scientists are busy with laptop computers) as well as such homey things as sewing and ironing needs, shampoo, conditioner, or anything else you might have forgotten. "I've even fixed people's cars," Michael says with a laugh.

The Paisleys are from Los Angeles, and they were looking for a nice mountain hamlet with friendly and accommodating people. This they have found in Los Alamos, but perhaps because they are so friendly and accommodating themselves! There are books to read, a dartboard to toss at, games of checkers to play.

There's a lot to do nearby, too, from the Larry Walkup Aquatic Center a few streets away to more rugged outdoor activity. "If you're any kind of outdoors person, you can do anything," Michael promises. "Great biking, ice skating, rock climbing at Bandolier National Monument, great trout fishing. . . ." What a grand place for an all-around vacation!

How to get there: From Central Street (in center of town) go west to Canyon Street. Turn left to Diamond Street (next signal), right on Diamond to Orange Street (next signal), right on Orange, and down the hill. The inn will be on your left.

Mesón de Mesilla
Mesilla, New Mexico
88046

Innkeeper: Chuck Walker
Address/Telephone: 1803 Avenida de Mesilla; (505) 525–9212
Rooms: 13; all with private bath, phone and TV provided as requested. Pets
  permitted by prior arrangement.
Rates: $45, single; $82, double; EPB.
Open: All year.
Facilities and activities: Restaurant open for lunch Wednesday, Thursday, and
  Friday, for dinner Tuesday through Saturday; Sunday brunch; banquet
  room for sixty-five people; swimming pool; bicycles. Nearby: Old
  Mesilla Plaza, with shops and restaurants, where Gadsden Purchase
  Treaty was signed and Billy the Kid was imprisoned.

Mesón de Mesilla is innovative in that it is solar heated.
Innkeeper Chuck Walker did research at nearby New Mexico Solar
Institute before building the inn.

Everything is new and fresh and bright. All rooms open off the
wide balcony that encircles the building. The painted tile work in
the entry is especially attractive.

The parlor has a fireplace (great for chilly New Mexican
evenings). A pile of towels waits by the door for guests heading for
the pool just outside.

Chuck left the insurance business to become an innkeeper,
and he is serious enough about his hosting to be very disappointed

when a guest declines the gourmet breakfast he takes pride in. He didn't have that trouble with me. My problem was deciding whether I would have the eggs Benedict or the lemon soufflé French toast! I chose the latter, and the plate was garnished with fresh fruit in a positively French manner.

"You have to love people to be in this business," said Chuck, "and I meet the most marvelous people in the world." He joked that when he was in the insurance business, people avoided him at parties, but now they don't run anymore. "I've turned eighteen years of total rejection into these years of total acceptance," he said happily.

He and his late wife Merci patterned their inn after California ones that they admired, those with "a fine restaurant, good food, small size, and an intimate atmosphere."

Chef Bobby Herrera, who has been with the inn since its opening, offers three specials for lunch each day. Lunch is either buffet or a la carte; the dinner menu features such specialties as fillet of salmon champagne, scampi *alla pescatora,* and beef Wellington, and Chef Herrera checks on diners to make sure they're happy and satisfied. No doubt about that, because reservations are a must. "We're offering more fish and seafood," Bobby says," and it's all fresh—no frozen, which always surprises people who think that's not possible in New Mexico." The all-you-can-eat Sunday champagne brunch is crammed with good food, and the inn offers full service cocktails.

Chuck delights in sending guests to "the best theater in the Southwest," the American Southwest Theater, directed by playwright Mark Medoff. The inn will also pack lunches for hikers to Aguirre Springs, a hiking trail overlooking the New Mexican missile range.

How to get there: Take exit 140 off Highway 10 or I–25 to University Avenue to Avenida de Mesilla.

Monjeau Shadows Inn
Nogal, New Mexico
88341

Innkeepers: Brenda and Joe Brittain
Address/Telephone: Bonito Route; (505) 336–4191
Rooms: 4, plus 1 2-bedroom suite; all with private bath; TV, no air condi-
tioning (elevation 7,000 feet). No smoking inn.
Rates: $60, double; $90, suite; continental breakfast.
Open: All year.
Facilities and activities: Dinner by reservation, picnic tables, hiking paths on
ten acres. Nearby: fishing on Bonito Lake; skiing at Ski Apache; Rui-
doso Downs horse races, shops, and restaurants.

Monjeau Shadows is the perfect answer to just what makes a
country inn different from a motel: There's a lot more ambience,
even if there's probably no swimming pool! One of the supreme
pleasures in this almost-perfect setting is to sit on the porch and
watch the hummingbirds; or hike down one of the nature trails to
the tree house.

The inn is famous for its hummingbird watch in summertime.
Joe sets up feeders, which also attract many other species, making
great bird watching. The sun deck and the porch beneath it offer a
gorgeous view of the mountains all around. The house, perched
high on a hill, is surrounded by 200-year-old junipers, as well as
piñon and ponderosa pine.

The charming Victorian-style farmhouse, nestled on a hill, was built as a private home before it was opened as a country inn. The two-story living room has a stained glass skylight; the bright colors shine with sunlight by day and are illuminated by lights at night. A lot of weddings take place here—"Do we ever have a lot of brides!" Brenda says—and one of the reasons might be the long staircase, which is a picture-perfect setting for a wedding gown and train. The balcony above has bookshelves and a French door leading to the sun deck.

There's also a lounge with more books and a television set. Down in the inn's lower level are a large game room with bar and pool table and a separate lounge with a sofa bed that can be put into service for extra guests.

I enjoyed the small basket of fruit I found in my room and the candy on my pillow, both welcoming touches. Newlyweds get complimentary champagne when the inn's two suites become the Bridal Suite.

"We make our own everything, just about," Brenda says. "I try to serve three homemade things for breakfast, like muffins, cheese-sausage ball, and a special bran bread that's been a family recipe for ages. The croissants, well, I have to confess they're bought," she says with a laugh. I took my breakfast outdoors to eat, but inside or out, it's delicious.

Complimentary afternoon refreshments are served. The Brittains will recommend restaurants in nearby Ruidoso, although Brenda confesses that they've taken pity on guests who have arrived hungry late at night.

How to get there: Highway 37 north of Ruidoso, between mile markers 15 and 16. Turn west at the inn sign.

Whistling Waters
Ranchos de Taos, New Mexico
87557

Innkeepers: Al and Jo Hutson
Address/Telephone: Talpa Route, Box 9; (505) 758-7798
Rooms: 3; all with private bath; no air conditioning (elevation 7,000 feet). No smoking inn.
Rates: $55 to $65, per room, EPB. No credit cards.
Open: All year.
Facilities and activities: Patios, picnic areas, sales gallery. Nearby: hiking; horseback riding; four ski areas within twenty-five minutes; mountain bike rental and many restaurants in Taos, approximately 5 miles away.

Whistling Waters' name comes from the clear cold stream running behind the inn. There are two little arched wooden bridges across to a narrow strip of land only wide enough for a birdhouse and a picnic table. This inn itself is a wonderful rabbit warren of bedrooms and social rooms wandering one into another like a maze. "Duck your head!" Al warns. "Every way we go you either step up, step down, or duck," he says with a laugh, explaining that the house is old: "Short people, short doorways."

At one time four separate pieces of property, the inn has been composed by Jo and Al into a delightful place to make yourself at home. They did much of the work themselves, Jo doing the plastering while Al was busy with wiring.

"We wanted to keep it old," Al says of the careful reconstruction and restoration work. "We have people in their eighties who were born here and remember the history. Near as we can find out, the buildings are two or three hundred years old; this was all land grant. There are just old deeds and titles; they didn't want to spend money for lawyers back in those days."

The Hutsons are from Kansas, and like many Taos newcomers they are in love with the area. "People just can't believe how quiet it is at night," they say. Both are creative people; the shop at the entry has chic clothing designed and made by Jo, as well as jewelry and pottery, and whimsical wire bird cages made by Al. They actually made the adobe bricks they used to rebuild "an old ruin" for Jo's pottery studio. Courtyards are abloom with bright flowers and fruit trees along rock terraces.

The soft pink adobe walls, low doorways, and dark beams are restful. The East Room and the North Room have their own private courtyards; outside the East Room there is a tree that cannot make up its mind whether it's apricot or peach. The Blue Room has a huge bathroom and an old handcrafted corner cupboard full of pottery. All seven fireplaces really work; ceilings are of authentic viga and latilla construction.

Both innkeepers cook, but Al confesses that "after biscuits and gravy or pancakes, I fizzle out. Jo is the fancy chef; she makes a sausage casserole that is just wonderful." I thought her baked cheese roll with jam was pretty special, too. While they do not serve meals other than breakfast, they rise to an emergency like maybe being snowed in. "We won't let people go hungry. We think they're just like family, and we give them a key to the front door. The house is theirs—we don't say 'off limits' to anyone," Al says.

How to get there: From Highway 68 on the outskirts of Taos, take Highway 518 east for approximately a mile and a half past Ranchos Elementary School, a cemetery, and the second not the first, school yard. Immediately past the school yard, turn north (left) on a semi-paved road. Where road branches three ways, take the one-lane road sharpest left. The inn will be on your right, and there is a sign.

Red Violet Inn
Raton, New Mexico
87740

Innkeepers: Ruth and John Hanrahan
Address/Telephone: 344 North 2nd Street; (505) 445–9778 or (800) 624–9778
Rooms: 4; all with private bath. No smoking inn.
Rates: $45 to $65, double; $10 extra person; EPB.
Open: March 1 through January 31.
Facilities and activities: Lunch and dinner by reservation; washer/dryer, iron, guest fridge, transportation from bus or rail (Amtrak). Nearby: historic downtown area, live performances at Shuler Theater, art gallery and antiques shops, golf, racetrack, hiking, and fishing; skiing 45 miles away.

The first thing I asked Richard was why the inn was called the Red Violet. He laughed. "We wanted our name to be memorable. There's no such thing as a red violet—but there's a Red Violet Inn!" And a good thing, too, since there's not another inn for miles around. "We're right between Denver and Albuquerque, and Santa Fe and Amarillo, a real good halfway stop for wherever you're going," he says.

The red brick Victorian home was built on the Santa Fe Trail in 1902 by the Reverend Orvil Eldridge and his wife, Eileen. She played the church organ, and in those days a lady was known by the hats she wore. "She left us a dozen hats," Ruth says, "and people actually send us more." They festoon the walls of the Hat Room.

Handsome Jacks Room is named for Richard's Pony Express rider great-uncle. "When I get my Dad in a silly mood," Richard says, "he tells stories . . ." So far he hasn't been telling them to guests—maybe you'll be luckier than I!

"Our policy is gourmet food and pampering," Ruth says, "especially since Raton hasn't any really great places to eat." Breakfast can be Mexican soufflés, quiche, crepes, cheesecake, muffins; the lunch menu (by reservation) presents such offerings as Colorado Mountain Chili, chicken asparagus crepes, garlic chicken with wontons, or a surprise called the Go For It Banana Split Lunch.

The pampering that comes with the inn includes fresh flowers, robes, candy, fruit, cookies, and sherry waiting in your room, coffee and tea trays available always, and a 5 to 6 p.m. social hour with hors d'oeuvres such as an artichoke dip with garlic toast points or a vegetable dip with mini-tostados, wine, and iced tea. Ruth can serve from two to thirty people, and she's generous with her recipes—I left with two: mushroom/bacon quiche and a flan garnished with orange peel.

Both Ruth and John, casual and relaxed hosts, are collectors of many things, all displayed somewhere or other in the inn. John's plate collection—old Norman Rockwell plates and a row of colorful Chinese children—surrounds the dining room. The stair landing boasts Ruth's bottle collection, and high on the walls of the Homestead Room you'll find an intriguing collection of washboards and other reminders of the hardships of pioneer life while you loll in the comfort of bright modern furnishings and linens. The entry hall is filled with many green plants. The twin sofas in the parlor, brightly Victorian, are an eyeful.

Ruth was a librarian at the University of Colorado, and John had a silk-screen manufacturing business. "We've worked together successfully as partners and friends for the past twenty years," they say, and it looks as though this team will go on together for a lot more than the next twenty.

How to get there: From I–25 coming from the north, take exit 455; from the south, take exit 450. Both exits form the I–25 Business Loop, which becomes 2nd Street in town. The inn is just north of the downtown historic district and on the west side of the street at the corner of 2nd Street and Parsons Street.

Chinguague Compound
San Juan Pueblo, New Mexico
87566

Innkeepers: JB (Joan) and Philip Blood

Address/Telephone: P.O. Box 1118; (505) 852–2194

Rooms: 3 casitas of from 1 to 5 rooms; all with private bath, kitchen, living area with kiva (Indian "beehive" fireplace), screened porch, TV. No smoking inn.

Rates: April 15 to October 15; $60 to $135; winter: $65 to $150; additional beds, $10 extra; EPB. Deposit for one night's lodging required. Reservations strongly recommended.

Open: All year.

Facilities and activities: Library, games, TV. Nearby: Indian events in the Eight Northern Pueblos; Santa Fe Opera House 17 miles south, July–August season.

You pronounce *Chinguague* "ching-wa-yea," which isn't hard at all—my difficulty was in remembering it! The name of the arroyo you have to cross to get to this fascinating inn means "wide place" in the language of the San Juan Indians.

Before I could cross the arroyo, I had to drive through the town of San Juan Pueblo and ask for help in finding it. The obliging switchboard operator at the town police station said they often send guests on their way with a police escort! But she called Philip Blood, who came and got me. (He was coming in to town to get the mail, anyway.)

By now I imagine you've tumbled to the fact that this is an unusual place. Situated close to the banks of the Rio Grande in the midst of the San Juan Indian Reservation, Chinguague Compound is an idyllic retreat of several adobe casitas. Contented guests take long walks along the river, go fishing, or bird watching, read the hundreds of books, play the classical music records, loaf, and watch the sunrise and sunset over the Sangre de Cristo Mountains.

"When people come here the first time, they don't believe it," says JB, who claims to be on perpetual vacation. Both she and Philip are fugitives from back East, delighted to be in the inn business.

"It's fantastic—we've met people from all over the world. We find bed and breakfast people just wonderful. We invite all our guests to breakfast, though they can cook their own; but we've even had a guest with dietary restrictions who would come—she'd just bring her own breakfast!"

It's hard to stay away. Aside from the good company, guests dine on JB's blue corn waffles or cornmeal pancakes with New Hampshire maple syrup, sausage, homemade granola and coffee cake, and fruit-and-yogurt parfait. Wheat and corn are freshly ground as needed for baking; JB and Philip grow their own corn and grow the fruit to make apricot and plum preserves or peach-flavored honey.

As if grinding your own flour is not enough, I caught JB actually ironing sheets. "I don't like polyester," she said firmly. "There's something about sleeping between freshly ironed sheets. . ." It all fits in with the salubrious atmosphere at Chinguague Compound, where the resident Doberman's, Hildi and Clio, are as friendly as their owners. And as relaxed.

How to get there: Take Highway 84/285 to Route 68 and exit at San Juan Pueblo. Turn right at the white water tank and ask for help at the police station on the right by the post office! (Or call, and help will be forthcoming.)

Alexander's Inn
Santa Fe, New Mexico
87501

Innkeepers: Mary Jo Schneider and Carolyn Delecluse
Address/Telephone: 529 East Palace Avenue; (505) 986–1431
Rooms: 5; 3 with private bath; no air conditioning (elevation 7,000 feet). No
smoking inn.
Rates: $65 to $125, double; $15 additional person; continental breakfast and
afternoon tea.
Open: All year.
Facilities and activities: Sun deck, patio, mountain bikes; guest privileges at El
Gaucho Health Club. Nearby: Santa Fe Plaza with shops, art galleries,
museums, and historic buildings is in walking distance.

Alexander's Inn is a surprise in New Mexico—it's not an adobe
hacienda. The two-story American country-style house is located in
a residential area on Santa Fe's historic east side. Built in 1903, it
has retained the cozy feeling of a family dwelling. With the help of
a resident gardener, the beautiful flower gardens, both front and
back, are filled with a riot of roses, tulips, lilacs, poppies, and
peonies most of the year.

"I'm a born hostess," Mary Jo says as she sets a plate of warm-
from-the-oven raisin oatmeal cookies right under my nose. "I love
setting the table, arranging flowers." She used to manage a restaurant, but managing the inn for Carolyn is better by far, she says
enthusiastically. "I love being at home, being a homemaker, nurtur-

ing people where it's quiet, intimate, where I can interact with guests."

At Alexander's Inn guests are encouraged to make themselves at home, make themselves coffee or tea, put food in the refrigerator, have friends over and visit in the cozy living room/dining area. The roomy entry, too, has a corner by a window where guests can relax.

There are plants and books and a collection of menus. Mary Jo herself is a fount of information. "I've lived here six years and I can help people really get around."

The quaint inn is full of nooks and crannies, skylights and eaves. The Master Bedroom has a four-poster king bed, a skylight, a large bricked bath, and a sitting area in front of the fireplace. Rooms 3 and 4 have four-poster queen beds and private baths. Up the narrow stairs, two guest rooms share a large bath; one has twin beds and the other an iron-and-brass queen bed.

Check-in brings tea and cookies, a nice afternoon pick-me-up. Both breakfast and afternoon tea are as often as not served outside on the patio to take advantage of Santa Fe's lovely weather. Homemade granola, blueberry muffins, cereals, and fruit—such as a mélange of pineapple, strawberries, and kiwi—are served for breakfast.

And the teatime plate of cookies I almost finished single-handed weren't just everyday oatmeal cookies. "They're pear, raisin, walnut oatmeal cookies," Mary Jo says, explaining the different taste I detect. "It's the pear."

Alexander's Inn guests can snack with impunity—they can work it off with swimming, indoor or outdoor tennis, exercise classes, and machines at the El Gaucho Health Club.

How to get there: Exit I–25 at Old Pecos Trail, which turns into the Old Santa Fe Trail. Turn right at Paseo de Peralta and follow around curve to Palace Avenue. Turn right and go 3 blocks. Alexander's Inn is the old brick-and-wood building on the left. There is a sign.

El Paradero en Santa Fe
Santa Fe, New Mexico
87501

Innkeepers: Ouida MacGregor and Thom Allen
Address/Telephone: 220 West Manhattan Avenue; (505) 988–1177
Rooms: 14, including 2 suites; suites with private bath and kitchenette, all
    with phone, some with air conditioning, 2 with TV. Pets permitted.
Rates: $50 to $125, double, EPB. No credit cards.
Open: All year.
Facilities and activities: Picnics by reservation; dinners for groups that fill the
    whole inn. Nearby: five-minute walk to historic Santa Fe Plaza, with
    art galleries, restaurants, and historic buildings.

El Paradero is Spanish for "the stopping place," a lovely name
for this warm and cordial inn. Innkeepers Ouida and Thom are professionals in the best sense of the word, dedicated to and loving the
work they have chosen for themselves.

The innkeepers have extensively remodeled this old Spanish
adobe farmhouse but have kept its rambling, rabbit-warren character. Santa Fe's Historic Styles Commission approved the plans to
leave the old structure a hodgepodge, and the effect is delightful.

The front part of the building is more than 200 years old.
Space was doubled circa 1850 with a Territorial-style addition. To
complete the charming polyglot effect, the front door is 1912 Victorian, with oval beveled glass. The walls are textured buttermilk and
sand, painted, and all is concealed behind a high adobe wall.

Inside, all is light and airy, with high viga ceilings, big windows, and Mexican tile floors. Green plants hang from the skylight in the breakfast room; the picture window opens the view to the patio; and through the serving window I could see the hand-painted tile decorating the bright, clean kitchen.

The inn has a recent addition, the small Victorian house next door. In it are two luxury suites, each with a fireplace, bedroom, bath, and kitchenette. This house, too, is on the state Historic Register.

There's a lot of common space in this inn: a main *sala*, a cozy television lounge, two dining rooms, patios, and the courtyard are available to guests all day and evening. Tea and treats are served, along with convivial company, in the afternoons. "A lot of our guests are artists and writers, and it's fun for them and fun for us," says Ouida.

Busy Ouida is active on the city council, but she still has time to be a gracious hostess. She also grows parsley and other herbs, and each breakfast is a gastronomical adventure. *Huevos avocado*, two poached eggs on an avocado half with salsa and cheese, take my vote. New is the Healthy Buffet "for the fruit, bran, and yogurt set," Ouida says. And there is always freshly squeezed orange juice, fresh fruit, freshly ground coffee—and for tea-sippers like me, forty-five varieties!

Santa Fe, a tourist town, has many fine restaurants. Ouida and Thom will gladly recommend their favorites, most around the Plaza, within walking distance of the inn.

How to get there: From I-25 south take the Old Pecos Trail exit into town. Take a left on Paseo de Peralta and turn right on Galisteo. The inn is on the southeast corner of Galisteo and Manhattan. From I-25 north take the St. Francis exit, follow it to Hickox, turn left before it becomes Paseo de Peralta, cross Cerrillos Road, and turn left on Galisteo.

TAYLOR

Grant Corner Inn
Santa Fe, New Mexico
87501

Innkeepers: Louise Stewart and Pat Walter
Address/Telephone: 122 Grant Avenue; (505) 983–6678
Rooms: 13; some with private bath; all with phone and TV; wheelchair
accessible. No smoking inn.
Rates: $50 to $125, double, EPB.
Open: All year except January.
Facilities and activities: Picnics, lunch, and dinners for 12 or more by reserva-
tion; afternoon tea, open to public; yearly bazaar between Thanksgiv-
ing and Christmas. Nearby: historic Santa Fe Plaza 1 block away.

On each guest room door of this handsome Santa Fe Colonial
home hangs a red-velvet-and-lace heart that says WELCOME. This
should give you a hint of the cordiality of this inn. But there's a
sense of humor at work here, too. The reverse side of the stuffed
velvet heart on your door will say BEWARE OF OCCUPANT.

"We can't really pamper our guests, but we can come pretty
close," says Innkeeper Pat. Close—like fruit, fresh flowers, and ice
water in your room, plus a terry robe if you're sharing a bath. Like
a personal welcome card from Louise, Pat, and Bumpy (young
Elena, daughter of the house). Like warm, personal care not only
from the Walters but from all the inn staff.

Begin with this truly outstanding tall blue-and-white house on
the corner of Grant Avenue. It's surrounded by a spanking white

picket fence and absolutely draped in weeping willows. Inside, blue and white walls, white drapes, and the warm woods of antique furniture meld with the large antique oriental rugs covering polished wood floors.

Guest rooms have antique pine and brass beds, and you can have twin, double, queen, or king (some of them four-poster), depending on which room you choose. Double Deluxe rooms— numbers 7 and 8—have their own porch, and four rooms have space for a rollaway.

Louise is an interior designer with a background in the hotel business, and Pat is a teacher of space planning and design, so you can see why Grant Corner Inn is pretty much of a masterpiece.

Pat also doubles as chef, creating eggs Florentine, banana waffles, and his special New Mexican soufflé. Louise compiled the *Grant Corner Inn Breakfast and Brunch Cookbook.* Need I say more?

Breakfast in winter is served in front of the blazing dining-room fire. Summers, you can have it on the front veranda, under the willows. In the evening complimentary wine and hors d'oeuvres are offered to inn guests.

The Walters are eager to provide guests with information on local events, such as the Indian pueblos and their dances and music and art festivals, as well as the renowned Santa Fe Opera with a July–August season. Santa Fe Plaza, practically on the inn doorstep, is lined with shops and restaurants, art galleries, and curio shops. Don't miss the art museum, housed in one more of Santa Fe's pink adobe buildings.

How to get there: The inn is on the corner of Grant and Johnson just south of Santa Fe Plaza. Grant is the street that borders the plaza on the west.

Inn of the Animal Tracks
Santa Fe, New Mexico
87501

Innkeeper: Daun Martin
Address/Telephone: 707 Paseo de Peralta; (505) 988–1546
Rooms: 5; all with private bath, phone, and TV; no air conditioning (elevation 7,000 feet). No smoking inn.
Rates: $85 to $110, double; $10 additional person; EPB and full afternoon tea.
Open: All year.
Facilities and activities: Patio, picnic lunches, dinner by reservation. Nearby: Sports Complex; Santa Fe Plaza with shops, art galleries, museums, and historic buildings; hiking, skiing.

You don't have to be Sherlock Holmes to discover that Innkeeper Daun is crazy about animals. Her inn's name speaks for itself—and I was greeted by Barney, Daun's sweet but huge black Bouvier and Newfoundland mix. Then there are the cats. "All of them are lovable," Daun says.

Even larger than Barney is the gigantic—but not real—bear installed near the fireplace. The mammoth teddy is J. Wayne the Banker Bear, and he changes his outfits with the season. He was decked out for gardening with sun hat, bandanna, work gloves, and a trowel. "He just got out of his ski clothes," Daun told me.

By now you realize that Daun has a great sense of humor. "J. Wayne was the only banker who believed in me; he loaned me money for the inn," she says frankly. "'You have a very impressive record,' he said." He was right: He was referring to Daun's ten years as innkeeper of the Britt House in San Diego, California.

The eighty-seven-year-old building that Daun bought for her new inn owes its name to a loose translation of the Spanish phrase *las anadadas.* Each room carries out the animal theme—and expresses her philosophy of innkeeping. Animals, Daun believes, can be our teachers in the ways of harmony. "Here I hope visitors may put aside all that robs them of their joy in life." She makes note of favorite foods and serves them to repeat guests.

The Sign of the Soaring Eagle has six large windows with a view of apple, pear, and honey locust trees and a corner fireplace to invite contemplative thoughts. The Sign of the Gentle Deer suggests a retreat to enjoy views of the resident squirrel busily gathering nuts outside. The Sign of the Playful Otter has handmade maple rockers for a soothing interlude, and the Sign of the Loyal Wolf faces west for a gorgeous sunset. The Sign of the Whimsical Rabbit is a cozy room with a private entrance off the garden. All rooms have Swedish platform queen beds, made for Daun by a friend, and featherdown mattresses. "My guests feel very coddled when they sink into that luxury," Daun says.

The common room, the Sign of the Bear, is where you can relax on overstuffed sofas and gaze at both the fire and J. Wayne the bear, whose bright eyes seem to take an interest in you. The dining area is the Sign of the Buffalo; here guests enjoy a full breakfast of perhaps spinach strata of eggs and cheese topped with sour cream and Parmesan (but Daun will fix low-cholesterol if you want), homemade yeast breads, and fruit.

In summertime there's breakfast and tea on the patio with Daun's Delight, a special fruit drink. Afternoon tea, Daun says, is coming back in, and hers is practically a full meal. Scones hot from the oven, salads, meat spreads, coffee cakes—the buffet was loaded with goodies.

How to get there: From Highway 40 north take the last Santa Fe exit (Old Pecos Trail), which turns into Old Santa Fe Trail. Turn right on Paseo de Peralta and follow around to number 707.

Preston House
Santa Fe, New Mexico
87501

Innkeeper: Signe Bergman
Address/Telephone: 106 Faithway; (505) 982–3465
Rooms: 15 share 14 baths; all with TV, 5 with air conditioning. No smoking
   inn.
Rates: $48 to $128, double, continental breakfast.
Open: All year.
Facilities and activities: Nearby: historic Santa Fe Plaza, with restaurants,
   shops, art galleries, and the Palace of the Governors.

   This charming house is the only Queen Anne in New Mexico,
Signe told me. "This house has been a real pleasure. It's different
from anything in Santa Fe, or in all of New Mexico, and the minute
I saw it I wanted to own it!"
   It was built in 1886 and has some wonderful features. The
large arched window halfway up the stairs faces west, and the window seat on the large landing is a favored spot for afternoon
refreshment.
   The staircase itself, all gold and black lacquer, is very unusual.
"It looks oriental," I said to the innkeeper. "It is," she replied. "It
was built by Chinese workmen who came to build the railroad. This
is the only way they knew to build."
   Signe, an artist, remodeled the house and turned it into an inn
because that seemed the perfect thing to do with it after it became

hers. Many of Signe's paintings grace the walls and are for sale.

With her artist's vision, Signe wanted guests to see her inn as an exciting experience, not just as a place to spend the night. My favorite room is number 1, whose fireplace is of tile with a built-in wood cupboard. The flowered wallpaper, high ceilings, and lacquered oval oriental nightstands on each side of the king-sized bed made a hit with me. From the third-floor room, another favorite, there's a wonderful view and an outside spiral staircase to the garden below.

The parlor has a communal television in case you want company, as well as an antique armoire, furniture upholstered in cool white, and a tile fireplace. Recently renovated and decorated is the adobe building adjacent to the inn with rooms furnished in traditional Southwest adobe style. "Now," Signe says, "guests have a choice of Southwestern architecture and furnishings, or Victorian in the main house!"

Breakfast is served in the large dining room, and it's generous. Pear streusel, bread pudding, sour cream coffee cake, four cold cereals, yogurt, and fruit salad are accompanied by homemade jams and jellies. New bread recipes are being added, alternating with standbys, continuously. An afternoon tea is also served between 4:30 and 6:30.

Signe's helpers bake in the evening as well as serve breakfast. "But mostly, everybody here does everything," she says. "They find that after a waitressing stint elsewhere, innkeeping is infinitely superior. This is such a different atmosphere—you get to know people instead of merely serving them." That pretty much sums up the spirit of innkeeping, I think.

How to get there: Take Palace Avenue 4 blocks east of the Plaza. Turn left on Faithway, just 1 block long, and the inn will be on your right. (There's Holy Faith Episcopal Church on the corner for a landmark.)

Territorial Inn
Santa Fe, New Mexico
87501

Innkeepers: Lela McFerrin, Joseph Moncada, and Penny Hughes
Address/Telephone: 215 Washington; (505) 989–7737
Rooms: 11; 10 with private bath, 2 with fireplace, all with TV; wheelchair accessible; no air conditioning (high elevation). No smoking inn.
Rates: $70 to $150, double, seasonal, continental breakfast.
Open: All year.
Facilities and activities: Hot tub. Nearby: Santa Fe Plaza with restaurants, galleries, and shops; health club; museums, Santa Fe Opera, Indian pueblos; hiking, fishing, skiing area, mountain bike and horseback rentals.

This lovely old inn just off the Plaza was built in the 1890s as the private home of a Philadelphian who came west. A blend of New Mexico stone and adobe, the sedate house with a pitched roof is surrounded by tall, old cottonwood trees. In the 1920s Santa Fe society was entertained here by merchant owner Levi A. Hughes. "They entertained their friends with a graciousness that we like to think you can still receive here today," Joseph, assistant innkeeper, says. The inn is in the last of the private homes that once lined the tree-lined street so close to the Plaza.

Each guest room is different: You have a choice of cozy and quaint or more formal and luxurious. Furnished and decorated by a local interior designer, the rooms have reproductions of fine antique furniture and refreshing linens. Interesting and unusual is the treatment of the ceilings: Every one has a centerpiece of draped fabric coordinated with the rest of the color scheme. "The building served as an office building for a while," Joseph says. "The ceilings had fluorescent lighting, and the decorator came up with this clever treatment to save tearing up the ceilings." It's not only clever, it's very attractive, adding even more to the luxurious air of the inn.

Breakfast might be fresh fruit in the form of poached apples or peaches in champagne, along with granola, bagels, croissants, muffins, and breads, served in the common room, or you can have breakfast in bed if you want it delivered to your door. Evenings, you're invited to mingle in the living room with wine and cheese from 5 to 7 p.m., and I agree with Joseph when he says "which is nice before you go to dinner." And all night you can help yourself to candy, brandy, and cookies from the minibar in the hall, as well as complimentary soda and mineral water.

Lela is a legal assistant, and she runs the inn with the help of Penny and Joseph. "I love it," Joseph says as his face lights up. "It's great meeting people from all over the world. People come here to Santa Fe and have a marvelous time." He thinks their personal service is the best in the city. "We make dinner reservations, send them on the guided tours we think are nice, make menu suggestions . . ." For special celebrations, the inn provides champagne.

The inn is surrounded by lovely gardens, including a rose garden, and the hot tub is situated in a gazebo in the garden. If it's chilly, there's a roaring fire in the living room, or you can retreat to your own room if you have one of the two having their own fireplaces.

How to get there: From I–25 take St. Francis exit north to Paseo de Peralta; then turn right on Washington to 215. There is a sign.

Water Street Inn
Santa Fe, New Mexico
87501

Innkeepers: Dolores and Al Dietz
Address/Telephone: 427 West Water Street; (505) 984–1193
Rooms: 6; all with private bath, phone, and TV; wheelchair accessible. Pets upon discretion of innkeeper. No smoking inn.
Rates: $85 to $130, double; $15 extra person; EPB.
Open: All year.
Facilities and activities: Nearby: Santa Fe Plaza with restaurants, galleries, and shops; museums, Santa Fe Opera, Indian pueblos, skiing.

What caught my eye upon walking into this award-winning adobe restoration was a bouquet of yellow tulips in such full bloom that they looked like peonies. Then I noticed full pots of flowers blooming everywhere, as well as a candy dish half full of Hershey kisses. "Yes, those are very popular," Dolores was delighted when she noticed my glance. "We're small, and we like to take care of individual needs." Nearby was coffee, tea, and soft drinks for guests.

Dolores and Al redid the building eight years ago as office space, and it gradually evolved into an inn. Al was born in his family's hotel in Louisiana and he had never lived in a house until he married Dolores. "He said he'd never have a hotel—and now we have this!" Dolores exclaims.

The whole family thinks it's a great idea, and youngest son Thomas works alongside his parents. "I made all the curtains,"

Dolores says, "and Thomas and I tiled all the new bathrooms." And Aurora, who is not a member of the family but fits in as though she is, helps with everything. "She retired from thirty years of nursing, but she just couldn't stay home," Dolores says. "Now she is everything here. If she ever leaves, I'm leaving too!"

The adobe inn has brick floors and oriental rugs, beamed ceilings, four poster and other antique beds, fireplaces, decks, and patios; some rooms have a sofa, trundle, or futons for extra guests. "This is a quiet, personal place," Dolores says. "Our guests enjoy one another as well as the inn. We have hors d'oeuvres at night, and many guests then go out to dinner together." She and Al run the inn the way they like to live: reading, relaxing, hanging loose.

Dolores does the cooking, but once in a while Aurora surprises her with bread and rolls, or shepherd's pie with potatoes and chili. Another breakfast might be eggs Benedict or eggs Dijon with muffins and breads, cold cereal and yogurt sent to your room on order. You can eat there in privacy or in the common room upstairs with comfy furniture, fireplace, and fabulous views. Evenings, wine and cheese or other snacks are served either downstairs or in the upstairs common room.

Rooms are spacious and fresh, bright with new furnishings, and there are blackout curtains if you want to sleep late and waste that good Southwestern sun! Room 1 is a large blue-and-white creation off the downstairs hall next to an interesting hat rack festooned with straw hats and canes. It opens off a patio, as does Room 2. Room 3 is a junior suite, with nice heavy shutters on the windows and a Louisiana cypress four-poster bed. "This is called either acorn or rolling pin," Dolores says of the four posts, and I'm not sure either; I just know it's attractive.

Room 6, upstairs, has pine twin beds and a balcony for breakfast, lounging, and sunset viewing.

How to get there: From I-25 take St. Francis exit (U.S. Highway 84–285) north 2 miles to Cerrillos Road. Go east to Guadalupe until you cross Alameda. Water Street is the next street to the left.

Bear Mountain Guest Ranch
Silver City, New Mexico
88062

Innkeeper: Myra McCormick
Address/Telephone: P.O. Box 1163; (505) 538–2538
Rooms: 15, including 2 suites and 2 cottages; all with private bath; wheelchair accessible; no air conditioning (high elevation). Pets permitted.
Rates: $59.50, single; $99, double; AP. No credit cards.
Open: All year.
Facilities and activities: Bird watching room, birding classes and nature clinic, bicycle tours. Nearby: Gila Cliff Dwellings, prehistoric Indian sites, ghost towns, fishing, rock hunting, horseback riding, hot springs.

Love of nature and care for her fellow humans mark Myra McCormick and her unique guest ranch. "Tell me your interests," she says, "and I'll plan a tour for you, guided or otherwise." Her list of suggestions encompasses geology, archaeology, caving, white-water rafting, wild-plant seeking, fossil hunting, fishing, hiking, birding (a favorite and a specialty of the inn)—Myra can tell you exactly what birds may be seen in the Southwest at each season of year), or just plain "soaking up sun on the front porch."

Children invariably want to go to the cliff dwellings. Another exciting excursion is to the Glenwood Catwalk: grilled metal rails, elbow height, forming a walk between vertical rock walls on the west side of Gila National Forest. Myra describes it as "this huge mass of rock, a mile and a half of it lining Whitewater Creek."

Peace, solitude, friendliness, and health are the watchwords of Bear Mountain. Myra has a care for the health of her guests, and food is all home cooked, down to the jar of granola I helped myself from at breakfast. A dinner of oven-baked chicken and scalloped potatoes is bound to have at least two vegetables, in addition to a delicious mixed fruit salad. Meals, cooked from scratch from all-natural foods, are served family style, all you can eat. After spending all day in the great outdoors, I worked up quite an appetite and really dug in.

"I used to think if the children didn't have hamburgers, they were in a bad way, but there's such a variety here, they seem to like it, and of course the sweets for dessert they think are okay!" Myra says. "So many who come here tell me that as they travel across the country they get fed up with baked potato and tossed salad, and they're hungry for vegetables."

My room reminded me of the 1920s and '30s: clean, comfortable, and not too fancy or fussy. Rag rugs are on the varnished floors, plants are everywhere, and the rooms are bright and sunny with the light from large, old-fashioned windows. Corner suites have sun porches with marvelous views of the surrounding mountains.

Myra provides sack lunches, with home-baked bread, to take with you on your explorations. "Very seldom do people stay in," she says. "The big thing for people who come here is to be out *all day long*," and they often enjoy participating in her Lodge & Learn programs. "There is no regimentation, though," Myra says. "Guests can be gone all day long, or leave after the morning classes and not be back until dinnertime." Myra also sets up five- and six-day bicycle tours to the mountains and the desert.

How to get there: From Highway 90 or 180, when you get to Silver City, take 180 to the fourth traffic light. Take the right fork, which is Alabama. Turn north and go 2.8 miles, cross the first cattle guard, and go left on the dirt road .6 mile. Don't worry; there are signs to guide you.

Eaton House
Socorro, New Mexico
87801

Innkeepers: Anna Appleby and Tom Harper
Address/Telephone: 403 Eaton Avenue; (505) 835–1067
Rooms: 4, all with private bath. No smoking inn.
Rates: November 1 to April 1: $85 to $95, double. Rest of year: $75 to $85, double. EPB except June to August continental.
Open: All year.
Facilities and activities: Lunch to take out. Nearby: historic town walking tour, Mineral Museum, New Mexico Tech Golf Course, petroglyphs, observatory, Bosque del Apache Wildlife Refuge, Alamo Indian Reservation.

"This is infinitely more fun than what I did before, and the people are wonderful," Anna says, but I think it works both ways: Both Anna and her inn are wonderful. The building, on the New Mexico Historical Register, was built in 1881 and is a cross between eastern Victorian and New Mexican Territorial. It was built by Colonel Ethan W. Eaton, who was an important figure in the $30-million Magdalene Kelly Mine back in the 1880s. The area is rich in silver, lead, zinc, and copper, as well as more ancient points of interest, such as the Piro Indian petroglyphs in nearby San Acacia.

Socorro in Spanish means "aid" or "help," and the town got the name back in 1598 when Spanish explorers received aid from the Piro Indians, who are believed to have been the area's first inhabitants. The climate, typical of high desert, is a great bird-watching area, and many of Eaton House guests have come for just that.

"We have hundreds of hummingbirds from April to September, as well as dozens of other species," Anna says. "I pack what I call my early-birder special for guests who want to go out before I serve breakfast. They go out with hot coffee, chocolate or tea, and sweet rolls, and they come back later for a full breakfast." Anna, who used to travel 200,000 miles a year in her field of marketing and interpersonal skills, wanted to live a higher quality of life than what she describes as a "bubble existence. You live in a car, office, plane—you have nothing to do with reality."

Now Anna is into the reality of making sure her guests are taken care of. She feels strongly about no-nitrate meats, range eggs, organic vegetables. Breakfast is a cheese soufflé with apricot topping, brioche, turkey sausage, fresh fruit in season. The lunches she packs to order have tuna or ham and cheese on homemade bread, fruit juice and bottled water, homemade cookies, brownies, fruit cobbler, and her celery-and-carrot "trail mix." Especially good and healthy are Anna's apple-and-raisin crispy cookies!

Guest rooms, bright and comfortable, contain Southwestern furniture, much of it made by a local artisan. In spacious Colonel Eaton's Room, though, there's a four-poster from Santa Fe and an antique 1859 desk and old liquor cabinet. A closet wall in Daughter's Room is all mirrors, and the twin beds were hand carved for twin daughters.

"We've had great-granddaughters and sons (of the original family) stay here," Anna says. The *trastero* (combined bench and armoire) in the Vigilante Room is an interesting piece. There's luxury in the down comforters and the huge bath sheets, but the iron bars in the windows of the hallway are a reminder of a 1906 earthquake—that's when the colonel put them in. The only thing changed of the original house are the added *portales* (covered walkways) so that each room could have its own entrance.

How to get there: From I–25 in Socorro, take Manzanares west to California. Turn south on California for 2 blocks to Church; go west on Church 4 blocks to Eaton, and then south on Eaton to 403.

American Artists Gallery House
Taos, New Mexico
87571

Innkeepers: Judie and Elliot Framan

Address/Telephone: Frontier Road (mailing address: P.O. Box 584); (505) 758–4446

Rooms: 6, including 1 suite and 1 cottage; all with private bath, 1 with kitchen; no air conditioning (elevation 7,000 feet). No smoking inn.

Rates: $65 to $95, double; $25 extra adult, $15 extra child; EPB.

Open: All year.

Facilities and activities: Contact with the art community, history, and culture of area. Nearby: historic Taos Plaza with restaurants, shops, and art galleries; hiking, horseback riding, skiing, tours, Taos Indian Pueblo, and museums.

American Artists Gallery House was one of the first fine inns in these parts, with bright, comfortable guest rooms decorated in pleasing Southwest style and hung with art by local artists. New innkeepers Judie and Elliot were guests at the inn when Judie overheard two of my favorite innkeepers, Ben and Myra Carp, say that they wanted to retire to travel and to spend more time with their grandchildren.

Judie was concerned at the time because Elliot's work as a project engineer for Cal Tech was taking him abroad, and she worried about him traveling out of the country. "Actually, I was spooked," she confesses, "and I wanted to find a way I could keep him at home."

Although at first Elliot looked at her as though he thought she'd lost her mind, she says, he soon came around to her way of thinking. "Retirement?" he now says with a laugh. "What retirement?" They both are dedicated to continuing in the American Artists Gallery tradition of showcasing local, regional, and national artists, as well as developing Elliot's photography. They are dedicated to hospitality as well, continuing the entertaining "happenings" involving guests in the local Taos art scene, which the inn's former owners were known for.

"I have changed Myra's New York Experience breakfast specialty to my New York/California Experience, since we're from California," Judie says. Now the dish is a wonderful mixture of avocados, jicama, and California red onions. Another delicious breakfast is Judie's quiche Florentine, with fresh spinach and mushrooms, whereas Elliot's specialty is blue corn pancakes with blackberries and syrup. Often served are fresh-baked pecan cinnamon rolls.

The sunroom has become a large dining room facing the inn's famous outdoor garden, thus enlarging the already good-sized common room. The Honeymoon Cottage is new, and Judie plans on having the cottage overlook what she hopes will be an English garden. "Well, an English-type garden, with lots and lots of flowers. We'll have to see what grows here," she says as a concession to the climate, "but I'm hoping for lilacs and roses." Now her interesting cactus collection graces the guest rooms, but she's looking forward to fresh garden flowers, too, as well as raising fruits and vegetables to be used in meal preparation.

"We plan to continue the tradition of making every guest a part of the family, and a friend," she says. "We're eager to learn, along with our guests, the lore and the magic that is Taos."

How to get there: Coming into Taos from the south on Old Santa Fe Road (the main highway through Taos), turn right on Frontier, located by the Ramada Inn. The inn will be on the right a short way down the road.

Casa Benavides
Taos, New Mexico
87571

Innkeepers: Barbara, Tom, and Jason McCarthy
Address/Telephone: 137 Kit Carson Road; (505) 758–3934
Rooms: 22; all with private bath and TV, some with kitchenette; no air conditioning (elevation 7,000 feet); wheelchair access to inn, guest rooms, and dining room. No smoking inn.
Rates: $80 to $175, double; $15 extra person; EPB.
Open: All year.
Facilities and activities: Hot tubs, patios. Nearby: historic Taos Plaza with shops and restaurants a half block away; Indian pueblos, museums, hiking, fishing, skiing area, mountain bike and horseback rentals.

Barbara Benavides McCarthy is a native *Taoseña* as is her husband Tom. She wanted to buy the inn property, a mélange of seven adobe buildings, because she had a very personal interest: Her father was among the carpenters who built them.

"Actually it was a whim," she says. "One of these was my family home; the others belonged to good friends of both our families. Tom said I could buy the property, but I had to make it pay for itself. (Tom has been the businessman in the family.)

"My cousin said, why don't you open a bed and breakfast, it's no work at all!" This is Barbara's supreme joke. She collapses in helpless laughter. "No work at all!"

Tom has three retail shops in Taos, and Barbara swears that

even so, she works harder than Tom does, "although Tom helps me here," she admits. "He helps me serve. I've never worked so hard in my life," she says; but it has turned out to be work she loves. She adds that the nicest thing is how different this is from meeting people in a shop. "They've already bought what I have, and we can just enjoy each other."

The guest rooms Barbara has designed are an interior decorator's dream yet authentically New Mexican, with kiva fireplaces for chilly nights, skylights, and Mexican tile. The inn started with fifteen rooms and keeps on a-building. A true-blue *Taoseña*, Barbara is proud that all her carpenters are Native Americans. "I've dedicated my Taos Pueblo Room to them," she says. Her favorite guest room, decorated in a western gambling and bordello style, is named Doña Tules.

"She was my kind of woman," Barbara confides with a twinkle. "The townspeople dress up in local costumes on Padre Martinez Day, and once a year I get to be her. She was the mistress of a former state governor." The padre, a Taos celebrity, brought the first printing press to the town, "but he had nothing to do with Doña Tules," she hastens to add.

Each guest room contains something from either Barbara's or Tom's family. In La Victoriana you'll find Barbara's great-grandparents' wedding certificate on the wall. The San Tomas Room's walls are hung with *retablos*, tin religious paintings from churches all over New Mexico. The Rio Grande Room has log furniture and red-and-black Indian weavings. Each room is a masterpiece, and you can tell that Barbara had a ball designing them.

Barbara also has a ball cooking, which she does with equal flair. Mexican eggs with green chilies and cheese, jalapeño salsa, homemade flour tortillas, pecan pancakes, French toast, and muffins, all family style. "You eat all you want," she says.

Casa Benavides means "the house of good life." I enjoyed the joy of life that radiates here. Even young Jason wants to be included as one of the innkeepers. He checked to make sure I was spelling his name right.

How to get there: The inn is located ¾ block east of Taos Plaza and the main intersection of Highway 68 and Kit Carson Road. There is parking, perfect for exploring the town on foot.

Casa de las Chimeneas
Taos, New Mexico
87571

Innkeepers: Susan Vernon and Ron Rencher
Address/Telephone: 405 Cordoba Road (mailing address: Box 5303); (505) 758–4777
Rooms: 3, including 1 suite; all with private bath; wheelchair accessible; no air conditioning (elevation 7,000 feet). No smoking inn.
Rates: $103 to $130, double, EPB.
Open: All year.
Facilities and activities: Hot tub. Nearby: trolley to Taos Plaza with shops, galleries, and restaurants; Taos Pueblo, museums and seasonal events, skiing.

Chimeneas is Spanish for chimneys, and the inn is named for the traditional New Mexico kiva fireplaces in each room. There are two in the Library Suite, one each in the Blue Room and the Willow Inn, and three more in the main house.

Susan and her assistant, Isabelle, are responsible for the delicious breakfasts served each morning: eggs Benedict or perhaps Ron's multi-grain corn pancakes; *huevos rancheros,* breakfast burritos—always a delicious hot dish following a fresh fruit course.

Guest rooms have French doors opening onto a grassy walled courtyard where fountains play and flowers bloom. Both innkeepers are avid gardeners and have planted more than two thousand bulbs. I have to agree with Susan when she says the results are spectacular! New near the hot tub are herb, vegetable, and rose gardens, with paths for strolling and enjoying.

Inside, designer linens, down pillows, skylights, and hand-carved furniture make for a luxurious stay. Unexpected are the color cable television sets and the ice makers concealed behind carved wooden screens.

The large common area is light, bright, and sunny. Paintings by Ron and other local artists' work enhance the thick adobe walls. Sodas and juices are complimentary, and so is the homespun treatment of guests, typical of the warmth of Taos.

"Although we don't serve either lunch or dinner, we did have a guest who got the flu, and we made him homemade chicken soup," Susan told me. "And of course, if anyone wants a cup of tea. . . ."

Susan is a Taos publicist and active community volunteer. Ron, who paints in both oil and watercolor, has work hung in galleries in Santa Fe, as well as in Taos and other parts of the country. "In Taos, most everyone usually does three things in order to be able to live here," she said with a laugh. She works with the Taos Chamber of Commerce and the Taos Ski Valley to promote tourism.

I noticed a rack of brightly colored quilts and learned they are all handmade, by Susan's mother, and are for sale. So is much of the art on the walls, not at all unusual for Taos, where almost every inn is also a gallery. Art with a capital A is king and queen in Taos; it seems to be something in the air!

How to get there: Going north on the South Santa Fe Road, turn right at the traffic light on Los Pandos and continue a short way, keeping a lookout for Cordoba, a small unpaved road to your right. The inn will be behind an adobe wall to your left almost as soon as you turn the corner.

Casa de Milagros
Taos, New Mexico
87571

Innkeepers: Helen Victor; Sylvia and Tony Celnik
Address/Telephone: East Kit Carson Road (mailing address: P.O. Box 2983);
(505) 758–8001
Rooms: 6, including 1 2-bedroom suite; all with private bath and TV, suite
with kitchen; wheelchair accessible; no air conditioning (elevation
7,000 feet). Pets permitted. No smoking inn.
Rates: $65 to $85, double; $125 to $180, suite; $15 extra person; EPB.
Open: All year.
Facilities and activities: Hot tub, sauna, sun deck; ski storage area. Nearby:
Taos Plaza with shops, galleries, and restaurants; Taos Pueblo Indian
Reservation, skiing, hiking, horseback riding, hot springs.

Casa de Milagros, "house of miracles," has taken over Gallery
West, and innkeeper Helen Victor promises such miracles as some
of Taos's notable artists dropping in for a friendly chat. Every day,
she says, is an adventure in Taos, and no one will argue with her
about that! Year round, things are happening—such as the Spring
and Folk Art Festivals, the Summer Fiestas, the Balloon Fiesta, the
Pow-Wows at the Taos Pueblo, Christmas Yuletide, and of course,
the eagerly-awaited-every-winter ski season.

Now the inn has a beautiful walled courtyard filled with very
attractive landscaping around a new hot tub. Guest rooms have different names: The Chimayo Room is decorated with tapestries and

weavings and has a kiva fireplace and a private entrance off the portico; the Pueblo Room is full of pottery and sculpture; the Taos Room is a treasure trove of local and historic memorabilia and books "both by and about notable residents of Taos," Helen says.

The spacious Cottonwood Room, close to the hot tub, has a skylight as well as a kiva fireplace. In addition to the twin beds (or king-size when pushed together) there's a sofa bed that sleeps one. The Milagro Suite offers two bedrooms, a large living/dining room with fireplace, and a complete kitchen. All the bathrooms are colorful, with Saltillo tile; the hand-carved doors are by noted Taos artist Clarence Vigil.

Helen has assistants, Sylvia and Tony, who are from Cardiff, Wales. "We emigrated for a warmer life," Sylvia confesses with a contented smile.

Breakfasts include homemade granola, bread pudding, pancakes, or crepes with sautéed fruit. Helen uses whatever's in season, like peaches, apples, or berries. "But blackberries are the favorite!" She often makes her special eggs Milagro, whereas Sylvia specializes in a meatless eggs Benedict. Sylvia also does the bread pudding. "You're English, you make the bread pudding," Helen told her. Sylvia laughs. "Then she gives me a Southwest recipe to follow!"

Helen spent an entire year searching for just her inn. Originally from Boston, she knew the Taos area from coming here on skiing vacations. Now she's delighted to be settled here. "What I love about it is the coziness and the fireplaces," she says of the inn.

"We have a casual atmosphere, and guests bring variety and joy into the house. So many different types, including a lot of people in the entertainment field, people from Los Angeles, from New York." Helen herself is a professional photographer, and the inn is decorated with many posters from her color shots.

There may be less room at the inn by now: Mabel the cat has been in the family way. "She's a sweetheart," says her owner. "I have people waiting in line for her babies," she adds with a laugh. Vinnie, the dog, is a delight too, but he has to stay outdoors.

How to get there: From the traffic light at Taos Plaza, go east on Kit Carson Road for approximately ½ mile. The inn will be on your left.

Casa Europa
Taos, New Mexico
87571

Innkeepers: Marcia and Rudi Zwicker
Address/Telephone: 157 Upper Ranchitos Road; (505) 758–9798
Rooms: 6; all with private bath, several with built-in bancos that convert to
   a twin bed; no air conditioning (elevation 7,000 feet). No smoking inn.
Rates: $70 to $120, double; $15 extra person; EPB and afternoon tea.
Open: All year.
Facilities and activities: Sauna, hot tub, three private courtyards for play, a
   special clubhouse. Nearby: historic Taos Plaza with restaurants, shops,
   and art galleries; hiking, horseback riding, and winter skiing; Taos Indian Pueblo and museums.

Marcia and Rudi would like to list young son Maximilian as
one of the innkeepers; he is such a fine small host when guests
include children. "They're all welcome to play with his toys," Marcia told me. Maxi also gladly shares a special place where children
can play. "Where Rudi comes from in Germany, everyone has a
garden house. Rather than putting a garden house here, we have
one on stilts—it's Maxi's private clubhouse."

Rudi and Marcia are the hospitable models their son patterns
himself after. Both are used to the public and enjoy entertaining.
Before coming to Taos, they were proprietors of a fine restaurant in
Boulder, Colorado, for many years.

"But," Rudi said, "I needed to do something with people
again."

"He needs to work about eighteen hours a day," Marcia added with a fond laugh.

"Well, we get our guests started, we introduce them, and then they are fine," Rudi said. I certainly was fine, my only problem being one of indecision at teatime; should I choose the chocolate mousse–filled meringue or the raspberry Bavarian? Or perhaps the Black Forest torte or one of the fresh fruit tarts? (I really wanted one of each, all made by chef Rudi, who was trained at the Grand Hotel in Nuremberg, Germany.)

Breakfast is another such feast prepared by chef Rudi. For the grownups, fresh fruit salad, a mushroom-and-asparagus quiche, lean bacon edged in black pepper, home-fried potatoes, and fresh homemade Danish that absolutely melted in my mouth. Children dive into the blue corn pancakes with bacon and eggs, "or they come into the kitchen to choose their own cereal. I've learned," Marcia said with a laugh. "Once I put fruit on cereal and the child said 'yuk!' so I leave it alone!"

The house itself is a treasure, with fourteen skylights and a circular staircase to the gallery above the main salon, displaying the paintings, pottery, and sculpture of local artists as well as wonderful Navajo rugs. The inn appears deceptively small from the outside; inside, the large common rooms (but very uncommon!), both upstairs and down, lead to six exceptionally spacious and elegant guest rooms. It's also very comfortable. The wood floors are graced with oriental rugs; the white stucco walls are hung with original art. The front courtyard is bright with flowers around the Spanish fountain; the European garden in back offers quiet relaxation.

How to get there: Driving into Taos from the south on Highway 68, take Lower Ranchitos Road left at the blinking-light intersection just north of McDonald's and south of Taos Plaza. Go 1½ miles southwest to the intersection of Upper Ranchitos Road, which will be on your right. (For a landmark, there's a James Mack Studio on the right-hand corner.

Casa Feliz
Taos, New Mexico
87571

Innkeepers: Bonnie McManus and India Northrup
Address/Telephone: 137 Bent Street; (505) 758–9790
Rooms: 3, plus 3-room cottage; all with private bath; no air conditioning (elevation 7,000 feet). No smoking inn.
Rates: $75 to $115, single; $85 to $125, double; $10 extra person; EPB.
Open: All year.
Facilities and activities: Large enclosed garden with picnic table, barbecue grill; parking. Nearby: Taos Plaza with shops and restaurants around the corner; public swimming pool across the street; mountain bike and snowmobile rentals; skiing, Indian pueblos, museums.

This warm and welcoming artistic inn has won the gratitude of local authorities for the restoration of Casa Feliz, bringing back the ambience of the days when Georgia O'Keeffe, Becky James, and John Dunn frequented the old adobe home. Now on the National Register of Historic Places, Casa Feliz is a treat, just off the Plaza right in the middle of town. And like many Taos inns, it's a gallery as well, showing works of many fine local artists. Bonnie's aim is to show in her main gallery the works of local artists who don't have a regular space, including the art of the Taos Indians who live in the Taos Pueblo.

While she runs the gallery, Bonnie also runs the inn, serving a very generous breakfast.

"One of the ideas when I started was that people should not feel they are being served; they should feel at home," Bonnie says. "I pile the tables with homemade breads, cakes and muffins, and New Mexican dishes as well." Delicious is Frittata Feliz with green chilies and Monterrey Jack cheese; different are the piñon-nut waffles, and wonderful are many of Bonnie's other dishes "that I don't even have names for," she says as she serves scrambled eggs with hominy and pinto beans. Her muffin repertoire is large, with ginger and blueberry ones both favorites.

There's also the thoughtful touch of a snack for tired travelers when they check in, usually with something cold and wet—wine, beer, soda—all welcome in this dry climate. Evenings, there's wine and cheese by the fire in the cozy sitting area of the gallery.

"I've wanted to create a calm, peaceful, and relaxing atmosphere here for my guests," Bonnie says. Guest rooms are spacious and uncluttered, with adobe walls of soft rose. And each has unique New Mexico style handcrafted furniture and queen-sized beds. The Romantic Room is romantic, the Vega Room, of course, has vegas on the ceiling, and the Desert Room's colors and cactus give it a light and airy feeling. The cottage at the back of the garden has three connecting bedrooms, all sharing one bath, ideal for a family or "a family of skiers," Bonnie suggests. "People can come and go."

All the rooms have electric blankets on the beds, a nice amenity in this mountain town, where people can be more concerned with keeping warm than being air conditioned. The large enclosed garden, perfect for picnics and barbecues, has a wonderful view of magic Taos Mountain. It's just a half-hour's drive up to the Taos Ski Valley for winter fun and the same amount of time to the Rio Grande for summertime river rafting.

Lately, Bonnie has become infected with the artistic atmosphere surrounding her. "I've started to dabble in little things, like bolo ties, made from found objects," she confesses. "There's a jewelry class here in town . . ."

How to get there: The inn is located on historic Bent Street, 1 block from the Plaza behind the northwest corner. There is parking in the rear.

El Rincon
Taos, New Mexico
87571

Innkeepers: Nina Meyers and Paco (Paul) Castillo
Address/Telephone: 114 East Kit Carson Street; (505) 758–4874
Rooms: 12; all with private bath, TV, VCR, and stereo; no air conditioning (elevation 7,000 feet). Pets permitted.
Rates: $45 to $125, per room, continental breakfast.
Open: All year.
Facilities and activities: Shop, art gallery, and museum are part of the property. Nearby: Taos Plaza, just around the corner, has restaurants, shops, and galleries.

El rincon means "the little corner" in Spanish, and this delightful inn is full of little corners. What began as a little house to be used as an art studio for Nina has become a delightful maze of rooms and stairways that just grew like Topsy. "The whole place started so that I could have a studio," says Nina, whose artwork and artistry are evident throughout the inn. "Then I decided to add a second story. People saw the rooms I decorated, and they wanted to stay—and, well, it just mushroomed."

A favorite is the La Doña Luz Room, named for a Taos lady who lived in the house more than a century ago. She was the sister-in-law of a famous Taos character, Padre Martinez. I'll let you history buffs find out more about this on your own.

The new Santiago Room is lovely European Spanish, with

decor collected in Spain by the innkeepers in the 1950s. Los Flores (the flowers) is a Garden of Eden: the Jacuzzi bath for two has murals all over the walls and ceiling!

The bed in El Sol is one that Brigham Young is reputed to have slept in—and that Nina was definitely born in. La Vista is the hot-tub room, and there's a balcony with a loft. The Tres Reyes (three kings) room is a bed/sitting room; La Luz (the light) is a little hide-away where you can lie in bed and watch the magical Taos Mountains. Most rooms have small refrigerators, and in the winding hallways there are several kitchen snack-fixing areas and a washer and dryer to use.

Nina is so talented that guests keep wanting to buy her work, yet she is quite modest about what she does. "I had a lot of art training, but I didn't know I could do all this. I've learned a lot. . . ." Her kitchen cabinet doors are hand painted, and a guest liked them so much that "I sold one of the cabinet doors!" She soon painted another.

Breakfast, out in the Mexican patio in summer, was fresh-squeezed orange juice, melon balls with lemon yogurt (sometimes strawberries and cream), blue corn or blueberry bran muffins, a fruit and fiber cereal, and of course coffee and tea. Winters, breakfast is warm and cozy in front of the fire. For honeymooners and anniversary celebrants, there's champagne in the guest room.

Nina's father was the well-known Taos Indian trader Ralph Meyers, and his widow, Rowena Martinez, still runs the Original Trading Post of Taos on the street in front of the inn. The Trading Post has been a mom-and-pop store since 1909, selling artifacts, jewelry, and silverwork. The inn's small museum has such objects of interest as Kit Carson's breeches and the first holy-water font in the United States.

How to get there: Follow Highway 68 north through town until you come to the traffic light at Kit Carson and Taos Plaza. Turn right and the inn is just around the corner to your right, behind the Original Trading Post of Taos.

Hacienda del Sol
Taos, New Mexico
87571

Innkeepers: Marcine and John Landon
Address/Telephone: 109 Mabel Dodge Lane (mailing address: P.O. Box 177);
(505) 758–0287
Rooms: 7; 5 with private bath; no air conditioning (elevation 7,000 feet). No
smoking inn.
Rates: $45 to $90, single; $55 to $115, double; $20 extra person; $10 crib;
EPB.
Open: All year.
Facilities and activities: Hot tub. Nearby: Taos Plaza with restaurants, art gal-
leries, and shops; Taos Indian Pueblo, Kit Carson Home, Millicent
Rogers Museum, Martinez Hacienda.

"I was in education for thirty years," Marcine says, "and John
was a traveling salesman. A long time ago, we decided we'd retire
at age fifty-five and do something together." They used to visit Taos
twice a year at least, and like so many happy innkeepers, once they
saw this inn, they fell in love with it.

"It's our home," Marcine says, "and that's how we treat it. We
don't come in the morning; we're already here." She likes to
recount how they moved in the door as previous innkeepers Carol
and Randy Pelton were moving out. "The Peltons made breakfast
Monday, and we made breakfast Tuesday."

The inn's story is part of Taos history. Mabel Dodge Luhan, the wealthy arts patron who brought Georgia O'Keeffe and D. H. Lawrence to Taos, bought the home as a hideaway for her Taos Indian husband Tony, so he wouldn't feel like a fenced-in bear. What's more, Georgia O'Keeffe painted her *Sunflowers* here.

The inn, like so many New Mexico homes, is an old adobe building hidden behind a wall. But it backs up to 95,000 acres of Indian land, with a beautiful view of Taos Mountain, the Magic Mountain of the Taos Indians. "Now I can't imagine living any farther from that mountain than I have to," Marcine says.

The Sala de Don was Tony's room; Escondido has two skylights; and my room was attached to another room just as large, in which the centerpiece, surrounded by windows, was a huge, dark-blue Jacuzzi. Talk about luxury!

Luxurious, too, is the outdoor hot tub, where you can loll back and let the magic of the mountains work on you. The Casita, a separate little adobe house, has two guest rooms, two baths, and fireplaces. It can be used as a suite or as two separate rooms, each with a bath.

"We both are people-oriented," John says. "This is pretty much a continuation of what we were doing." Marcine adds, "Except that I'm cooking more!" A guest convinced them of the joy of a bread machine, and you can imagine how delicious the inn smells in the morning. As for which one is the chef, "If it comes out of the oven, I do it," Marcine says, "From the top, John does." Guests rave about John's "elegant" stuffed French toast or Marcine's porridge topped with vanilla ice cream—how's that to start the day? There's a social hour that often lasts much longer, giving guests a chance, as Marcine says, "to show, share, and tell," while enjoying cheese and crackers with nuts or fruit and wine and mineral water. And for you coffee hounds, know that the brew is their own special blend, Cafe del Sol.

How to get there: The inn is 1 mile north of Taos Plaza, on Highway 64/Paseo del Pueblo Norte. Turn right on unpaved road immediately alongside the Southwest Drum and Moccasin Company, and the inn will be on the left, hidden behind a tall "latilla" fence that surrounds the inn's 1.2 acres.

La Posada de Taos
Taos, New Mexico
87571

Innkeeper: Sue Smoot

Address/Telephone: 309 Juanita Lane (mailing address: P.O. Box 1118); (505) 758–8164

Rooms: 5, including Honeymoon House; all with private bath, Honeymoon House with skylight loft bed; no air conditioning (elevation 7,000 feet). Pets permitted.

Rates: $58 to $85, single; $65 to $95, double; $12.50 extra person; EPB. Two-night minimum May 1 to October 31. No credit cards.

Open: All year.

Facilities and activities: Nearby: Taos Plaza, art galleries, museums, restaurants within walking distance; downhill and cross-country skiing, hiking, rafting, fishing, horseback riding.

Innkeeper Sue Smoot has the reputation of knowing what she wants and wasting no time getting it. A few years ago she breezed into town from New York City with an architecture degree under her belt, bought an old adobe hacienda, and practically restored it herself.

The result is a cozy mix of Southwest style and items Sue brought with her from New York. Mexican carved headboards set off batik tapestry; oriental carpets cover both polished wood floors and blue linoleum. And now there is a Japanese garden with a trickling fountain in the entry courtyard.

"Outside the walls it all looks very New Mexican," Sue says, "but once one enters the courtyard, then one senses the Japanese garden . . . East meets West."

Sue's boundless enthusiasm is very catching. Two young guests from New York came in, beaming, while I was there. Sue had helped them plan their day.

"Lovely day! We went out to the Taos Pueblo, and I rode a horse for the very first time!"

Sue flashed her wide smile. "I can keep them busy! I send them to horseback riding, I plan day trips that may culminate in long or short hikes . . . art galleries, paintings, pottery, jewelry."

Energy and enthusiasm begin at breakfast, at which Sue serves egg burritos (eggs, beans, and cheese wrapped in a soft tortilla); hot red salsa (on the side); cantaloupe boats filled with grapes; and apples and oranges. Delicious odors of thyme and marjoram emanate from the kitchen.

"We all eat together; that's where the fun is," Sue says. "My guests really enjoy it." The long dining room faces French doors opening onto the east garden and the sunshine. Behind, in the lounge, bookshelves are stacked for a good read by the tile fireplace. Several of the rooms have wood-burning stoves or fireplaces, and the Honeymoon House has a loft bed under a skylight. Little notes in the rooms ask if guests prefer other than black coffee, and are they vegetarian?

Sue tackled her architecture degree after a career in modern design and advertising. At first she thought of opening a New England inn, but not finding one that matched her means, she went West like many a pioneer before her. "I take what I'm doing seriously, but it's what I want, so I'm also having a great time!"

Pearl, the Australian sheepdog, is long gone to her reward; but "we love her new sweet successor," says Sue, "a golden retriever I've named Jan.-Two, short for January 2, which is the date I got her, but people are still always asking me, what happened to Jan.-One?"

How to get there: From the traffic light at the Plaza and Kit Carson, go west on Don Fernando for 2 blocks, then left on Manzanares, and take the first right onto Juanita Lane. The inn will be on your right at the end.

Old Taos Guesthouse
Taos, New Mexico
87571

Innkeepers: Tim and Leslie Reeves
Address/Telephone: 1028 Witt Road (mailing address: P.O. Box 6652); (505)
    758–5448
Rooms: 9; all with private bath; no air conditioning (high elevation). No
    smoking inn.
Rates: $50 to $95, double; $10 extra person; continental breakfast.
Open: All year.
Facilities and activities: Hot tub. Nearby: Taos Plaza with restaurants and
    shops; Indian pueblos; museums; hiking, fishing, skiing area; moun-
    tain bike and horseback rentals.

The moment you walk through the extra-wide front door, late
of the old Taos post office, you'll be caught up in Tim's enthusiasm
for anything and everything Southwestern. "We just want to
accomplish what we set out to do," he says, "renovate this wonderful 150-year-old adobe hacienda, using imagination—but retaining
the old Southwest flavor." He and Leslie (and daughter Malia,
although she's a little young to contribute much yet) are renovating
the house at the same time they're running the inn, but you'd
never know everything wasn't already completed. Each guest room
is different, and Tim loves to tell of the stern professor who unbent
enough to say upon departure: "I have to tell you I've traveled this
world, and this is one of the neatest places I've been."

Neat is right, and Tim's enthusiasm is contagious. "Look!" he says of Room 6. "Everything everybody wants in the Southwest—stained glass, vigas, *latias*, sculptured posts, adobe showers, Mexican tile, kiva fireplace, log furniture . . ." I had to holler "halt!" and he laughed. "It's so great when you complete a project and people ooh and ah," he confessed. "And we take it personally when someone's not happy." It would be difficult to be unhappy in such congenial circumstances and in such well-thought-out and complete guest rooms. It's a casual, homey, comfortable kind of place, where you can do your own thing or mingle with the other guests. A group of doctors was staying while I was there. As soon as they came back from their happy outdoor pursuits, they began to plan an evening barbecue on the patio.

The split-level traditional hacienda with Territorial windows was a guest house back in the 1940s. Situated on a rise over Taos, it presents a fabulous mountain scene. "Our view makes our hot tub have the best in the Rockies," Tim says with his usual verve. The Reeveses' next project is to enlarge the kitchen because "the kitchen is the place where people get together. So we want to build an even larger one."

While Tim is busy being the master builder, Leslie is the cook, quite a change from her previous life with the ski patrol in Santa Fe. "My fresh-baked breads and muffins are always different," she says, "but—always healthy." She also serves hot cereal and fresh fruit.

The small Shi Tzu, Sachi, greets guests with a welcoming bark, but the older, more sedate Pomeranian named Princess may not even deign to raise her head.

"Princess was deeded us with the place," Leslie says with a good-natured laugh. There is also a calico cat named Tony.

Surrounded by lovely trees so old they almost hide the inn, and on seven and a half acres of land with fabulous vistas, the Old Taos Guesthouse is already so delightful I can't imagine what future improvements Tim and Leslie have in mind. It'll be interesting to see what they come up with next.

How to get there: Take Kit Carson Road east for 1.4 miles to Witt Road. Turn south on Witt Road for .7 mile. The inn will be on the right, and there is a sign.

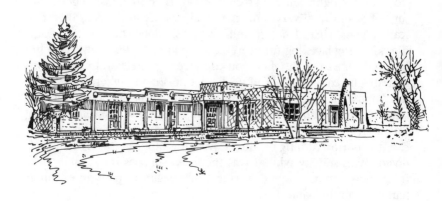

Rancho Rio Pueblo
Taos, New Mexico
87571

Innkeepers: Yolanda Devereaux and Judd Platt
Address/Telephone: Karavas Road (mailing address: P.O. Box 2331); (505) 758–4900
Rooms: 9; all with private bath, phone, and TV; wheelchair accessible. No smoking inn.
Rates: $85 to $150, double; $25 extra person; continental breakfast.
Open: All year.
Facilities and activities: Putting green, sauna, and Jacuzzi. Nearby: Taos Plaza with restaurants and shops; Indian pueblos; museums; hiking, fishing, skiing area; mountain bike and horseback rentals.

Yolanda's family has been in Taos for many generations, which makes her somewhat unique among many of Taos's innkeepers. "I'm a true Taoseña," she says. "My father was a local doctor, and he actually made house calls here," she says of the sprawling pink adobe she and Judd have lovingly restored. "He loved this place."

Built in the late 1800s by the Riviera family to house their twenty-two children, the Platts were able to buy the hacienda when Mrs. Riviera died at the age of 100. Standing on twenty-two acres bordering Indian land and the Rio Pueblo, which gives the inn its name, the long, low adobe house is half-hidden under a stand of cottonwood and willow trees. The grounds are green and well cared for. "The land belongs to the Indians," Yolanda says, "but they're only interested in it for grazing. We get a permit from them so we can irrigate."

The walls are almost 3 feet thick, and the inn has twelve fireplaces. In keeping with the Spanish heritage of the home, the fireplaces have been built by Taos artist Carmen Velarde, whose work also is in the Smithsonian. Another well-known artist who has contributed to the inn's ambience is Taos artisan Miguel Chavez, who made much of the inn's furniture. Throughout the inn you'll find *bancos, nichos,* carved beams, *latillas,* vigas, Mexican tile floors—everything the Southwest has to offer that sets it apart from the rest of the country. Enhancing this are the colors that Judd and Yolanda chose: soft peach for the walls and teal blue for the tilework. Guest rooms are large and restful, with thoughtful touches such as terry robes, and alarm clocks for those who might want to go skiing early in the day (the Taos Ski Valley is right at hand).

And the view from the large living room windows along two sides of the large room is magnificent. The Taos and Sangre de Cristo Mountains on the western horizon make for spectacular sunsets. Not to mention snow-covered peaks in the winter and an occasional rainbow after a spring shower.

In winter a breakfast buffet is spread in the sunny dining room; in summer there are three courtyards for alfresco meals. Off the back patio is an apple orchard dating from the building's construction, and it's now full of weathered, gnarled old trees. Breakfast is a feast of fruit and granola, waffles and omelets, oatmeal and croissants, cheeses with French bread.

Yolanda's background is public relations, and Judd is an attorney-turned-ski instructor—and innkeeper, of course. "We've adopted just about everybody we've had as guests," they both say. "We just sit around and talk over fresh coffee—and they decide to stay another day!" That's how relaxing it is at Rancho Rio Pueblo.

How to get there: From the McDonald's corner on the Santa Fe Road (Highway 68), turn west to Ranchitos Road. Go south on Ranchitos Road for 1.4 miles to Upper Ranchitos Road. Go north for .5 mile, and turn west on Karavas to the inn.

Salsa de Salto
Taos, New Mexico
87571

Innkeepers: Mary Hockett and Dadou Mayer
Address/Telephone: P.O. Box 1468, El Prado 87529; (505) 776–2422
Rooms: 8; all with private bath; no air conditioning (elevation 7,000 feet). No smoking inn.
Rates: $85 to $160, double; $10 extra person; EPB.
Open: All year.
Facilities and activities: Swimming pool, hot tub, tennis court, croquet. Nearby: hiking trails, fishing in Rio Hondo, skiing in Taos Valley, Indian pueblos; 10 miles to historic Taos with shops, restaurants, mountain bike rentals.

El Salto is the big mountain on the horizon, and lovers of spicy food know how lively salsa is; and that, says Dadou Mayer, is how they gave this inn its name. To wallow in luxury beneath the rugged peaks of the Sangre de Cristo Mountains makes for quite a contrast: outdoors the wild mountains, the mesas, and the high blue sky; indoors an elegant home with finely crafted New Mexican furniture and gourmet food prepared by a Frenchman trained in a hotel school in Nice.

Dadou is also a skier, a former member of the Junior National French Ski Team. In one year's Grand Marnier ski race he won the love of his life, a shining chrome convection-and-steam oven that he keeps polished to a fare-thee-well.

148

Of innkeeping, "It's my profession; I love it," he says with a most charming smile. Past owner of the Hotel Edelweiss up in the mountains, where he had a cooking school, he likes the change to a small inn.

"The inn is so much more personal than the hotel business," he says. "My guests say, 'How nice of you to welcome me into your home.'"

Mary is an architectural student who always wanted to "do" a bed and breakfast inn. A native New Mexican, she knows the answers to all the questions guests might ask—"or you can bet that if I don't, I'll find out for you!" she says. "I can direct guests to all the 'shouldn't miss' galleries, fishing holes to cast your fly for a native trout, the Pueblo dances and ceremonies, quaint shops, and the best restaurants."

The huge square lobby and dining area, with big windows open to the far vista of mountain and mesa, is furnished with soft beige leather sofas begging you to sink into them. The room is divided by a giant fireplace made of rocks from an old Taos Ski Valley copper mine. I asked Dadou about the row of sleigh bells on the rough wood mantel, and he shook them impishly. "I just found them somewhere and I like them," he said, grinning like a boy.

Guest rooms are large and uncluttered, with lounge chairs and tables on which to put things—a necessity, I think. Down comforters and nightly mints are nice features. There is a token television area, mostly used by hopeful amateurs to view ski and tennis tapes.

Breakfast you can bet will be grand—perhaps eggs Catalan and, on the buffet, yogurt, fresh fruit salad, cardamom and piñon-nut dill bread, cereals. Special is Chanterelle Omelette. "The chanterelle mushroom is abundant in the Southwest," Mary says. "We freeze them and love to serve these souvenirs of the summer in the winter." There's a refrigerator where guests can help themselves to ice, soda, or glasses of wine.

Great fun in July is the annual croquet tournament, with participants all bright in tennis whites and white lace dresses. Guests, "of course," may participate.

How to get there: Take Highway 68 north out of Taos; at the blinking light turn right on Highway 150, the Taos Ski Valley Road. One mile past the small town of Arroyo Seco, you'll see the inn on the right; there is a sign.

Stewart House Gallery and Inn

Taos, New Mexico
87571

Innkeepers: Mildred and Don Cheek
Address/Telephone: 46 Ski Valley Road (mailing address: P.O. Box 2326); (505) 776–2913
Rooms: 4; all with private bath; no air conditioning (high elevation). No smoking inn.
Rates: $75 to $120, double; $15 extra person; EPB.
Open: All year.
Facilities and activities: Hot tub, picnic grill area, art gallery. Nearby: Taos Plaza with restaurants and shops. Indian pueblos; museums; hiking, fishing, skiing area; mountain bike and horseback rentals.

If you're looking for a really funky, unusual, and different inn, you'll love the Stewart House. Innkeepers Mildred and Don will be the first to tell you so. "We were out in Carmel (where Don had an art gallery), and we thought, what's the funkiest house we know?" Don says. "I'd been representing Charles Stewart for twenty years, and Mildred told me, 'Why don't you just buy Chuck Stewart's for an inn and a gallery?'"

Mildred chimes in, "We had never discussed it, and Don said 'What? An inn and a gallery?' I said I thought an inn would be fun, and he said, 'When do we move in?'" They closed the deal and moved out to Taos thirty days later. But Don hadn't seen the house in three years.

"It looked terrible," he says good-naturedly. "Weeds everywhere, so abused, took us six months to clean up." But in cleaning up they discovered all kinds of wonderful things Stewart used in the house. All sorts of old wooden doors, iron grills, glass, and shutters were used in odd ways as part of the house. A Victorian oval-windowed front door has become wall-and-window in the nook off the common room. The bathtub in the bathroom of the Artists' Room sports an old claw-foot tub that originally belonged to famous Taos artist R. C. Gorman. Stewart remade most of the inn's doors, some of them from doors 225 years old. He hauled stone from the Rio Grande, hung longhorns over his bed. "I still find new things, and I've lived here since 1989," Mildred says in wonderment.

"Evidently Stewart never threw anything away; he scavenged everywhere for interesting objects to incorporate into his house—and his work," Don says. Each room, guest or common room, is unique, individual, and full of surprises. Don and Mildred didn't want sterile motel rooms, and this is as different as you can get! In addition, the Cheeks live by the rule of good beds, good pillows, and good baths.

"We have two real strict rules here," Don says. "First, everybody's known by their first name, and second, if you want something and don't ask for it, it's your fault." Mildred adds that there's something special about having hot muffins and breads in the morning. "Where else can you get it?" she asks as she begins slicing three yummy loaves of wheat-and-honey bread.

Breakfast went on to include blueberry/walnut pancakes, breakfast burritos, granola with bananas and yogurt, fresh orange juice, tea, and coffee. Other mornings you might have green chili and corn pancakes or sausage and egg casserole. It's usually a buffet, and you'll be well insulated in case it's winter and Don invites you out for a snowball fight in ten-degree weather.

For other meals, four of Taos's most highly rated restaurants are within 2 miles of the inn.

How to get there: Take Highway 68 north to the blinking light at the intersection of highways 64, 522, and 150. Turn right onto 150 (old Taos Ski Valley Road) for .6 mile. The inn will be on the left, and there is a sign.

Willows Inn
Taos, New Mexico
87571

Innkeepers: Estella Enrique and George de Kerckhove
Address/Telephone: Kit Carson Road at Dolan (mailing address: Box 4558);
(505) 758–2558
Rooms: 5; all with private bath; limited wheelchair access. Pets boarded
down the street. No smoking inn.
Rates: $110 to $125, double, EPB.
Open: All year.
Facilities and activities: Lunch and dinner by reservation. Nearby: Taos Plaza
with restaurants, shops, and art galleries; Taos Indian Pueblo; muse-
ums; hiking, horseback riding, skiing; tours.

This lovely inn is on a corner, hidden behind high pink adobe
walls. Once the home of artist E. Martin Hemmings (one of his
paintings hangs in the White House), the inn is now a quiet retreat
for George, an artist, and Estella, who makes sure that serenity
reigns. "We have a lot of professionals who don't want to be both-
ered by ringing phones," she says. In the courtyard a fountain
sparkles in the quiet, and even the cat, Bravo, is unobtrusive. "He
came and sat under my car for three days, and I was going to throw
him out. But he's such a love I kept him."
The inn is decorated in Southwest style punctuated with interesting antiques. Every room has a New Mexican kiva fireplace and
a Mexican tile bath, fresh flowers, and whatever amenities guests

152

may need—bottled water, chocolates from Italy, complimentary refreshments—everything, says Estella, done with special thought in mind. The comfortable overstuffed sofas and chairs in the living room are covered with Laura Ashley fabrics, and there are books and magazines scattered about. The dining room is long, with two tables, one of which is an original Duncan Phyfe. The hutch dates from 1690. "We tried to blend European and Southwest together," the innkeepers say, and they have done so refreshingly.

Estella, born and schooled in Las Cruces, was teaching in California, and George, brought up in Brussels, was painting, when they decided to stop vacationing in Taos and live here instead. George found the property and was initially charmed by the two large willows in front. "They're the oldest in Taos," he claims. Next they decided to add on four rooms in a courtyard setting, engaging a local architect. The main house was built in 1926 by Taos Indians for Hemmings, with his studio a large, light room at the back of the courtyard.

"The architect we chose was a member of the historical society, so he knew everything had to be in keeping with the main house," Estella says. And it all fits right in, doing nothing to disturb the historical marker alongside the front door.

George is versatile: He was trained in Brussels in the hotel industry and came to this country because an uncle who worked for the railroad lured him to California. "But he always told me about Santa Fe [New Mexico], and his stories fascinated me," George says. Now he uses Hemmings's studio for his work, which is hung in the inn as well as in a gallery in town.

Estella is the chef, with George helping to serve, and served might be Belgian waffles (of course!) or German puffed pancake or a Southwestern dish such as an egg-and-cheese or egg-and-sausage casserole. Homemade breads and muffins and fresh-ground coffee, too. "You'll find no plastic, no paper, here," Estella says. "It's all linen, cotton, and china." She laughs. "Even a can of Pepsi looks foreign here!"

How to get there: From U.S. Highway 68 turn east onto Kit Carson Road (the traffic light just east of the Plaza) to Dolan. The inn will be on the right.

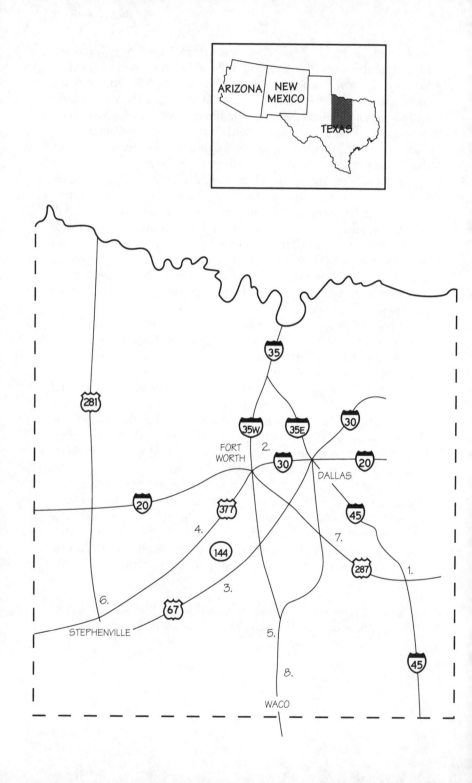

North Texas

Numbers on map refer to towns numbered below.

Raphael House
Ennis, Texas
75119

Innkeeper: Danna K. Cody
Address/Telephone: 500 West Ennis Avenue; (214) 875–1555
Rooms: 6; all with private bath; TV available. Smoking in sun room and on porches.
Rates: $65 to $88, double; $10 less weekdays; corporate rate with light breakfast $52, otherwise EPB.
Open: All year.
Facilities and activities: Lunch, dinner, tea, receptions by reservation, cooking classes spring and fall. Nearby: Colonial Tennis Club, shopping area's twenty-five antiques shops, Landmark Commission driving tour, spring Bluebonnet Trail.

The Raphael House has stood in central Ennis since 1906, and since 1988 Danna Cody has restored it to all its former glory, which was glorious indeed. Now listed on the National Register of Historic Places, Raphael House follows the precept of fine hotels "to provide the very best," Danna says. Now president of the Heritage Society, Danna also is on the board of the Ellis County Historical Society and a member of the Historic Landmark Commission. Yet she confesses to acquiring the house as a sort of lark. Visiting her family after a buying trip to New York (she was a buyer for several Austin stores), she came to look at the house "before it was torn down or burned. Once Ennis Avenue was lined with big houses like this, but this is the only one left." She returned three times and finally made an offer to buy from the last of the Raphaels, a patient in a nursing home. Before she knew it, she was the new owner of the wonderful old house and was fortunate to be able to buy much of the original furniture.

"I feel like I've adopted a family," she says as she shows off the many family photographs that she "inherited." The walls are covered with Raphaels, one of the first families in Ennis back at the turn of the century, when they built the first department store, the Big Store. Rooms are named for the Raphael family members who lived in them. Julia's Room has its original set of white French furniture from 1918, bought by sister Wilhelmina, but kept by her parents. "They wouldn't let Wilhelmina take the set with her because they didn't like the man she married," Danna is delighted to explain.

Ernest's Room has a beautiful tiger oak chest, hidden under a coat of paint when Danna acquired it. "I was having it stripped—I was going to sell it. But the strippers called me and said, 'I think you ought to have a look at this.'"

The Library is stocked with old books as well as new ones, magazines, a television, and a VCR. The entry is so huge that it holds a large grand piano, which Danna encourages guests to play. "Sometimes they'll sing," she says, "and it's so nice to come in at night and hear them."

Breakfasts are as rich as the house, with French toast stuffed with strawberries and cream cheese or what Danna calls her Tex-Czech breakfast with local Kolabasse sausage and marvelous strudel stuffed to the rim with apples, pears, pecans, and coconut.

How to get there: Ennis is on Highway 287, which becomes Ennis Avenue. Raphael House is at the northwest corner of Ennis and Preston Street.

Miss Molly's
Fort Worth, Texas
76106

Innkeepers: Susan and Mark Hancock; Kay Kilgore
Address/Telephone: 109¹/₂ West Exchange; (817) 626–1522
Rooms: 8, 1 with private bath. No smoking inn.
Rates: $60 to $110, single or double; $10 extra person; continental breakfast.
Open: All year.
Facilities and activities: Out the front door: Stockyards Historic Area with rodeos and cattle auctions, restaurants and shop, monthly special events. Nearby: Fort Worth museums, water garden, botanical and Japanese garden, zoo, Sundance Square.

Set right in the center of the authentic Old West area of Fort Worth, Miss Molly's has a partial address because the inn is upstairs, with the front door framed between two storefronts. One is the Star Cafe, a classic cowboy place to eat in Fort Worth. When you reach the top of the steps, you'll be in what was once a popular bordello, and you might even meet the ghosts of Butch Cassidy and the Sundance Kid. No kidding, Fort Worth was a favorite breathing spot for the outlaws, as well as for other gunslingers, rodeo cowboys, and drovers, who weren't too proud to mix with cattle barons and wealthy oilmen at "Miss Josie's," as Miss Molly's once was called.

Before that, the historic inn was a prim and proper hotel and boardinghouse. Once again it has been returned to respectability—although there's still plenty of lively entertainment around this Wild West area with its saloons, Western gear shops, and mounted policemen.

Miss Molly's guest rooms reflect the glory days, with the Cowboy Room done up in boots and saddle and the Cattlemen's with longhorns mounted on the wall. The Gunslinger has a rogue's gallery of photos, but Miss Amelie's is all prissy, with lace curtains and hand-worked linens from her boardinghouse days. As for Miss Josie's, her room is decorated in elaborate Victorian, complete with draped ceiling and red velvet hangings.

There's a marriage certificate in Miss Amelie's room. "If she knew that her room was next to Miss Josie's, Fort Worth's most famous madam . . ." Susan rolls her eyes in mock alarm.

Bathrooms are complete with old-fashioned claw-foot tubs, pedestal basins, and pull-chain toilets. But something new has been added: "Hot baths used to cost extra," Susan says, "but since we moved the plumbing indoors, they're included in the rate."

The continental breakfast is homemade, with hearty specialty breads and muffins and lots of fresh fruit. It's served beneath the stained glass skylight in the parlor, and then it's off to one of the monthly events in busy Fort Worth, whether it's February's Last Great Gunfight, June's Chisholm Trail Roundup, or December's Texas Circuit Rodeo Finals. Fort Worth boasts, "Here is where the West begins," and Miss Molly's is just the sort of place to put you in the mood to relive those "good old days."

How to get there: Take I–35 north from downtown Fort Worth and exit at 28th Street at the Fort Worth Stockyards sign. Go to North Main and turn left to West Exchange (the third traffic light). Turn right, and inn will be on the left; there is a sign over the Star Cafe.

Stockyards Hotel
Fort Worth, Texas
76106

Innkeeper: Mike Davis
Address/Telephone: P.O. Box 4558; (817) 625–6427; outside Texas (800) 423–8471
Rooms: 52, including 4 suites; all with private bath, phone, and TV.
Rates: $95, single; $105, double; EP.
Open: All year.
Facilities and activities: Restaurant, bar. Nearby: Fort Worth Historical District with restaurants, bars, Western shops, Cowtown Coliseum (rodeos), Livestock Exchange Building (livestock auctions); horseback trail rides at Cowtown Corrals; outstanding museums and botanical gardens a short distance away.

Fort Worth may be known as Cowtown, but this historic hotel isn't for just any wrangler coming in off the range. Elegant Western opulence are the words for this hostelry down the block from the horses and cattle of the Exchange.

"Our style is 'Cattle Baron,' classic cowtown comfort," says Mike Davis. But I can't help wondering if cattle barons get a cowboy poem and a homemade praline on the pillow at home on the ranch as they do here at the hotel!

The hotel was built by Colonel Thomas Thannisch in 1907, when thousands of head of cattle were making Fort Worth rich. It exemplified fine Western hospitality then, and the restored (in

1983) hotel is truly elegant and hospitable.

Most elegant is the lobby, with leather Chesterfield sofas and antique chairs upholstered in speckled hide. Bronzes and prints by Western artists Frederic Remington, Charles Russell, and Jack White complement the mirrored doe-hide mantel hung over with massive antlers. It's a real eye-catcher.

Most fun is Booger Red's Saloon, where I sat on the saddle bar stools and nibbled on the happy hour (5:00 to 7:00 p.m.) chicken *fajitas*, nacho chips, and salsa to the tune of soft background country-western music.

Each room has one of four decorative motifs: Western, Indian, Mountain Man, or Victorian. Each also has a view of either the historic shops and saloons of Main Street or the skylighted indoor atrium. I liked relaxing in the wicker settee in the upstairs sitting area, a space surrounded by green plants and bathed in sunlight.

It's also fun to take a ride in one of the classic carriages for a horse-drawn tour, because you have only to step outside the door to be in the middle of the Wild West. You'll see horses being ridden up and down the street, and even the policemen are mounted. And at the Livestock Exchange Building down the block, you can watch cattle being auctioned off just like in the good old days. Fort Worth isn't called Cowtown for nothing; cattle built the West, and they're still big business in Fort Worth; the town's motto is "Where the West begins."

Cowtown Coliseum is also the location for the many rodeos that take place in Fort Worth. You just might be in town to catch one. You can also take a trail ride in the land of the Chisholm Trail, beginning at Cowtown Corrals on 23rd Street before you sashay on over to Billie Bob's, the world's largest honky-tonk, to Texas two-step—if you can! (It's an easy step to learn.)

How to get there: From Highway 820 take North Main exit 13 (Highway 81/287) south to Exchange Avenue. The hotel is on the northeast corner of Exchange and North Main.

Inn on the River
Glen Rose, Texas
76043

Innkeepers: Nancy and Michael Rosenthal
Address/Telephone: 205 Southwest Barnard Street; (817) 897–2101
Rooms: 22, including 3 suites; all with private bath. No smoking inn.
Rates: $70 to $140, single or double, EPB.
Open: All year.
Facilities and activities: Lunch and dinner for groups by reservation; meeting
house for conferences and retreats. Nearby: historic small town square
with restaurants, shops, and galleries; Dinosaur State Park with
renowned dinosaur tracks; Fossil Rim Wildlife Center; Texas
Amphitheater June through October.

The inn is on the river, all right—the beautiful Paluxy River,
framed along the spacious back gardens by three famous old oaks.
The oaks are "The Singing Trees" of an Elvis Presley recording, and the
lyrics were by a guest of the inn when it was the Snyder Sanitarium.

Located in the center of Glen Rose, this interesting building
began life as a sanitarium for good health—Glen Rose was known
for its salubrious mineral waters back in 1919 when the inn was
built, and Nancy and Michael are proud of the Texas Historical
Commission's marker in front of the building. A large square structure, the inn has a wonderful spacious lobby with furnishings of
comfortable overstuffed pieces and light wicker. This lobby certainly
makes an inviting gathering place for guests.

Each room and suite is individually decorated with a refreshing choice of wallpaper, custom bedding, antique wardrobes, and white-tiled bathrooms, creating pleasant dreams. There is a ceiling fan in each room. A small museum on the second floor tells the history of the house; it's a repository of photographs and other memorabilia from when it was the Snyder Sanitarium, as well as details of the building's renovation in 1984.

Breakfast in the sunny, sparkling dining room "means bountiful," Nancy promises, and she certainly lives up to it. You'll be served at least three courses, a feast of Nancy and Michael's specialties, beginning with freshly squeezed orange juice followed by a fruit course changing daily, depending upon what's in the local market. Next come scrambled eggs with chives or homemade sausage baked with eggs and cheese—Nancy's recipe from her innkeeping days at Martha's Vineyard. Michael might make potato pancakes or cheese grits. Breakfast at Inn on the River is an honest-to-goodness meal, and coffee's always out for the early birds.

The rest of the day and night, beverages and cookies are always available in the dining room.

One of the best things is the river. "It's always cool down here, even on the hottest nights," says Michael. During the day there's fishing for sand bass and bluegills. At night I sat outside and watched the moon rise over the tops of those three 250-year-old trees, and I could see how the river and the trees enticed Nancy and Michael into innkeeping at this spot.

The Great Blue Heron Meeting House overlooking the river is a delightful place for a meeting or a retreat. "We're here for our guests," the Rosenthals say, "a quiet and peaceful retreat."

How to get there: The county courthouse on the square faces Barnard Street. With the courthouse on the right, go on down Barnard 2 blocks, and the inn will be on the left.

The Nutt House
Granbury, Texas
76048

Innkeeper: Sylvia "Sam" Overpeck
Address/Telephone: Town Square; (817) 573–5612
Rooms: 15, plus 1 2-bedroom, 2-bath cottage; 6 with private bath, 9 share 2
baths, 1 with wheelchair access.
Rates: $39 to $85, double, EP.
Open: All year.
Facilities and activities: Restaurant open for lunch every day except Monday;
dinner Friday and Saturday nights only; wheelchair access to restau-
rant. Nearby: the entire town square is on the National Register of His-
toric Places; water sports on nearby Lake Granbury.

Everybody loves to say that they've stayed at the Nutt House.
A visit here is always good for a laugh as well as for a good inn and
dining experience.

The house was built in 1893 for two blind brothers, Jesse and
Jacob Nutt. I could tell it was originally a store (a grocery) by the
storefront windows, now attractively hung with drapes and plants.
The building became a hotel in 1919, and it owes its present fame
to Mary Lou Watkins. A great-granddaughter of one of the brothers, she opened the Nutt House Restaurant in 1970. Texans came
from all over the state to dine here on such good country fare as
chicken and dumplings, hot-water cornbread, fresh peach cobbler,
and buttermilk or pecan pie. (There are also several good restau-

rants on the square.) The lobby, where old-fashioned screen doors lead to the restaurant, has wooden floors and the largest Norfolk pine that I've ever seen indoors. Sam told me that it has been there since the early 1970s.

This is a real comfortable country place. The Nutt House is just like home used to be, back in "the good old days," and as informal as life was back then. "If they're coming in late, we just leave their key in the mailbox, with their name on it, and they can let themselves in," says Sam. Coffee's always in the pot in the lobby and in the upstairs hall of the annex. Whoever gets up first plugs them in.

"People just come out in their robes to sit and visit, or play cards and dominoes," Sam says.

The rooms in the hotel, all upstairs, have screen doors and ceiling fans, reminders of an earlier time, although the hotel is now air-conditioned. They're furnished as though it's still 1919, and the upstairs parlor has old ledgers and such for browsing.

The newer rooms in the annex are on the second floor, in what used to be the law offices of the Granbury lawyer who erected the building in the early 1890s. Four connecting offices form four guest suites, and their double transom doors are left intact in case guests want connecting rooms. "The doors were just too lovely to remove," Sam says, and I agree with her.

Sam gives credit to Madge Peters, the former innkeeper, for assisting with the annex decor. She designed the window treatment for the 9-foot-tall windows, a combination of shutters and lace curtains, the latter all handmade by her.

The Nutt House Inn, a log cabin on Lake Granbury just 1 block from the hotel, has a deck overlooking the lake and not-too-distant woods. The two-bedroom, two-bath cabin has antique furnishings, including wrought-iron beds. Guests share a living area, dining room, and kitchen.

How to get there: The inn is on the northeast corner of the square, directly across from the opera house.

Tarleton House
Hillsboro, Texas
76645

Innkeepers: Barbara Jean Rhodes and Charles Rudy
Address/Telephone: 211 North Pleasant Street; (817) 582–7216
Rooms: 9; 7 with private bath, 8 with TV. No smoking inn.
Rates: $68 to $125, double, EPB.
Open: All year.
Facilities and activities: Nearby: Hill College Civil War Museum, and Research Center, Katy Railroad Station and Museum, Historical County Jail, historic homes, Aquilla and Whitney lakes.

You're apt to be welcomed by Bo, a snowy-white bulldog formally known as the Duchess of Tarleton, who is delighted to see guests arrive at this slate-blue and maroon Victorian mansion 60 miles south of Dallas. "We bought this as a retirement project," Charles says. The peace and quiet of Hillsboro is quite a change for this ex-Dallas police officer who used to police South Dallas. "It's a rough neighborhood and there were lots of fights." Now he says how good it is to see people "kind of let down and relax. It's like a Time Machine here, some say it's like going back to their childhood, when they visited Grandma and Aunt Sally."

Charles and Jean have restored and remodeled this old house with its beautiful stained glass windows and eight old fireplaces, called aptly by Charles "works of art." Now, antique Radiant stoves warm and light some of the rooms. "These old stoves give a red and blue glow and a nice heat. They can run you out of here."

Before Charles and Jean retired, they called this their giant getaway house. "In Dallas I had access to lots of junk yards and found old bathtubs, other finds. My wife loves building projects, and she's always rebuilding." Jean has retired from managing Weight Watchers studios in South Texas and is pleased with the work they have done on the house. "The woman who had the house before us liked to strip wood, and we're lucky much of it was never painted," she says. Charles laughs. "The house used to be known as the Green House because it was a yucky shade of green." But he says that Jean always paints her houses blue with cranberry trim, and that's what you'll find.

Charles says he's always liked to cook, and both innkeepers share in kitchen duty, serving Jean's special Corpus Christi eggs, a delicious concoction of eggs, onions, tomatoes, and cheese in tortillas. You'll also have Czech sausage or smoked bacon from nearby West, a town known for this and for *kolaches*, delicious Czech pastries. Breakfast is served promptly at 9:30 A.M., with morning coffee on an hour before.

All the guest rooms are spacious and have either king or twin beds, except for the Green Duck Room. "It has a double bed because it's a very small room," Charles says almost apologetically. "It's like being in a barn—but with all the luxury of air conditioning and heating, and a full bath with a shower." Rooms are light and bright with lots of windows—many rooms have bays and more than one view.

How to get there: From I–35 take the cutoff to Hillsboro to the courthouse. From there go east on Franklin to Pleasant, then north on Pleasant; the inn will be on the right.

The Oxford House
Stephenville, Texas
76401

Innkeepers: Paula and Bill Oxford
Address/Telephone: 563 North Graham Street; (817) 965–6885 or 968–8171
Rooms: 4; all with private bath. No smoking inn.
Rates: $72, double, EPB.
Open: All year.
Facilities and activities: Lunch, dinner, and afternoon tea by reservation.
Nearby: use of the Oxfords' swimming pool five minutes across town;
tour of bronzing factory; Fossil Rim Wildlife Preserve and Glen Rose
dinosaur tracks forty-five minutes away; local festivals.

When Judge W. J. Oxford, Sr. was paid the sum of $3,000 in
silver coins for trying a case back in the 1890s, he knew just what
to do with such a treasure. Between 1890 and 1898, he built the
Oxford House. The judge's third wife told stories of how it took one
thousand loads of fill dirt, at 75 cents a load, even to make a start
on the foundation, and how the lumber was brought from Fort
Worth across the Bosque River.

It was a busy time at the judge's back then, and you'll still find
a busy whirl at the Oxford House, what with weddings, receptions,
luncheons, and dinners, as well as breakfast for inn guests.

"We even do an English tea," Paula Oxford says. "Three courses: dainty savory sandwiches, then piping hot scones and nut
breads topped with butter, jam, and lemon curd, finishing with a

dessert course of moist cakes, strawberry tarts, truffles, and pastries."

Bill Oxford is a third-generation Oxford attorney with close ties to the judge and the judge's interesting home. Paula and Bill live across town, and, as Paula says, "Nobody was using the old house, so it was my idea to make it into a bed and breakfast inn." There's much family history bound up in the tall Victorian manor. Marie's Suite, named for a child who grew up in the house in its early days, contains an antique seven-piece bedroom suite from the 1890s. Aunt Mandy's Room is decorated with photographs of an aunt who was "a real pill," Paula says. "She expected to be waited on hand and foot, so they always put her in the room that was hot with sun in the summer and cold in the winter, hoping she wouldn't stay long!"

Each guest room has a private bath with antique claw-foot tub. Bubble bath and special soaps encourage you to soak and meditate—very relaxing. The Victorian charm of the inn includes a sleigh bed built in the 1890s, beveled glass mirrors, and antique armoires. Porches, reaching three-quarters around the house, are made of cypress with hand-turned gingerbread trim.

"Zandra McElmurray Coweth helps me out, and she's responsible for the good food that keeps the inn humming," Paula says about Zandra's pear in brandy with crumbles on top, sausage yeast biscuits, German cinnamon rolls, or fruit swirl coffee cake. They start the day out just fine. Other meals are by reservation; if you order dinner, possibilities are chicken breast in wine sauce or seafood crepes, perhaps served with rice/apricot pilaf, mandarin orange salad, and cheesecake with praline sauce.

If you park in the back, you'll enter under an arbor. The wide back lawn has a big old swing, and there are white chairs and tables under the trees.

How to get there: Highway 108 becomes Graham through town, and the inn is 2 blocks north of the town square, on the east side of the street. There's a sign out in front.

The Bonnynook
Waxahachie, Texas
75165

Innkeepers: Bonnie and Vaughn Franks
Address/Telephone: 414 West Main; (214) 938–7207
Rooms: 4; all with private bath, 2 with Jacuzzi. No smoking inn.
Rates: $60 to $70, double; $15 extra person; EPB.
Open: All year.
Facilities and activities: Coffee nook with small refrigerator, lunch and dinner by reservation. Nearby: downtown with restaurants, shops, antiques, and craft malls; historic square with famous courthouse.

Driving up to the Bonnynook, you'll be amazed at the garden that takes the place of a lawn. Green plants all year, and, in season, flowers, flowers everywhere—bachelor buttons, carnations, daisies, roses, chrysanthemums—and planted in the center, a plaque that reads: "Historic Waxahachie Incorporated recognizes this property built in 1895 as worthy of preservation."

"Both Vaughn and I were brought up in old houses," Bonnie says. "We had old furniture that didn't work in modern houses, so we said, 'why don't we look for an old home that needs restoration? If nothing else, we'll have a home.' Soon as we walked into this house, Vaughn and I turned to each other and said, 'I think we're home.'"

The first thing that caught my eye in the double parlor was what Bonnie says is an Austrian cozy corner, a huge piece of furniture that's a sofa built into a bookshelf and a chest of drawers, with a pull-out table/desk, alongside. All sorts of interesting collectibles surrounded the cozy upholstering, and the piece fits beautifully in a corner of the room, a cozy corner indeed.

Most of the inn's furnishings are in keeping, giving it a distinctive European air. Bonnie is a sociologist and Vaughn an engineer, and I think neither of them has never disposed of anything that's a legacy from their Austrian and Welsh heritages. Which makes the Bonnynook practically a museum, and a comfortable and entertaining one at that.

The antique clawfooted table in the Sterling Room was rescued from Bonnie's grandmother. "She was folding linen on it," Bonnie says in amused dismay while explaining that the room is named for her favorite nephew. The Morrow Room has her granddad's trunk, still with its labels from Wales, and with Uncle Wiggly books spilling from its bottom drawer. "I grew up on Uncle Wiggly books," Bonnie says nostalgically. "As for the trunk, it's been to college five times."

Bathrooms are like greenhouses, large and bright with green plants surrounding the bathtubs. More plants bloom on the porches, both upstairs and down.

Candy, fresh flowers, evening snacks from cheese and crackers to cookies and brownies, encourage guests to comment in the comment book, "which is a lot of fun." Breakfast is a combined effort because Vaughn loves to cook as much as Bonnie does, except that he has his recipes written down whereas Bonnie's are in her head. "When we get in the kitchen, anything goes!" they confess. Anything, as in special crepes, shoo-fly pie, applesauce pancakes, ginger pears. . . .

"It's such a nice feeling, when people who were all stressed out are ready to leave, and you get a nice hug," Bonnie says. "They seem to say, 'I'm all relaxed, ready to get back.' I like to think that when people walk away from us, they have a sense of who we are, as we have a sense of who they are. I want to know people, let them know me."

How to get there: From I–35 take Business Route 287 (West Main) east; from I–45 to Ennis, take 287 west 11 miles to Waxahachie.

The Zachary Davis House
West, Texas
76691

Innkeeper: Marjorie Devlin
Address/Telephone: 400 North Roberts; (817) 826–3953
Rooms: 8; all with private bath. No smoking inn.
Rates: $40 to $60, double, EPB.
Open: All year.
Facilities and activities: Nearby: historic town with restaurants and bakeries,
antiques and craft shops; Playdium Swimming Pool; festivals; hunting
and fishing at Lake Whitney.

In her youth, Marjorie says she was bitten by the hotel bug,
going to school mornings and in the afternoons working in the
largest hotel in her home town of Laredo. She went on to bigger
and better things in the hotel industry, and you can be sure she
knows how to take good care of her guests. Turn-down service,
sweets on your pillow, complimentary wine, all combined with a
lovely old home decorated with perfectly color-coordinated bed
linens, towels, and comforters. "We had a lot of fun picking out the
linens," Marjorie says of the family who lured her back to her home
state after years in California.

"They all wanted me to move back to Texas, for one thing, but
I didn't want to just sit around." Marjorie, beginning such a new
career, has eight grandchildren and twelve great-grandchildren,
from age two up to nineteen, and it was a granddaughter who said,

"Grannie, there's a nine-bedroom house here in West that would make a wonderful bed and breakfast—and we really need it!" They convinced her that with all her hotel experience, having an inn should be right up her alley.

In remodeling the house, which was built in 1890 for an early settler of West (originally named Bold Springs), Marjorie at first was baffled by the problem of adding a bath to each room. But it was solved very cleverly: Each room has the necessary fixtures concealed behind an attractive screen. (All except two have showers, not bathtubs.)

There's a sense of humor here. The Quack Room has a border of wallpaper ducks around the ceiling, ducky linens, and a wooden duck, and "I have several doctors who ask for this room," Marjorie says with a twinkle. The Southwest Room, the smallest (a single), has the largest bathroom in the house, and the Downstairs Room, with oriental furnishings, is called that not only because that's where it is, but, says Marjorie, "I couldn't decide whether to call it the Chinese Room or the Emperor's."

Each room is different, and it's hard to make a choice. The Poppy Room has white wicker furniture to set off the bright poppy linens, whereas the Bluebonnet Room, blue and white, celebrates the Texas state flower. Mary's Room is named after a previous owner's daughter, who said, "Oh, Mrs. Devlin, I would love to have it named after me!"

Breakfast usually features Nemecek bacon or sausage—they've been in business in West since 1896—as well as all kinds of eggs in casserole or out. The full country breakfast also alternates with French toast, chicken or beef *fajitas* (sautéed meat wrapped in flour tortillas), and hotcakes. West, known for its Czech heritage, also is famous for *kolaches,* and Marjorie is sure to serve them, but you'll probably want more from some of the town's good bakeries!

Marjorie sponsors two Little League teams on the three back acres of her land she calls her "back forty." "I like to be part of the community," she says. In the entry just beside the door is an authentic Czech costume. "It's what everybody wears, come West-fest over the Labor Day weekend."

How to get there: From I–35 take exit 353 in West and go east on Oak Street to Roberts. Turn north 1¹/₂ blocks, and the inn will be on the right.

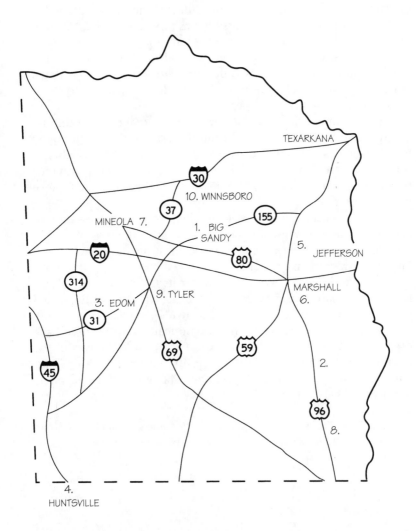

TEXARKANA

30

10. WINNSBORO

37

MINEOLA 7.

1. BIG SANDY

155

5. JEFFERSON

20

80

314

9. TYLER

MARSHALL
6.

3. EDOM

31

69

59

2.

45

96

8.

4.
HUNTSVILLE

East Texas

Numbers on map refer to towns numbered below.

Annie's Country Inn
Big Sandy, Texas
75755

Innkeeper: Les Lane
Address/Telephone: 101 North Tyler Street; (214) 636–4355
Rooms: 13; 8 with private bath, all with phone, 1 with TV. No smoking inn.
Rates: $38 to $115, EPB, except Saturday continental breakfast.
Open: All year.
Facilities and activities: Restaurant (closed Saturdays), gift shop, needlecraft gallery. Nearby: Needlecraft Fair in July, Quilt Show in September, and Annie's Pecan Festival in November.

This spanking gray-and-white dollhouse of an inn looks like one Queen Victoria might have played with in miniature. The rooms, except for the Queen Anne Room downstairs, are small, but I found them charming in every detail. Some rooms have lofts, perfect for kids.

The walls, with striped or floral wallpaper, are wainscoted; lace curtains frame the windows; fluffy, frilled, and lacy spreads and pillow shams cover the beds. Each room has a copy of an antique safe. (It's really a refrigerator; on Saturdays, when the inn and restaurant staff have their day off, your breakfast is in the safe instead of in the tearoom.)

I loved the atmosphere of camaraderie I found in the parlor when I arrived. It was early evening, and everybody was gathered around the television set, watching a vital football game. "Come join the party," they called out, waving glasses in the air.

"Looks pretty crowded to me," I answered."There's always room for more," they said, and sure enough, space was made for me on the antique sofa and I joined them with a glass of wine.

It's always a treat to relax in a rocker on the porch or visit in the parlor with other guests, invariably interesting people. I also love the treat of the gourmet breakfast served in the tearoom across the road (except Saturday, when it's continental style). There's a terrible choice: Should I indulge in the cream-cheese-and-pecan-stuffed French toast, or should I have the strawberry crepes? Both begin with either fresh-squeezed orange juice or a delicious cold strawberry soup and a muffin.

The tearoom, with its white picket fence and circular verandas, is in one of Big Sandy's oldest homes, built in 1905. In 1982 it received the town's first official Texas Historical Marker. And yes (everyone always asks, says the innkeeper), there really is an Annie; she founded a very successful needlecraft mail-order company, Annie's Attic, which operates right out of little Big Sandy.

Both the Attic and the Tea Room have delightful displays of pretty arts and crafts. The rag dolls, the aprons, the quilts and place mats—beware, you may be inspired to begin some needlework of your own. There even are patterns to make old-fashioned clothes for costumes and, I guess, for just plain fun.

How to get there: Big Sandy is on Highway 80 between Dallas and Longview. The inn is right in the middle of town, where Highway 155 crosses 80.

Pine Colony Inn
Center, Texas
75935

Innkeepers: Regina Wright; Marcille and Pershing Hughes
Address/Telephone: 500 Shelbyville Street; (409) 598–7700
Rooms: 12; 2 2-room suites with private bath, 8 share 2 whole and 2 half-baths. No smoking inn.
Rates: $27.50, single; $45 to $55, double; EPB.
Open: All year.
Facilities and activities: Art shows, yearly quilt show. Nearby: restaurant, nineteenth-century courthouse; use of swimming pool, fishing, hiking, and hunting at family's Caddo Pass Lodge; Sabine National Forest; Toledo Bend Reservoir and Pinkston Lake.

This old hotel has been lovingly restored by daughter Regina and parents Marcille and Pershing, who pride themselves on being natives of Shelby County, one of the oldest in Texas. "Dustin is the eighth generation in the country," Regina says of her young son. "Suddenly people are into genealogy, and they come to consult with Mom; we go back more than one hundred years." Marcille writes a nostalgia column for the local paper, telling family stories like Thanksgiving in 1874 when her grandfather was a young man.

"We don't put on any front," she says, "we're all family. Guests tell us, 'We'll be back in two weeks, can we unload our car?'" There's a storeroom kept for just such a contingency. You'll find Pershing wearing his overalls, maybe sweeping the front porch.

"He's just a little old country man," says his daughter fondly. As for feeling at home, "At first people want to make sure they have their room key. After a while they realize there's no need." If the front door is locked, guests can come and go at will up the side stairs to the front balcony and into the large sitting room, complete with overstuffed sofas and a television set.

The rustic hotel has dark-red Mexican tile on the first floor, what seems like acres of it, all laid by Regina and Marcille, who'll be glad to tell you how much work it was! Upstairs, they've kept the beautiful pine floors. Originally the Halley Hotel, the building was closed for seventeen years and was in bad repair. "Mom and Dad kept saying something should be done about this nice, big, old building," Regina says with a laugh, "and finally we broke down and bought it."

All rooms have ceiling fans, and a fascinating touch is the network of white pipes snaking all along the ceilings. "Can you believe that's a sprinkler system?" Regina says. "It cost $20,000 even that long ago!"

Breakfast might be pancakes with homemade ribbon cane or blueberry syrup, eggs "any way," bacon, sausage, or you might be asked, "What *can* you eat?" With enough notice, Regina says, "We can run to the grocery store."

Rooms are small and simple but comfortable, with touches that make each one individual. Miss Barnhart's Room honors the woman whose bedroom suite furnishes it. The Indian Room has both pottery and paintings done by Regina. An old spinning wheel decorates the entrance hall, and a bank of old-fashioned brass mailboxes, one for each room, is set into the wall by the front door. If guests stay long enough to receive mail, they get to use one.

How to get there: Highway 87 becomes Shelbyville Street, and the inn is on the corner of Pine Street.

Red Rooster Square
Edom, Texas
75754

Innkeepers: Doris and Bob Moore
Address/Telephone: Route 3, Box 3387, Ben Wheeler 75754; (903) 852–6774
Rooms: 3 share 2 baths; wheelchair accessible. No smoking inn.
Rates: $55, double; EPB. No credit cards.
Open: All year.
Facilities and activities: Nearby: Edom has pine-scented country lanes for hik-
    ing; craftspeople; East Texas antiques stores; famous Canton First
    Mondays Trade Days half an hour away.

    Quite a surprise is this large rural-Victorian home, in a town so
small it doesn't even have a post office! The original family Red
Rooster was an antiques shop owned by Bob's grandfather back in
Eton, Ohio; this Red Rooster is really in the country, because you're
out of town as fast as you're in it. This is "real country," and I recommend lazy hours on the long front porch alternating between
swing and rocking chair. But little Edom also has a lot of happy festivals, which Doris and Bob will be happy to tell you about.
    The guest rooms are comfortable, new and bright, just about
what you want your home to look like, and the downstairs bath
has a luxurious Jacuzzi. The Moores have gone into the inn business because, Doris says with a laugh, "We built a too-big house!"
Their children are grown, and when Doris planned the large home,
her husband kept pointing out that "the kids won't be home every

weekend." Nevertheless, "I built the house just like I like it," says a happy Mrs. Moore, who completely enjoys her guests. So now they are an inn, and a very spacious, welcoming one indeed.

They're close to Canton with its famous First Mondays Trade Days. "If you go to Canton," said Doris, "you have to have show and tell. We've had a bunch of women sitting on a sheet I spread on the floor." But be sure to reserve ahead, because "that's our biggest weekend," she cautions.

The full breakfast is served family style, spread out on the bar dividing the large kitchen and den. "We always decide the night before what time to serve breakfast"; the innkeepers consult their guests, and the majority rules. Then it's your choice whether to pile your plate up and sit in the breakfast room or to relax in the den, watching television.

Either place, delicious is the sausage strata—layers of egg, cheese, sausage, and mushrooms—served with orange juice, melon and grapes, cinnamon twists, and blueberry muffins. The blueberries are grown in Edom, and big, juicy ones they are, too. They are a big crop for the area. If you don't believe it, come to the Blueberry Festival at berry harvest time.

If you're still hungry, there's also oatmeal with brown sugar and raisins, ideal for the cholesterol-conscious and "very healthy for everyone," says the chef.

And for dinner, Edom may be a *very* small town, but Doris recommends The Shed, a little restaurant serving "good home cooking."

How to get there: The inn is 2¹/₂ miles south of Highway 64 on Highway 314. Go south off I–20 (Van exit), take Highway 314 south to Edom, and the inn will be on the left.

Wild Briar,
The Country Inn at Edom
Edom, Texas
75764

Innkeepers: Mary and Max Scott
Address/Telephone: P.O. Box 21, Ben Wheeler 75754; (903) 852–3975
Rooms: 6; all with private bath. Smoking permitted in public room ("the snug").
Rates: $100, per room, MAP. No credit cards.
Open: All year except for Tuesdays and Wednesdays when holidays fall on those days.
Facilities and activities: Dinner by reservation; gift shop of East Texas crafts. Nearby: hiking paths, craftspeople, East Texas antiques stores, Canton First Mondays Trade Days.

Wild Briar is a two-story manor-style brick house almost completely hidden in the trees surrounding it: oaks, sweet gum, pines, cedars, and holly. Although the inn is named for the wild berry vines on its twenty-three acres, indoors it's as British as Mary and Max can make it.

"We travel in England, and when we go, we like to visit many of the inns our rooms are named for, as well as seeking out new places. We want to be a true country inn, where people can stay and feel welcome." The "snug," where smoking is permitted, copies the coziness the Scotts enjoyed in British pubs. There are videos of old movies, and dinner orders are taken.

Mary taught junior high school for twenty years, and she'll teach you a great deal about England and its inns. The Wild Briar presents a mix of English, Welsh, and Scottish country inns the Scotts have stayed at. Each room is named for one of their favorites. Whether you stay in Sturminster Newton, Bonthddu, Harrogate, Glebe, Thakeham, or Tresanton, you'll be glad you did.

"What do most people come and do?" I asked Mary. "Nothing!" was her mirthful answer.

The morning begins with a mug of coffee in the kitchen or on the patio, but at breakfast you'll have to exchange the mug for a cup in Mary's Spode Summer Palace pattern to match the breakfast china. Juices, fruit like grapefruit and strawberries or the huge Edom blueberries, strawberry bread, zucchini muffins, all go with "any eggs to order" and bacon or sausage. Mary often makes quiche ahead so Max won't have a problem feeding guests if it's her turn to teach Sunday school. On weekends Max makes gravy for biscuits, "his forte, not mine," Mary said.

Dinners are delicious full-course meals, perhaps starting with gumbo or broccoli-cheese soup; next comes a green or fruit salad, followed by rolled tenderloin with cornbread dressing or buttermilk-pecan breast of chicken. Family-style vegetables might be a selection of green beans, new potatoes, corn on the cob, squash, sliced fresh tomatoes, all "from our farmer friends down the road." Dessert? How about profiteroles, or mystery pie, so called because you can't tell which fruit's in it.

The Scotts are civic-minded folk; Mary serves on the city council of Edom (with a population of 300), and Max is on the water board.

How to get there: Take Highway 314 south off I–20 (Van exit) to Edom. Turn right on FM (Farm Road) 279 to FM 2339 on your left. Wild Briar is the first driveway on the left on FM 2339.

The Whistler
Huntsville, Texas
77340

Innkeeper: Mary T. Clegg
Address/Telephone: 906 Avenue M; (409) 295–2834 or (713) 524–0011; or
catch Mary on her digital pager (713) 788–8672
Rooms: 5; 4 with private bath. No smoking inn.
Rates: $85 to $100, double, EPB. No credit cards.
Open: All year.
Facilities and activities: Lunch and dinner by reservation, three acres of
wooded land. Nearby: restaurants and shops on Town Square, Sam
Houston's home, the Woodlands and Steamboat House, historic ceme-
tery, scuba-diving school in old quarry.

When Mary Clegg says she is inviting you into her ancestral
home, she's not fooling: This 130-year-old mansion has been in the
family for six generations. Mary's great-uncle built the home
around 1859. Mary's mother, Marguerite Thomason, was born in
the house and lived here for most of her ninety years. "When
Mother passed away, none of my two brothers or my sister wanted
the house. Bulldoze it, they said."

But Mary's husband said, "You love that house." They began
restoration in 1986, and it's unbelievable what they accomplished.
Now Mary is a widow, and she takes pleasure in showing the many
family mementos, old photographs, and portraits. She is particularly
proud of the framed proclamation from the Heritage Land Program,

signed by Texas's past governor Dolph Briscoe, attesting to the fact that the land was in constant use for agricultural purposes in the same family for over one hundred years. The inn also boasts a Texas Historical Marker.

Mary named the inn The Whistler in honor of her mother's father. "My grandfather, he was happy, he whistled all the time, and we all loved to hear him." Mary's downstairs bathroom claims the distinction of having the first indoor plumbing in Huntsville. There is wonderful furniture in the inn, much of it on a scale to match the heroic proportions of the house. A great deal of it was made in the past by inmates of Huntsville's penitentiary, but the dining-room table has a different story. It's from the Deep South, Mary says as she tells how during the Civil War its owner went down on her knees to beg Union soldiers not to damage her rosewood piano. That must have been some piano, because what is left of it is now the inn's large dining table.

Guest rooms are on the same generous scale. A surprising contrast, although on the same expansive scale, is the huge, modern cathedral-ceilinged common room and kitchen added to the rear of the house. Mary says that guests "all love this room and say they're going home to build one just like it! The party always ends up here."

Mary's breakfast specialty is a dish she calls Julia's, named after "my sister, my daughter, my grandmother, and my granddaughter," she says with a laugh. "If I disclose my special seasoning, people go home to make it, then call me to say it doesn't taste the same!" The meal also includes ham, sausage, or bacon; "always grits"; homemade biscuits; and oat bran, blueberry, or pecan muffins. There are pecan trees all over the place, and Mary picks the nuts herself. She picks the blueberries, too, at the Texas Blueberry Farm nearby.

Guests, Mary says, mostly like to sit on the long front porch and vegetate. She has a photograph of the house taken in 1899 showing the exact same lineup of chairs sitting on the porch.

How to get there: Take exit 116 off I–35; go east about 1 mile on Highway 30 (11th Street) to signal light on Avenue M. Turn left and drive 2 blocks; driveway of inn is on the left, and there is a sign.

The Captain's Castle
Jefferson, Texas
75657

Innkeepers: Marian and Pete Sorensen
Address/Telephone: 403 East Walker Street; (903) 665–2330
Rooms: 8 (5 in main house, 3 in Carriage House on grounds); 6 with private
  bath, all with TV. No smoking inn.
Rates: $75 to $95, double, EPB.
Open: All year.
Facilities and activities: Sun deck, gazebo. Nearby: restaurants, antiques
  shops, historic homes, riverboat ride, surrey ride, Mardi Gras, Jefferson
  Historic Pilgrimage, Christmas Candlelight Tour.

In the early 1870s Captain Thomas J. Rogers combined two
houses: one of Texas Planters architecture, which he had oxen roll
on logs across town from down on the riverfront, and one that was
already on this site. The more imposing one he attached to the
front, and this is what you'll see.

"He was trying to make his house antebellum," Marian says
with a delighted laugh. Well, I don't know how antebellum The
Captain's Castle is, but it certainly is impressive, with tall white
columns, spacious grounds, and both American and Lone Star flags
flying. Impressive on the inside, too, it was a popular feature on the
Jefferson Historic Home Tour even before the Sorensens acquired it.

"We were on the way to a wedding in Longview," Pete says,
"and just on impulse we walked into the chamber [of commerce]

office and asked, 'Do you know of a business for sale? We are bored to tears.' I had retired from the oil business and we were looking for something to take up the slack time." The Sorensens are from Louisiana—Cajun country—but thanks to his ancestors Pete looks more like a Danish sea captain, white beard, tattoo, and all, than a retired oil man. Even more surprising is that he is quite artistic. He paints, or rather, he did before he became a busy innkeeper!

Both Pete and Marian are delighted with this "impulsive" turn in their lives. "What's nice about it," says Marian, "is that you get into the mainstream, even though you're retired." People, she says, bring the world to them. Adds Pete, "We pamper the daylights out of them!"

Breakfast is served on a massive claw-foot table, and Pete is the chef. There may be scrambled eggs, bacon and sausage, cheese grits or hashed brown potatoes, and homemade sesame biscuits, as well as fruit and orange juice. Afternoons, the social hour brings wine and chili cheese dip or Cajun meatballs. Pete learned to cook early on. "I was the next-to-youngest of twelve children, and I would go to learn in Cajun restaurants in New Orleans," he says.

The bustle-back chairs in the parlor, says Pete, "came from the town's very popular house of ill repute," which flourished down by the river when Jefferson was a wild and raucous riverboat town before the Civil War. Today things are more sedate.

Guest rooms are large, comfortable. Rachel's Room downstairs has Marian's great-grandmother's white linen Second Day dress in a corner, and the furniture is all Jefferson Antique. Melissa's Room upstairs has a trunk overflowing with old toys, a stand hung with straw garden hats, and a white wicker cupboard stocked with old dolls. "Women and girls alike try on the hats and play with the dolls," Marian says with delight.

The new Carriage House has a full-length covered porch overlooking a cool fountain and the huge old pecan trees in the garden. Carriage House guests get to enjoy breakfasting in the air-conditioned, glass-enclosed gazebo in the garden.

How to get there: Go east at the intersection of Highway 59 and Highway 49 and drive 2 blocks to Alley Street; turn right, go 2 blocks. The Captain's Castle will be on your right on the corner of Alley and Walker.

Excelsior House
Jefferson, Texas
75657

Innkeeper: Gloria Bennett
Address/Telephone: 211 West Austin Street; (903) 665–2513
Rooms: 14; 12 with private bath.
Rates: $40 to $80, double, EP. No credit cards.
Open: All year.
Facilities and activities: Breakfast served ($4.75). Nearby: restaurants, antiques shops, museums, historic homes, horsedrawn carriage rides, riverboat rides, Mardi Gras, Jefferson Historic Pilgrimage in May, Christmas Candlelight Tour.

The Excelsior House has quite a reputation, especially because railroad magnate Jay Gould signed the register "End of Jefferson, Texas." He was angry because the town fathers wouldn't give him a right of way for his railroad.

Other, more contented guests, like Ulysses S. Grant, Oscar Wilde, Jacob Astor, and W. H. Vanderbilt, signed the register, too. If you're wondering what they were doing in this sleepy East Texas town, then you need to know that once Jefferson was Texas's second-largest city.

But with the end of the steamboat and with the absence of a railroad (shades of Gould), Jefferson declined into a small country town. It seemed likely to stay that way until a group of local women raised enough money to restore the Excelsior House and to extol the historic aspects of the town. Today the Excelsior, with other historic Jefferson hostelries, is a favorite tourist goal.

The hotel is lovely, a treasure of antiques. Oriental carpets cover the polished wood floors, heavy draperies grace the windows, old portraits hang on the walls. The Sevres chandelier in the dining room has never been wired for electricity, although no candles are burned in it nowadays.

Many of the rooms have names, including—what else?—the Jay Gould Room. The Sleigh Bed Bedroom has a fine example of this piece of furniture; the Grant Room has a ceiling-high four-poster bed. The Rosewood Room is dedicated to Lady Bird Johnson, who donated objets d'art to the room: a clock given by her father to her mother, and two rose glass vases. The Diamond Bessie Suite is named for a beautiful "lady of the night" who was murdered by her handsome gambler lover. His murder trial is enacted every year during the Jefferson Pilgrimage.

The lobby has exhibits of Jefferson memorabilia in glass cases and on the walls. The ballroom has a pressed-tin ceiling, large oriental rugs, a grand piano, and a crystal chandelier.

Breakfast is the only meal served, but it's a full one. Ham, eggs, grits, and the Excelsior's famous orange-blossom muffins are the hotel's interpretation of a proper plantation breakfast.

How to get there: From Highway 49 (Broadway) take Polk or Line Street south to Austin. The hotel is equidistant from either.

Hale House
Jefferson, Texas
75657

Innkeeper: L. D. Barringer
Address/Telephone: 702 South Line Street; (903) 665–8877
Rooms: 6 share 4 baths. No smoking inn.
Rates: $65 to $90, per room; rollaway $15; EPB.
Open: All year.
Facilities and activities: Nearby: Jefferson Historical Museum, Jay Gould's private railroad car, historic home tours, riverboat and surrey rides, Mardi Gras, Pilgrimage in May, Christmas Candlelight Tour.

Hale House is yet another example of the Victorian charm of Jefferson, the East Texas town that practically invented breakfast inns for Texas. The inn is furnished with antiques of oak and pine and made cozy with family heirlooms. An antique melodeon (forerunner of the pump organ) sits in a corner of the parlor paying silent tribute to May Belle Hale, whose parents built the house between 1872 and 1884. May Belle was a local musician and composer. In 1923 she had a waltz published by a New York music house: "Twilight Memories," subtitled "A Texas Lullaby."

The inn is on quiet, residential Line Street across the street from City Park. A brisk stroll around the block-square park is a fine way to start the day.

Jefferson was once Texas's second-largest city, in case you were wondering about all the historical excitement in the air year round. In 1873 Eastern financier and railroad magnate Jay Gould put a "curse" on Jefferson because city fathers refused to grant right of way for his rolling stock. Believe the curse or not, Jefferson declined when the natural dam keeping Big Cypress Bayou at navigable level collapsed, putting a finish to the town's main source of prosperity, river shipping.

But today things are hopping, and the innkeeper is very helpful about guiding guests to Jefferson attractions. It's a good idea to make reservations not only at the inn but at fine restaurants like the Galley Pub or the Stillwater as well.

Four of the inn's guest rooms have names that begin with the letter D. I was hard put to decide between Dana's Room, with cool white wicker; Diane's Room with its sideboard from England, circa 1890; Donna's Room, furnished with fine American oak; and Denise's Room, of Pennsylvania Dutch decor, with a handmade quilt on the double bed and hand-painted French oven breadboards on the walls.

If D is not your favorite letter, there's Lacey's Room, all fancy with a queen-sized bed draped in floor-length lace and walls finished in a French glazed wash. Or Chrisi's Room, with a matched set of antique burled-oak-and-walnut furniture made in Germany. Hale House is nothing if not eclectic, and you'll have a wonderful time admiring all the variety.

The cheerful sun porch has a large-screen television, and there's also a gazebo for a serene retreat. The elegant three-course breakfast, served in the formal dining room complete with crystal and silver, begins with hot breads and fresh fruit of the season. Early, early risers will find not one but two morning coffee areas: at one end of the hall on a French washstand from the 1850s, and at the other end on a German walnut cabinet.

How to get there: Go east on Highway 49 (Broadway) and turn right on Line Street. The inn is on your left in the center of the block across from City Park.

McKay House
Jefferson, Texas
75657

Innkeepers: Peggy and Tom Taylor
Address/Telephone: 306 East Delta Street; (903) 665–7322; in Dallas (214) 348–1929
Rooms: 3, plus 2 suites in main house, 2 in rear cottage; all with private bath. No smoking inn.
Rates: $80, double, EPB. Discount on weekdays.
Open: All year.
Facilities and activities: Nearby: Jefferson restaurants and antiques shops, museums, historic homes, horse-and-carriage rides, riverboat rides, Mardi Gras, Jefferson Historic Pilgrimage in May, Candlelight Tour at Christmas.

The McKay House has undergone all sorts of changes and enlargements; for starters the Taylors have raised the roof to make two lovely new suites. Still imbued with the spirit of old times, Peggy continues to dress in period costume to serve breakfast, and Tom wields hammer and nails to continue refurbishing the historic house. The dining area has been restored, and a conservatory designed for both dining and relaxing now overlooks a lovely garden.

"McKay House is one of the oldest houses in Jefferson," Peggy says, "and the oldest operating as a bed and breakfast, so we want to be as authentic as possible; we want things to be as they were back then." Television? Don't be silly, they didn't have television in the 1800s, Peggy says with conviction.

If this sounds like hardship, you couldn't be more mistaken. Peggy and Tom travel extensively, and Peggy says she tries to take notes on ideas that will make her guests comfortable. Things like designer linens, Crabtree & Evelyn toiletries, fresh flowers in the rooms, and custom-made Amish quilts on the beds—she sent wallpaper samples to Indiana to have them made to match.

The Taylor imagination and sense of fun are at work everywhere. The Keeping Room in the rear guest cottage is patterned after the room where Peggy says pioneers did everything—cooking, eating, sleeping, bathing. The footed tub is in the dormer, the dresser is an old icebox, a chopping block is an end table; and the commode is enclosed like an outdoor privy in a little house of original wood shingles, complete with half-moon peephole. The cottage's other room is a Sunday Room, like the parlor used when farmers cleaned up and went to town for the Sabbath.

When I opened the clothes cupboard in my room and found two garments hanging there, I thought the last guests had forgotten them. But no, each guest room is complete with Victorian nightwear: a woman's nightgown and a man's sleep shirt. Peggy hopes they are used.

"We want our guests to know how it was back in the 1850s," she says. They have fun wearing the vintage hats at the full sit-down breakfast in the conservatory. "When all the ladies wear their hats, you've never seen so much picture taking," Peggy says with a laugh. And what a conversation starter, to get people acquainted!

Peggy's "Gentleman's Breakfast" of Chicken a la McKay or honey-cured ham, cheese biscuits, and homemade strawberry bread with cream cheese and strawberry preserves is something to write home about. Hospitality, says Peggy, is the hallmark of McKay House, and you may be called to breakfast with a tune on the old Packard pump organ. "Or better yet, just pull a few stops yourself," says Peggy.

How to get there: The McKay House is located 2 blocks east of U.S. 59 and 4 blocks south of Highway 49 (Broadway).

Pride House
Jefferson, Texas
75657

Innkeeper: Ruthmary Jordan
Address/Telephone: 409 East Broadway; (903) 665–2675
Rooms: 10, including 1 suite (6 in main house, 4 in annex); all with private
bath; 1 room for handicapped.
Rates: $65 to $100, double; $10 extra person, EPB.
Open: All year.
Facilities and activities: Front porches, swings, rocking chairs, and reading
material everywhere. Nearby: historic homes to tour, Jefferson Muse-
um, railroad baron Jay Gould's railroad car.

Jefferson is the part of Texas that most seems like the Deep
South, and the hospitality of the Old South is what comes naturally
to innkeeper Ruthmary Jordan. She finds innkeeping to be a life of
"sharing, serving—and receiving. Wonderful people come through
my life. They share with me their family, their insights, their interests—as I do in return."

They also share an inn that is one of the prides of Jefferson.
Pride House was the first bed and breakfast inn in Texas, and a
national magazine has called it "one of the twenty-three most
romantic spots in America." Stained glass windows in every room
of the house—red, blue, and amber framing the clear glass cen-
ters—together with ornate woodwork, long halls, and gingerbread
trim on the porch make this house a treasure.

The parlor has an antique piano that the Historical Society asked Ruthmary to keep for them. Over it she has hung a wonderful old gilt mirror from her husband's family, "who were riverboat people, you know." Riverboating was big business on Jefferson's Big Cypress Bayou until the Civil War.

The main house has six guest rooms. The Golden Era Room next to the parlor commemorates the era of the town when more than 30,000 people lived here instead of today's 2,300. It's a lovely golden room with a romantic 9-foot half-tester bed and a large stained glass bay window. I was equally happy in the large Blue Room with its Victorian slipper chairs and king bed. The Green Room has antique white wicker furniture; the West Room is imposing, with rich Victorian red walls and an Eastlake walnut full bed. The Bay Room, which Ruthmary calls her "lusty Victorian," is furnished with Eastlake Victorian furniture and has gold stars on the ceiling.

The other four guest rooms are at the rear in the saltbox house that Ruthmary calls Dependency—because it was the servant's quarters, and "the folks in the main house were dependent on their work."

A refreshing contrast to the Victoriana of Pride House is the common room at the rear, large and bright, with a window wall lighting up the chic black and white tile floor and the green plants all around. When her daughter suggested this decor, Ruthmary says she couldn't see it, until daughter Sandy said the magic word, "green plants." Now it's the most popular gathering place in the inn.

Breakfast always includes one of Ruthmary's famous recipes from when she also had a restaurant downtown. Oh, her crème brulee fruit parfait! Indescribably delicious! With it, perhaps bran muffins delicately redolent of almond, croissants with strawberry butter and melon preserves, and two kinds of sausage. Another morning you might be served Ruthmary's special baked pear in French cream sauce. If you catch Ruthmary in a whimsical mood, there may be Not Eggzactly Benedict, a wonderful takeoff on you know what.

How to get there: Highway 49 becomes Broadway as it heads east into town. The Pride House is on the northwest corner of Broadway and Alley Street.

Stillwater Inn
Jefferson, Texas
75657

Innkeepers: Sharon and Bill Stewart
Address/Telephone: 203 East Broadway; (903) 665–8415
Rooms: 3, plus 1 cottage; all with private bath, cottage with phone and TV.
   No smoking inn.
Rates: $75 to $85, double, EPB.
Open: All year.
Facilities and activities: Restaurant open for dinner Tuesday–Sunday (reservation appreciated); lunch served to groups of fifteen or more; bar. Nearby: pets boarded reasonably; restaurants, antiques shops, museums, historic homes, horse-and-carriage rides, riverboat rides, Mardi Gras, Jefferson Historic Pilgrimage in May, Candlelight Tour at Christmas.

"It's very gratifying to have guests who appreciate what we're trying to do," Sharon Stewart says earnestly, speaking both of the thoughtful yet simple decor—a complete contrast to nostalgic Victoriana—and of the restaurant, which has become an East Texas dining tradition. These innkeepers in the 1890s Eastlake Victorian home have earned a reputation for fare such as I enjoyed: grilled breast of duck served with wild rice or potatoes pureed with garlic and cream; a carrot terrine; zucchini with herbs; and for dessert, Concord cake.

Sharon and Bill pride themselves on their fancy desserts like the Concord cake, a tasty confection of chocolate meringue, choco-

196

late mousse, whipped cream, and almonds, and on homemade ice creams like cappuccino and macadamia nut. I relaxed on a cool beige-and-white-striped sofa before the parlor fireplace and had a big delicious dish of the macadamia.

The inn's color scheme is a restful pale blue and cream. Downstairs are the bar and restaurant; upstairs are the guest quarters, constructed from light Salado pine, with dramatically pitched ceilings, skylights, and a comfortable sitting place with books and Sharon's sewing machine. The small cottage adjacent to the inn was moved onto the property and restored with the same spare lines and cool blue-and-cream color scheme, the same pencil-post pine bedstead.

In the cottage the innkeepers replaced the low ceiling with high structural beams "to give a feeling of more space," Bill says.

Breakfast is hearty and goes way beyond croissants and coffee. Added are scrambled eggs with fresh chives—"We've got an herb garden in the back," Bill says with typical enthusiasm—and Pecos melon. Everything's made from scratch by these two enthusiastic gourmets, including fresh-ground coffee.

"Not to brag," says Sharon, "but we're the only restaurant in East Texas with an espresso machine with two heads!"

They also have a light and sunny inn—clean-cut is the word that comes to mind, or maybe uncluttered. The few antiques, like the coffee table–cum–old Dutch bellows ("Hey! Where can I get one of those?" a delighted guest asked) and the furniture in the Victorian Room, all contribute to a getaway that helped unclutter my crowded mind. The white picket fence is also Sharon's pride. "It sets the house off, makes it seem so nice and 'cottagey'. . . . If you knew how many times I've moved before settling here!"

A cookbook with Bill's Stillwater Inn recipes is now in print.

How to get there: Highway 49 becomes Broadway as it enters town. The inn is on the northeast corner of Broadway and Owens.

Cotten's Patch Inn
Marshall, Texas
75670

Innkeepers: Jo Ann Cotten and Lonnie Hill
Address/Telephone: 703 East Rusk Street; (214) 938–8756
Rooms: 3 share 2¹/₂ baths; all with TV.
Rates: $75 to $85, double, EPB.
Open: All year.
Facilities and activities: Nearby: Marshall Pottery Factory, museums, Stagecoach Days in May, Fire Ant Festival in October.

Cotten's Patch looks like an old farmhouse set somehow in the middle of town. The pink-painted wooden house has the sort of tall narrow windows, peaked roof, and front screened porch that can be seen in many a house on the prairie.

But inside, what a surprise! The home is filled with lovely antique furniture, decorative objets d'art, and paintings. Everywhere I looked I discovered new treasures, things like the old ironing board and iron in the dining-room alcove, or the china that Jo Ann paints.

Innkeeper Jo Ann is an artist, and she has painted delightful trompe l'oeil decorations on many walls. The front hall has a painted hall tree on the wall; the kitchen has a painted rug and a latticed apple tree. I really laughed at the broom and mop painted on the pantry door. Not to be outdone by Jo Ann's artistry, Lonnie, a musician, enjoys treating guests to both organ and accordian recitals.

198

I had trouble picking a favorite room, a choice not made easier by Jo Ann's policy of first come first choose. "The first one here gets to see all the rooms," she says. "I always let them tour the house before others get here."

Jo Ann finds that the gentlemen often like to drink their coffee on the porch before the ladies get up, so the first one up gets to plug in the coffee. There are two pots, "one leaded, one unleaded," Jo Ann points out with a smile.

It's perfectly all right to eat in the lovely large dining room, but like most of Jo Ann's guests, I preferred to eat in the sunny country kitchen. "Most everybody just loves to eat in the kitchen," she says. Most likely to get closer to the fresh coffee cake, say I. Jo Ann enjoys having breakfast with her guests.

If she has a group, she says she "gets carried away" into the spirit of the thing, making individual quiches or sausage balls. "When I have my homemade bread coming out of the oven, they say it drives them crazy. Homemade bread and jelly: I have a neighbor who makes mayhaw jelly just like my grandmother used to make."

Touches like ice water and magazines in the rooms, turned-down beds with candy on the pillow make Cotten's Patch a real treat. Jo Ann also provides plastic "litter bags" filled with pamphlets describing what to do in historic Marshall.

The spa on the back porch has more of Jo Ann's fun art, a painted apple tree climbing the wall and spreading on the ceiling overhead. For real is the pailful of bright red apples alongside. "I tell my guests that if they get bored in the spa, they can bob for apples," Jo Ann says with a twinkle in her eye.

How to get there: From Highway 80 go south on Alamo to Rusk. Turn right and the inn will be on the left in the middle of the 700 block.

Munzesheimer Manor
Mineola, Texas
75773

Innkeepers: Sherry and Bob Murray
Address/Telephone: 202 North Newsom Street; (903) 569–6634
Rooms: 7, 3 in Country Cottage; all with private bath; wheelchair accessible.
    No smoking inn.
Rates: $65 to $90, per room, EPB.
Open: All year.
Facilities and activities: Dinner by reservation. Nearby: Texas Forest, Azalea
    and Dogwood Trails, Mineola Junction with antiques, gifts, and arts
    and crafts.

"We tried to create the atmosphere of when the house was built," Sherry and Bob say of the 1898 manor house that they bought, completely gutted, and put back together again. The photo album in the parlor chronicles the horrendous task they set themselves. When they began the project, Bob says, their entire family thought they were crazy. "That's nothing," Sherry chimes in. "All our friends did, too." They even got comments from strangers such as: "It is amazing that your marriage seems to be still intact!" "But," Bob says, "we've always liked to entertain and have people in the house . . . and Sherry always wanted an old house."

The large house has two parlors, a huge dining room, and guest rooms named in honor of former owners. I was in the Blasingame Room, which had both English and American antiques;

the bath had a footed tub; and my armoire had a bullet embedded down low inside the door. Bob said he's darned if he knows where it came from—it came with the armoire. A Victorian nightgown and nightshirt were provided, in case I really wanted to get into the turn-of-the-century mode. Each guest room comes so equipped, which is one of the things that make staying at this inn an adventure. I also found a tray with a bottle of St. Regis Blanc (wine without the alcohol) cooling in my room when I returned from dinner, as well as after-dinner mints.

For breakfast you'll have a full feast: perhaps fruit cup (for the Fourth of July it was red raspberries, white pear, and some of the area's huge blueberries); Bob's special scrambled eggs; pepper-cured lean bacon; and peach and blackberry jam to spread on fresh biscuits. Also on the menu are chilled blueberry soup, German pancakes, and almond French toast.

It was fascinating to hear the story of how the house was reborn; Bob spoke the truth when he said, "We'll wind up sitting in the parlor and talking about it till all hours." The Cowan Room, named after Dr. Cowan, the dentist, has his black leather dental chair as an entertaining point of interest. Bob collects all sorts of memorabilia such as shoe lasts and dinner bells. Other interesting features are the stained glass windows, the seven fireplaces, and the wraparound porch, where morning coffee and the Sunday paper made it perfect to be outdoors.

Added to the inn are three more charming rooms, which have not changed the exterior of the historic house. The Engineer's Room and the Conductor's Room foster memories of Mineola's great railroad days, and the Tack Room, built where the stable used to be, is complete with a hay loft and a "two-holer." (Indoors, for modern guests; old documents indicate that back in the good old days, the house had "a two-holer in the alley.")

How to get there: Mineola is located approximately 70 miles from Dallas and 80 miles from Shreveport at the intersection of U.S. 80 and U.S. 69 (it is also midway between Houston and Tulsa, Oklahoma).

Capt. E. D. Downs Home
San Augustine, Texas
75972

Innkeeper: Dorothy B. Fussell

Address/Telephone: 301 East Main Street; (409) 275–2289

Rooms: 5; 1 2-room suite with private bath, others share 2¹/₂ baths; mobile telephone available; wheelchair access to downstairs rooms and dining room. No smoking inn.

Rates: $55 to $70, double, EPB.

Open: All year.

Facilities and activities: Nearby: restaurants, historic homes and churches, El Camino Real Trail, Sabine National Forest, Toledo Bend Reservoir and Pinkston Lake.

San Augustine calls itself "the Cradle of Texas," vying with nearby Nacogdoches for the title of the oldest Anglo town in Texas. It certainly is full of Texas history, and the Capt. E. D. Downs Home is one of the reasons. This is the East Texas Pine Woods area, and lumber for the house was cut from the timberlands of the Downs family, floated down the Sabine River to a mill, barged back upstream, and transported to the site by oxen. It's still big lumber country today, and you'll see huge logs stacked alongside the road as you drive by.

The Fussells bought the house in 1976. "The house, vacant, looked so sad," innkeeper Dorothy says. "The camellias outside were so pretty; I said, 'This house needs to be used.'" It was built at the turn of the century by Captain Downs, grandfather of local celebrity Ed Clark, ambassador to Australia under Lyndon B. Johnson. Clark's mother was the last of the family to live in the house.

The spacious house is bright and friendly, furnished with some antique pieces but mainly with comfortable furniture. Guest rooms are large and as cool as their names imply: The Blue Room, the Green Room; the Yellow Room. There are three fireplaces, but today they're just for show, since the house is centrally heated and cooled. Pink and red camellias surround the sun room with its white wicker furniture, books, magazines, and television.

People love to sit in the sitting room and rock and read, and there's a piano in the parlor. Dorothy says she begs her guests to play. Dorothy does not stay on the property, but her aunt, living just next door, is always available. "We all, even our guests, call her Dear Ima," Dorothy says. "It started when my children were small. We lived in Virginia, and when they wrote to her, they began their letters 'Dear Dear Ima—they thought that was her name. She's a dear person; this whole town loves her."

So do guests, and Mary Ann, the cook, as well, by the time they leave. "She has worked for me for more than twenty years," Dorothy says. "She is such a great cook; we pride ourselves on our breakfast: sausage, bacon, eggs, our delicious biscuits and gravy." Dorothy sets her breakfast table, serves orange juice and coffee, and visits with her guests. "I've met so many lovely people. I have commercial travelers who love to sit at the kitchen table and work. I have no problem with long-distance calls; they always leave money for them—inn people are wonderful!"

Small as San Augustine is, Dorothy says she can recommend three good restaurants: Doodles, San Augustine Inn, and Faustos.

How to get there: Highway 21 becomes Main Street; the inn is 2 blocks from downtown on the corner of Congress and Main.

Rosevine Inn
Tyler, Texas
75702

Innkeepers: Bert and Rebecca Powell
Address/Telephone: 415 South Vine Street; (903) 592–2221
Rooms: 4; all with private bath. No smoking inn.
Rates: $65, single; $75, double; $10 extra person; EPB.
Open: All year.
Facilities and activities: Hot tub, game room. Nearby: Tyler Rose Gardens, Brick Street Shoppes, Carnegie History Center, Caldwell Zoo, Rose Festival, Azalea Trails, Historic Homes Tours.

Tyler is the "Rose Capital of the World," and Rosevine Inn is named both for the famous roses, which are shipped all over the world, and for the street it's located on. Bert is in real estate and was eager to snap up the half acre where the Pope House burned down long ago, leaving something most unusual for Tyler (and the rest of Texas): a basement. "Back in the '30s they must have built basements. I designed the house, Becca and I both decorated it, and we built it right on top of the basement of the Popes' English Tudor house, which had been vacant for a long time." Bert has turned the basement into a game room with shuffleboard, backgammon, and many a hotly contested board game.

The guest rooms are named for the flora of the area, beginning with the Rose Room, which has a high-backed antique bed, a cozy rocker, and its own small fireplace. The Bluebonnet Room, named for the Texas state flower, has a white iron bedstead and a comfy blue couch. The Azalea Room, peachy like the flowers, has a brass bed. The Sunshine Room? "Well," says Bert, "it's named for the daughter of the man who built the house that burned down, what else?" I'm not sure I follow his logic!

Becca and Bert had a great time combing the small towns of East Texas—Canton, Quitman, Tyler—to furnish the inn. Canton, 30 miles away, is famous for its First Mondays, a huge country flea-and-produce market spread out under the trees outside the small town.

Breakfast at Rosevine is hearty and delicious. There's always a hot entree like sausage quiche or French toast or omelets, served with toast and perhaps both blueberry coffee cake and applesauce muffins, along with a fruit-of-the-season cup, orange juice, and coffee and tea.

Between the welcome with wine and cheese and the delicious morning odor of fresh-brewed coffee outside in the hallway, Rosevine gives you a happy pampered feeling. "We try; what more can we say?" Bert asks with a smile.

I say that the landscaped grounds of Rosevine are so lovely that it's a difficult choice whether to laze in the hot tub under the pavilion or to play volleyball and croquet on the velvet lawn beyond the fountain in the back courtyard. Bert is the hard-working gardener. The inn is set on a slight rise of smooth green lawn; nine steps lead up to the flowerpots that mark the opening in the arched white picket fence. The path then winds across more green lawn to the front door of this charming red brick house with its backdrop of leafy trees.

How to get there: Tyler is the crossroads for many highways. Follow Highway 31 east into town to Vine Street, turn right, and the inn is the house on the right.

Thee Hubbell House
Winnsboro, Texas
75494

Innkeepers: Laurel and Dan Hubbell
Address/Telephone: 307 West Elm Street; (903) 342–5629
Rooms: 5, including 2 suites; all with private bath. No smoking inn.
Rates: $65 to $150, per room, EPB.
Open: All year.
Facilities and activities: Dinner by reservation. Nearby: Lake Bob Sandlin, Cypress Springs Lake, and twenty-two other lakes within a 20- to 30-mile radius; Autumn Trails Festival, Christmas Festival, spring and summer festivals.

East Texas was more pro-Confederate than not, back in Civil War days, and quite a few mansions testify to the antebellum influence. A true East Texas Southern belle is Thee Hubbell House, its white Georgian Colonial facade catching your eye as you drive down the street. The porches and upstairs gallery sport swings and rockers, and, as Dan Hubbell says, "It's amazing how people love to sit out and rock.

"If they're my age, or older, they remember what it was like to sit out on the porch and rock. Our guests seem to enjoy staying around, and we enjoy it, too," Dan continues. Part of the pleasure stems from the fact that Dan is the mayor of Winnsboro. "We meet and greet our guests on a kind of official level," he says with a chuckle. "It seems to add a sort of prestige to our guests, to have the mayor serve them coffee."

The Hubbells chose *Thee* instead of *The* for their inn name because "it sounds cozier," they say. The inn has five charming guest rooms. There are some lovely English antiques, and Dan's grandmother's sewing chair and Laurel's grandmother's washstand testify to their native Texas roots. Two of the guest rooms are suites: the Magnolia Suite and the Master Suite, which is the inn's largest guest room, with a dining room and its own veranda.

Nostalgia reigns at Thee Hubbell House, where you can walk the 2¹/₂ blocks downtown to antiques shops and at least three churches. The front door is open so that guests can come and go as they please. The Hubbells take their peace and safety for granted and are amused when guests ask, "Is it safe to walk?"

"We tell them, of course you can walk here, even at night. Then they take off like little school kids, giggling," Dan said with a twinkle.

The century-old mansion has pine floors, square handmade nails, and the original wavy-glass window panes. Cabinets now surround a solid oak pie safe that was so heavy it took three men to lift it. The banister posts were made at onetime owner Colonel Stinson's sawmill; his daughter Sallie married Texas's first governor, Jim Hogg.

Breakfast is bountiful, to say the least. Begin with a baked apple stuffed with mincemeat. Next have shirred eggs, baked ham, buttermilk biscuits, grits and cream gravy, wheat raisin muffins, coffee, and juice. "We call it a Plantation Breakfast," said Laurel. "We serve in the dining room at 8:30, and sometimes our guests don't rise from the table until 11:00!" They join their guests if there are fewer than eight; if there are "more than we can handle, we don't eat at all, but we have coffee with them."

Talk about Southern hospitality: Mondays all Winnsboro restaurants are closed, so the Hubbells may say, "If you enjoy a good stew, with just crackers and a glass of milk, well, come and sit down."

How to get there: Winnsboro is on Highway 37 between I–30 and I–80. Highway 37 becomes Main Street. Turn west on Elm to 307.

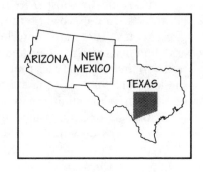

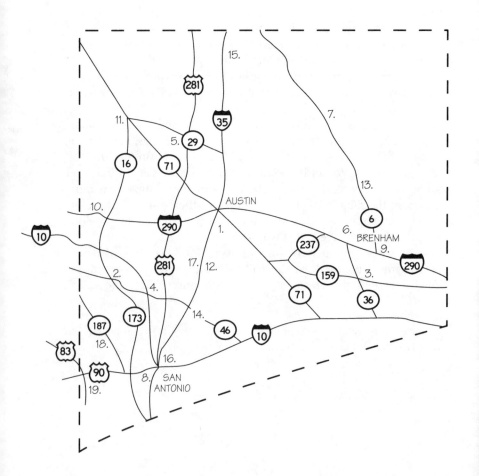

Central Texas

Numbers on map refer to towns numbered below.

Carrington's Bluff
Austin, Texas
78705

Innkeepers: Gwen and David Fullbrook
Address/Telephone: 1900 David Street; (512) 479–0638
Rooms: 8; 6 with private bath, all wilth TV. No smoking inn.
Rates: $60 to $85, double; $15 extra person; EPB.
Open: All year.
Facilities and activities: Kitchen and laundry facilities open to guests, hammock, picnic tables. Nearby: University of Texas campus within walking distance, Town Lake, Lake Travis, museums, LBJ Library.

Gwen and David, favorite innkeepers, are back in town after a several-year interlude in a cold climate. "I had this burning desire to go to New England," Gwen confesses. But although they loved their New England inn, Gwen got cold, homesick—and pregnant. She wanted baby Nicholas to be a Texan, too—no offense to New England!

So they are back home and happily innkeeping in this delightful house with a wonderful side garden and a view over wooded Shoal Creek Bluff. "David and I have been innkeepers for more than six years," Gwen says, "and we hate rules; we don't have a lot of rules. We open up our home and our guests just wander around, go into the fridge for a glass of wine, or use the kitchen—just not when I'm fixing breakfast!" she adds with a laugh.

Breakfast offers Gwen's homemade granola, ham-and-cheese

soufflé, chocolate chip banana muffins, gourmet coffee and teas, fresh fruit, and juice. After this feast all you'll want to do is lie in the hammock under the 500-year-old ivy-covered oak tree and contemplate the white clouds in the blue Texas sky.

The 1877 Texas farmhouse is situated on a 1-acre tree-covered bluff. Once a 22-acre original outlot of the Republic of Texas, the property was purchased by L. D. Carrington from David Burnet in 1856. L.D. owned a general store downtown, as well as the water company and the newspaper. He also served as city alderman and county commissioner. His true love was being commander of the brigade that guarded Austin from the Indians. His farmhouse, along with its 35-foot front porch, was built facing Shoal Creek Bluff. This was the perfect lookout point to watch for the Indians that lived west of Austin.

Guest rooms are named for Carringtons as well as for family members of the second owner, an Englishman who had been a vicar. In the Vicar Molesworth Room there are photos of the English vicarage on the walls. David is English, and the inn has a lovely air of an English country inn and garden. You'll know you're there when you see both Old Glory and the Union Jack flying from the side porch.

Gwen drew on her background in design to decorate in soft blues and beiges, inspired by the colors of the lovely Vermont quilt David gave her for a birthday. She has gone into quilting herself, and each guest room has an example of her art spread on the bed. The L. D. Carrington Room has a four-poster bed and a hunting horn to match the hunting-scene wallpaper; there's an antique pedal-operated sewing machine in the Martha Carrington Room. The Kathleen Molesworth Room upstairs has a view of the old oak tree and, through the boughs, Shoal Creek. (When booked with the Vicar Molesworth Room, it becomes the Molesworth Suite.) Across the street is the new Carrington's Cottage. Originally a dairy barn, the cottage displays the same decorating touches that make the inn so special.

The Fullbrooks have been busy gardening, making a lovely setting for the new gazebo on the "back forty," says Gwen.

How to get there: From I–35 go west on 19th (Martin Luther King Boulevard) all the way to David Street, a small street on the right just before you reach Lamar Boulevard. Go up the short hill, and the inn is on the left just as the street curves around to the right.

211

La Prelle Place
Austin, Texas
78704

Innkeepers: Barkley Alford and Lee Pate
Address/Telephone: 2204 Lindell Avenue; (512) 441–2204
Rooms: 5; all with private bath, phone, TV, and VCR. No smoking inn.
Rates: $49 to $79, double, continental breakfast.
Open: July through Labor Day.
Facilities and activities: Dinner by reservation, deck, hot tub. Nearby: restaurants, shops, Town Lake, Texas state capitol, University of Texas, LBJ Library, museums.

This fine old 1912 house has undergone a complete facelift to match the lovely interior. "People in North Austin think South Austin is a bit uncivilized," Barkley says with a laugh. "We chose to change that!" Nothing could be more civilized than these large rooms, exquisitely furnished with fine antiques and decorator wallpaper and fabrics.

"A lot is family, others collected since we started restoring the property six years ago," Barkley says of himself and his friend Lee. "We're in the antiques business, and we filter the best pieces to the inn." Striking are the striped scoop-backed fireside couch and the pewlike hall bench with carvings like ship figureheads on the arms. So are the tall-backed authentic Chippendale chairs in the dining room. The walnut Victorian magazine stand is another unusual find.

Barkley is a native of Central Texas with a background in fine arts. He says that "I don't have any excuse for being in this business, but I love old things and meeting people from all over the world."

An unusual feature of the house is the staircase. As I was admiring the way the two flights meet halfway in the middle and join to reach the second floor, Barkley informed me that it's called a "Good Morning" staircase. Why? "The momma just had to walk to the landing and call up to get everyone up!" Clever, and beautiful besides, with gleaming dark wood banisters that look as though they've been polished daily for years and years.

The large downstairs Master Suite has a private entrance. It's furnished with Eastlake Victorian, and the bath has an old-fashioned claw-foot tub.

The Peach Room is feminine, with French antiques and a pressed-tin ceiling; the Blue Room has a king-size bed and an enormous bathroom. Terry robes are provided for guests' comfort in all the rooms. The Green Room has two white-painted iron beds and a huge antique oriental rug that covers the entire floor. The Pink Suite has as a sitting room an enclosed porch that runs along the entire front of the house. I spied a fascinating collection of hobby horses in a corner, collected by horseman Lee. "Yes," Barkley says in answer to my delighted exclamation, "but our rule is no stick horse riding in the house after midnight." He says this with a perfectly straight face.

Across the back of the house upstairs is another closed-in porch that serves as a snacking place, with soft drinks and other refreshment in the refrigerator and steps leading down to the deck and hot tub below.

Breakfast is orange juice, fresh fruit, gourmet coffees, delicious pastries from Sweetish Hill or other famous Austin bakeries, and cold cereal, enjoyed either in the dining room on the fabulous Chippendale chairs or in casual comfort upstairs.

How to get there: Take South Congress to Live Oak; turn right and then left sharply because Lindell is immediately to your left across a narrow esplanade. The inn is just up the street on the right.

The McCallum House
Austin, Texas
78705

Innkeepers: Nancy and Roger Danley
Address/Telephone: 613 West 32nd Street; (512) 451–6744
Rooms: 5 (3 rooms, 2 suites); all with private bath and kitchen, 4 with private porch. No smoking inn.
Rates: $45 to $70, single; $60 to $85, double; $15 extra person (lower rates are for three nights or more and for any night Monday through Thursday); EPB. Monthly rates available. Visa and MasterCard to secure deposit only.
Open: All year.
Facilities and activities: Nearby: many fine local restaurants, University of Texas campus, LBJ Library, state capitol, Zilker Park with Barton Springs and Japanese Garden, other Austin sights.

The McCallum House was built in 1907 as the home of Jane Y. McCallum, an early suffragist, her husband, Arthur, and her five children. The Danleys now have a marker from the Texas Historical Commission to authenticate the building's history. McCallum was careful to make the distinction—she was not a militant suffragette—but she had definite ideas all the same. Some of the inn furniture, such as the Blue Room set with the oval-mirrored dressing table, came with the house and reflects her taste. In the attic Nancy found the big yellow suffragette banner that now hangs in the hall: 8,000,000 WORKING WOMEN NEED THE VOTE!

The Danleys took the old house and turned it into a charming inn. Roger is a remodeling contractor, and Nancy has done some construction too. Wait until you see the dollhouse in the entry, just below the stairs.

"We did that in moments of insanity," both the Danleys say with a laugh. I would call it artistry, not insanity. It's perfectly beautiful, with downstairs ceilings decorated with molding, a hearth of real brick, and even rugs needlepointed by the talented builders and decorators.

Roger's latest life-size triumph is Jane's Loft, a beautiful new attic room with 12½-foot ceilings and wonderful etched glass doors. A Victorian pattern done by hand by the Danleys decorates both the huge triangular window in the gable and the long etched panels on either side of the door leading to the big open porch.

Many guests, especially long-term ones (the Danleys often have professors visiting the University of Texas who stay for several weeks), are pleased as punch with the Garden Apartment in the back. This suite, decorated in deep rose and blue, with white wicker and a white iron daybed in the living room, has a bedroom with queen beds and a kitchen equipped for real cooking. "We've had lots of families, physicists doing research and lecturing at the university; it's a lot of fun," the Danleys say.

It's a house of porches. Adjoining the Blue Room and running along the entire side of the house is a screened porch fitted with white-wicker-and-blue-chintz furniture; I can see why folks want just to sit here and enjoy the breeze. There's a lot of sitting around the breakfast table too—that's one of the high spots of innkeeping, Nancy says. "We sit around the table and talk for *hours.*"

Nancy's special dish of scrambled eggs with shaved ham, sharp cheddar, onions, and parsley is served with streusel-topped blueberry bran muffins and a fruit cup of black cherries, bananas, and peaches. Roger's specialty is a quiche with a crunchy shredded-potato crust. The filling can be ham or sausage, spinach or mushrooms, depending upon the whim of the resident chef. Also on the menu are some wonderful low-fat and no-cholesterol muffins, sweet breads, and coffee cakes.

How to get there: Exit I–35 at 38th Street and go west to Guadalupe. Turn south for 6 blocks to 32nd; turn west on 32nd. The inn will be on your left.

Southard House
Austin, Texas
78703

Innkeepers: Regina and Jerry Southard and daughter Kara
Address/Telephone: 908 Blanco Street; (512) 474-4731
Rooms: 5; all with private bath. Smoking permitted in public rooms.
Rates: $52 to $99, double, EPB weekends, continental breakfast weekdays.
Open: All year.
Facilities and activities: Nearby: four-star restaurants, shops, and galleries within 4-block walking distance; Town Lake, Texas state capitol, University of Texas, LBJ Library, museums.

A fascinating thing about the Southard House is that the second floor was once the first floor. A photograph in the entrance hall, taken in the 1890s, shows how the house looked before the original owners hoisted it up and built a new first floor underneath around 1906. It is a very interesting Victorian Greek Revival home.

Another fascinating thing is the large world map that Regina and Kara showed me in the office; it's dotted with colored pins showing the many places in the world Southard guests come from: Europe, the length and breadth of the United States, China, New Zealand. "We've had guests from thirty-eight countries, including Russia!" Regina says with delight. So you're apt to meet with pretty interesting people. The University of Texas recommends the inn to visiting architects, lawyers, and visitors to the school's Huntington Art Gallery and School of Performing Arts.

The Southards have gathered antiques from all over. The Treaty Oaks room and suite, once the parlor, has a fireplace and a bathroom sink fitted into an antique washstand. There are old-fashioned transoms over each bedroom door. I liked the antique-looking (though new) tile and the original narrow-slatted wood walls in the bathrooms. In the dining room, a nineteenth-century English oak refectory table seems 7 miles long.

While weekday breakfasts are delicious ("I call them Gourmet Continental," says Kara, who may fix home-baked peanut butter-orange bread or strawberry yogurt muffins), it's the weekend breakfasts, prepared by Regina, that are spectacular. Mexican breakfast quiche, Belgian waffles, apple pancakes, or an especially yummy egg-cheese-grits dish, served with orange juice, just-ground coffee, and hot buttered yeast bread for toast, are eaten in the shade of a green-bordered patio.

Lately Regina has been specializing in scrumptious homemade cinnamon rolls, and even Jerry has been getting into the breakfast act, fixing a fabulous fruit smoothie with a secret ingredient. Dare I tell that it's champagne?

Recommended restaurants for lunch and dinner are within walking distance—Sweetish Hill, an Austin classic, is just down the street on the corner of Blanco and 6th—and take-out food may be brought in.

The Southard House offers airport pickup, caters to special diets when requested, and takes calls for business guests. A honeymoon package includes champagne, fresh flowers, and chocolates on a silver tray. One time a guest overslept; he was awakened by Jerry, who rushed him to the airport just in time for his plane. "He says we saved his life," Regina told me with a laugh, "and he comes back to us every time he's in town."

How to get there: Take the 6th Street exit off I–35 and go west on 6th until you reach Blanco Street on your right. The inn will be on your left.

The Wild Flower Inn
Austin, Texas
78705

Innkeepers: Kay Jackson and Claudean Schultz
Address/Telephone: 1200 West 22 ¹/₂ Street; (512) 477–9639
Rooms: 4; 2 with private bath. No smoking inn.
Rates: $59 to $69, double; $15 extra person; EPB.
Open: All year.
Facilities and activities: Nearby: restaurants, shops, Caswell Tennis Courts, Shoal Creek Hike and Bike Trail, University of Texas campus and LBJ Library.

Bright flowers lead up to this spic-and-span square white clapboard house, flowers lining the flagstone path, flowers blooming in containers on the green lawn. Indoors, fresh flowers bloom in pots, and painted flowers bloom in the stencils Kay and her crew painted on walls and up the stairs. The effect is of light and air, of sunshine pouring in.

"I used lace curtains because I didn't want to close us in," Kay says. "I wanted to bring the outdoors in." She also likes to show her guests the outdoors; one guest from Czechoslovakia wanted to see farm and ranch land, and Kay said, "Well, get in the car," and they covered about 100 miles to see Central Texas's famous wildflowers. "Heavens, so many miles!" he exclaimed. "At home we'd be in Bohemia already!"

Kay is a rather rare thing, a native Austinite, and from an old

Texas family to boot. Rooms are named for members of her family: The David G. Burnet Room is named for her great-great-grandfather, and I loved the white iron half-canopied bedstead. Dodie's Room contains the furniture of a great-aunt, and Carolyn Pearl Walker Room is furnished with pieces given to Kay's grandmother for her thirtieth anniversary. Unusual is the old daybed; there's a four-poster, too. White stenciled flowers march along the pale blue walls under the ceiling.

Kay has set some sort of record—she's gone for five and a half weeks without repeating a breakfast menu! It became a challenge, she says, when she overheard a British guest bragging to a newcomer that Kay had not served the same thing twice in the two weeks she'd been at the Wild Flower.

"She stayed for almost six weeks, and I didn't repeat." So of course I had to ask how on earth . . . ? "I alternate sweet and savory, for one thing," she says, "and always with juice, coffee, tea, and fresh-baked bread or muffins." A favorite is Eggs Goldenrod, white sauce with hardboiled egg whites over a croissant, the yellow yolk crumbled on top—that's a savory. A sweet might be French toast stuffed with ricotta cheese, with a syrup of zest of orange, orange marmalade, and brown sugar.

The house, on a quiet, tree-lined street near the University of Texas campus, was built in 1936 for a professor. It's a dead-end street, so there's no through traffic. "Restoring it, we did the work ourselves," Kay says, making it sound easy as daughter Angela, home from college, laughs. "Easy! We moved walls," Angela says. "We discovered a covered-up inside staircase (there's an outside one up to the small porch outside the Texas Country Room), took a kitchenette out of the upstairs . . ." She helped, in between her college studies, as did son Jay.

"I stayed at an inn on a business trip," says Kay. "Claudean and I had a woodcrafts shop, and when I went back to work, I told her 'I'm going to open a bed and breakfast.' And I have to say, it all just came together."

How to get there: From I–35 take Martin Luther King Boulevard (19th Street) west to the end at Lamar; turn right and go to the first traffic light (24th) and turn right again, staying in the right-hand lane. Turn right at the second street (Longview) to 22½ Street. The inn will be on the right on the corner of Longview and 22½.

Woodburn House
Austin, Texas
78751

Innkeepers: Sandra and Herb Dickson
Address/Telephone: 4401 Avenue D; (512) 458–4335
Rooms: 4; all with private bath and phone. No smoking inn.
Rates: $65 to $70, $15 extra person; EPB.
Open: All year.
Facilities and activities: Exercycle. Nearby: restaurants, shops; Shipe Park with
    pool, tennis, basketball; Elisabet Ney Museum, many other museums.

Woodburn House, built in 1909, has earned Austin City Landmark status for its architectural features. "Besides the Governor's
Mansion, there's only one other home in Austin like ours," Sandra
says. "The double-wrapped gallery, the woodwork of the Craftsman
style, which evolved from Victorian . . ." I was convinced the
moment I saw the beautiful old house, with its wide flagstone path
flanked with flowering shrubs and neatly bisected at the curb by a
huge, old elm tree. The name comes from Bessie Hamilton Woodburn who lived in the house for many years. Her father, Alexander
Hamilton, (not the Founding Father) was Texas's provisional governor after the Civil War.

Although the Dicksons are new to Austin, Herb is a Texan, and
they have wasted no time becoming active in the community. "We
like to belong where we belong," Sandra says. Guests have the feeling of belonging right from the start, when they're welcomed

sedately by Budges the Shar-Pei, whose complete canine name is Mr. Ka Budges. Very well behaved, he minds every nuance of Sandra's voice.

The inn, as promised from the exterior, is very spacious, with 12-foot ceilings and beautiful woodwork. There are two common rooms. One, the living room, has two large maroon leather sofas and a matching chair, which you absolutely sink into—lace curtains at the windows, polished dark woodwork, oak floors, an armoire, a bookshelf as tall as the room around a corner and up to the ceiling—it's a lovely room. On the dining room's built-in corner cupboard sits an old clock that has been in Herb's family for generations. The home is filled with antiques from the Dickson family. I especially admired the dozens of handmade quilts left to the family by Grandmother Dickson.

"Guests love to bundle up in them if it gets chilly while they're enjoying the upstairs gallery," Sandra says. It was a delight to curl up on the old glider, surrounded by huge old oak and pecan trees, and watch the squirrels, the woodpeckers, the jays, and the mourning doves go about their business.

Sandra, whose family was from Guadalajara, Mexico, likes to serve a Mexican breakfast, "*Real* Mexican, not TexMex," she says. She makes her own salsa and raises her own Mexican spices. "We bake our own breakfast breads and alternate Mexican cuisine with Belgian waffles, quiches, and fluffy French toast, which are more Herb's specialties. He does all the cutting and chopping—I do all the baking," she adds. For picnic lunches she sends guests down the street to the 100-year-old Avenue B Grocery. "Owner Ross Mason is just a delight. He loves our guests and makes wonderful picnic lunches for them."

One of the nicest things about the guest rooms, aside from their spaciousness, are the tall lace-covered windows opening off the gallery in front and shaded by old trees in the back. The wide halls, the front and back stairs, the butler's pantry, the large kitchen—everything about this inn is bright and gleaming.

How to get there: From I–35 take 45th Street west to Avenue D. Turn left, and the inn will be on the left at the corner of Avenue D and West 44th Street.

Dixie Dude Ranch
Bandera, Texas
78003

Innkeeper: Clay Conoly
Address/Telephone: P.O. Box 548; (512) 796–4481 or (800) 375–9255
Rooms: 19 guest rooms and cottages; all with private bath and TV; wheelchair accessible.
Rates: $70 to $80, single; $60 to $70, double; children under 2 free, 2 to 5 $25, 6 to 12 $40, 13 to 16 $55; AP.
Open: All year.
Facilities and activities: Family activities: horseback riding, hayrides, cookouts, swimming, poolside parties, barbecues, cowboy entertainment.

Clay Conoly's grandmother, Rose (Billie) Crowell, has had the Dixie Dude for so long she doesn't need an address. The postman knows just where to find her. "This is not a resort ranch," she says. "This is an old-time Western stock ranch that has, through fifty-six years, become a guest ranch."

Now she's the grande dame of the ranch, according to Clay, fourth-generation co-owner of the ranch, who with his family has taken over the management and updated the accommodations. He is carrying on Billie's tradition of calling the Dixie Dude "your home on the range." You get a warm welcome and real Texas hospitality, as though you're part of the family.

Clay has instituted some lively goings-on at Dixie Dude, including delicious barbecue outdoors every Saturday night, a cowboy breakfast on the range, and pool parties featuring *fajitas* and "juke boxes blasting away and everybody dancing, even the kids," Clay says. Hayrides, bonfires, and marshmallow roasts keep both parents and offspring busy—there will even be a piñata party if you tell Clay there's a birthday child on the premises.

Especially attractive to the youngsters is the cowboy trick-roping exhibition; Clay has a wrangler in to show off his expertise, and you can imagine how that captures young imaginations—everybody wants to see if they can do the same.

"You can do just whatever you want to do at Dixie Dude," is the family motto. One of the things I wanted to do was take the two daily trail rides. The ranch offers a beautiful view, and it's pure pleasure, on good saddle horses and led by experienced cowboys, to cover some truly scenic hill country.

Back at the ranch, after a wonderful dinner of fried catfish, green garden beans with new potatoes, tossed salad, and cornbread topped off with chocolate cake and ice cream, I was more than content to fall apart for a while in front of the fireplace in the huge Round-Up Room. I let the other guests play the piano or the juke box or sit around playing card games. Like Lobo the dog, who lay peacefully under the cedar log bench on the front porch, I was doing just whatever I wanted to!

After a while, I went out back and inspected the ranch's vegetable garden. Then I inspected the tack room, as if I knew something about horses. Well, I knew enough to be impressed; that's the cleanest tack room I've ever seen. Last but not least, I took a cool swim in the underwater-lighted swimming pool. And what with all the fresh air and exercise, I sure slept like a top! And why not? Fifteen hundred acres of beautiful Texas Hill Country, great food and hospitality have been making guests from all over the world happy since 1937!

How to get there: Dixie Dude is south of town, on FM (Farm Road) 1077 west of Highway 173 to Hondo. Drive approximately 9 miles and the ranch entrance will be on the right. There are signs to guide you.

Mayan Dude Ranch
Bandera, Texas
78003

Innkeepers: Judy and Don Hicks
Address/Telephone: Box 577; (512) 796–3312
Rooms: 60; all with private bath.
Rates: $90 to $95 per day per adult; $595 to $630 weekly (single occupancy add $10 per day); children 12 and under $40, 13 to 17 $50; AP. Ten percent service charge in lieu of tipping.
Open: All year.
Facilities and activities: Cocktail lounge, television room, horseback riding, hayrides, cookouts, swimming in pool and Medina River, tubing in river, tennis, daily activity schedule for adults and children.

Except that it's for real, Bandera's Mayan Ranch could fill in for anybody's dream fantasy of a true Western dude ranch. Stone cottages, furnished with Western furniture right off the ranch, nestle under old cedar trees. Down by the corral, wranglers (one of them a Hicks son, Randy) saddle up the horses for trail rides twice a day. The cool, clean Medina River winds along the bottom of the ranch, begging for you to lie back on an inner tube and just float along. . . .

Guests, says Judy, just can't believe the quiet. "They get on the tubes and just float down the river." If you keep on going, maybe you won't have to go back to the same old grind!

The Mayan is run by an entire herd of Hickses—Judy and Don

have thirteen children, several of whom have already produced grandchildren. The family has been running the Mayan for more than forty years; experts at making you feel at home, they invite everyone to "join the family."

Everybody always wants to know how come the name is pronounced "May-ann" instead of "My-un," like the Indians of the Yucatán. Could be because the Mayan ranch started life in the early 1930s as a Girl Scout camp, and that's what the Girl Scouts called it.

I loved the cowboy breakfast served on a bluff above the river—but you have to ride to it first. I signed up for a horse, but another option is the wagon, which goes faster—my mare kinda liked to lag behind. I guess she knew she wasn't going to get any of the delicious food that was busy sizzling on the fire for us.

Great fun was the softball game before dinner, between the Cowboys and the Indians. We were Indians, and our team won! Win or lose, all the players won a hearty appetite for the barbecue at the river and the Western sing-along. (But you still get to eat even if you prefer just to watch the game.)

From the large glass-windowed dining room, the view goes on for miles and miles of Hill Country. Watching the sunset from the deck outside the dining room and bar is a renewing experience. So is just sitting there with a cold drink in your hand, enjoying the cool breezes blowing over the trees. And the food, served buffet style, is hearty and plentiful, with new additions of lots of Mexican goodies.

At lunch the "health nuts" among the new cowpokes can enjoy mountains of salads, fresh fruit, and other cool concoctions. For water babies, lunch is served poolside as well as in the big dining room.

The Mayan is world-famous, and I loved meeting folks from all over the globe: England, Germany, Italy, and Japan. For many guests, like me, the Mayan is great for "lots and lots of loafing!" But for the energetic the days are packed with horseback rides, zany contests dreamed up by that lively Hicks imagination, feasts like the steak fry at Ghost Town, and fiestas like Irish Night or the Mexican Fiesta when we all came in costume—senoras, senoritas, and senors alike.

How to get there: From Highway 16 turn north onto Main Street, then west on Pecan; then follow the Mayan signs to the ranch, which is 1.5 miles northwest of Bandera.

High Cotton Inn
Bellville, Texas
77418

Innkeepers: Anna and George Horton
Address/Telephone: 214 Live Oak Street; (409) 865–9796 or (800) 321–9796
Rooms: 5 share 2¹/₂ baths. No smoking inn.
Rates: $50, double, EPB. No credit cards.
Open: All year.
Facilities and activities: Dinner for groups of ten or more; special Thanksgiving and New Year's Eve dinners for inn guests only; small swimming pool in back yard. Nearby: boarding facilities for pets, spring and fall festivals, Historic Home tour in April, Antiques Show in October, Austin County Fair.

Anna Horton says, "We're not pretentious," but the house itself is a grande dame, a beautiful home in the best Victorian manner. It's the largest house in town and was built by a very successful cotton broker back in 1906 when cotton was king. The name High Cotton comes from a Southern expression meaning everything's rosy, which is what I can't help but feel when I visit this wonderfully relaxed inn.

Check-in time, Anna says, is "when you get here," and check-out time is "when you leave." If there's a wait, well, guests can relax by the small backyard swimming pool.

I loved the informality of choosing my own room—guests, on arrival, get a choice of the rooms that haven't been spoken for yet.

This is a great way to have a tour of the inn. The rooms are named for old family friends as well as Horton antecedents. (George Horton IV is a member of the fourth generation of Hortons from Houston, 65 miles away.) I chose Uncle Buster's Room, a large corner room with lace curtains, an antique wardrobe, and two gilt-framed portraits of a stern-looking Victorian man and woman.

There's a lovely formal parlor downstairs, and by the door to the upstairs wraparound porch (there's one downstairs, too), a cheerful sitting area always has a cookie jar filled with the Hortons' famous cookies. The chocolate chip ones are something to write home about!

The furniture is all family-antique, and I love Anna's sense of humor. "Lots of it is dead relatives," she says. "George and I got married just when all the aunts started dying, and they're all upstairs waiting to scare any guests that get out of line."

The dining-room table, however, is a back-East piece from Lancaster, Pennsylvania, a real conversation piece 66 inches wide, with twelve leaves. It vies for attention with the built-in china cabinet, whose huge plate-glass door slides up the wall—and probably, I think, overhead into the ceiling as well, it's so large. (But I haven't figured out yet how it bends.)

Breakfast might be real country, with grits, bacon, scrambled eggs, bran muffins, and biscuits. Then again, there might be a sophisticated rum-soaked cake and Anna's new whole wheat "Zen" pancakes with homemade syrup. And always Anna's special blackberry preserves that she puts up herself.

Summer dinner was perfect—chilled cucumber soup, marinated chicken salad, fresh rolls, and snow pudding with custard sauce for dessert. Winters it's apt to be roast beef and Yorkshire pudding.

There are always animals on the inn grounds; the Hortons are soft-hearted animal lovers. Last time I was there the menagerie consisted of two dogs and two cats, and now I hear there's a pregnant pygmy goat named Lucy. She'll no doubt be a mother by the time you get there. But the animals are not allowed in the house, so if you want to see them, ask young Anna Horton.

How to get there: The inn is on Highway 36 South, on the edge of Bellville.

Ye Kendall Inn
Boerne, Texas
78006

Innkeepers: Sue Davis, Connie Bien, and Rick Villereal
Address/Telephone: 120 West Blanco; (210) 249–2138 or (800) 364–2138
Rooms: 6, including 1 suite; all with private bath and TV, 1 with wheelchair access. No smoking inn.
Rates: $80 to $125, double, continental breakfast.
Open: All year.
Facilities and activities: Cafe serving breakfast, lunch, and dinner. Nearby: Agricultural Heritage Center; Cascade Caverns; Cave Without a Name; Guadalupe River State Park.

Back in the early days of Texas, there was no hotel for travelers to these parts until Erastus and Sarah Reed bought a parcel of land for $200 in 1859. They began renting out their spare rooms to horsemen and stagecoach travelers, and from being known as The Reed House, the building changed its name through the years to The King Place and the Boerne Hotel. It wasn't called Ye Kendall Inn until 1909. Today the old two-story building, of Hill Country stone, fronted by white-railed porches, 200 feet along its length on both upper and lower floors, is alive again as an inn, facing the large open spaces and white gazebo of the town square.

The old place is full of mysteries. "The cellar goes into a tunnel," says Sue. "It goes to the building way down on the corner; I guess it was for stagecoach passengers to hide from the Indians."

(But too bad, it's not open to the public. Never mind, there's another mystery.)

"We have a ghost who lives here," Sue confided. "I haven't seen it, but my mother says she has. She heard boots and a man's voice, and then she saw a floaty shape going up the stairs."

Perhaps it's the quiet that leads to fanciful—or real?—visions. "Guests like us mainly because it's so quiet," Sue says. "It's the Hill Country quiet—there's not even dances here on Saturday night." But there's plenty to do all the same, with quite a few festivals held in Main Plaza out front, like a yearly Fun Fair with arts and craft shows, dances and pig races in town, and famous Hill Country caverns nearby.

High up along the walls in the upstairs rear of the building are what Sue calls "shoot-out" windows, possibly used to defend against those same Indians the stagecoach passengers were hiding from in the tunnel.

The entire lobby and rooms opening off it contain boutiques with antiques and designer clothing, but the huge upstairs hall is for inn guests, with comfortable lounge chairs, a large dining table, and double doors opening off the long porches both front and back. The view to the front is of the green square; in the back there's a large courtyard with white tables and chairs.

Guest rooms are furnished with English and American antiques, and each has a unique personality. The Erastus Reed Room is masculine with trophy heads mounted on the wall; the Sarah Reed Room is feminine in soft yellow and white. Fascinating are the old-fashioned bathroom fixtures, right there in the rooms, although the footed tubs and the commodes are screened off; Sarah Reed's screen is of white lace.

Breakfast is juice and coffee, fresh fruit, sweet rolls, and quiche, so it's more than plain continental. And the Cafe at Ye Kendall Inn has more gourmet fare, from fettucine Alfredo to chicken cordon bleu. (Or try the Boerne Special, chicken-fried steak with country gravy.)

How to get there: I–87 goes right down the middle of Boerne, and the inn is at the west end of Main Square, on Blanco, which crosses the highway.

Rocky Rest Inn
Burnet, Texas
78611

Innkeeper: Fannie Shepperd
Address/Telephone: 404 South Water Street (mailing address: P.O. Box 130);
   (210) 756–2600
Rooms: 3; 1 with private bath, 1 with TV. Pets permitted.
Rates: $45 to $55, single; $55 to $60, double; special rates for added guests;
   EPB. No credit cards.
Open: All year.
Facilities and activities: Lunch and dinner served by request; common room
   with television, piano, and books; antiques shop on property; thirty
   acres stocked with peacocks, goats, and cattle. Nearby: restaurants in
   town and near lake, Longhorn Caverns, Inks Lake State Park, Lake
   Buchanan, Vanishing Texas River Cruise, historic Fort Groghan.

   Fannie Shepperd is a most gracious and accommodating
innkeeper. "Some guests like to talk," she says, "and others are tired
from the trip. I see how they feel before I engage them in conversation or invite them for an evening glass of wine with me." This historic house has been Fannie's home for more than twenty-five
years, and guests soon feel as much at home here as their hostess
does.

   Now a widow, Fannie collected many beautiful things with her
husband during their years together. The parlor has both a piano
and an organ, and in the dining room you'll count no less than four

cabinets displaying a fine collection of china and glass. Fannie owes much of her interest in antiques to her late mother-in-law. "I had the patience to carry her around," she says, "and after a while, I began to like it."

The home was built in 1860 by Adam R. Johnson for his bride. Sadly, Johnson—allegedly the youngest general in the Civil War— was blinded as a result of his injuries.

You enter the spacious mansion by way of a large entry hall. Across an expanse of gleaming parquet floor there's a view past the polished wood staircase to the wide windows of the den at the back of the house. "Rocky Rest" is a misnomer; rest here is anything but rocky. All the rooms, including the guest rooms, are exceptionally large. All have antique furniture, and the master bedroom downstairs and one of the upstairs rooms sport canopied beds. On the large landing upstairs, a beautiful antique sofa and chairs upholstered in bright yellow brocade are particularly inviting.

Breakfast might be Fannie's Dutch Apple Baby, a sort of popover pastry filled with fruit, or if you prefer, scrambled eggs and sausage. Fannie can recommend several restaurants in the vicinity, but she will also cook lunch or dinner for you if you wish.

Burnet is the "Bluebonnet Capital of Texas," and in the spring the wildflowers are glorious. The inn is within walking distance of Town Square with its little shops, friendly people, and the town museum.

How to get there: Water Street is also Highway 281. The inn is on the highway 4 blocks south of the intersection of 281 and Highway 29. The inn will be on your right. A white fence and a sign are at the driveway into the inn.

The Knittel Homestead
Burton, Texas
77835

Innkeepers: Donna and Doug Hutchinson
Address/Telephone: 502 Main; (409) 289–5102
Rooms: 3; all with private bath; TV available. No smoking inn.
Rates: $75, single or double; $15 extra person; EPB. No credit cards.
Open: All year.
Facilities and activities: Dinner by reservation, bicycles. Nearby: National
  Archive Center for Cotton Ginning; tours of historic cotton gin; oldest
  operating Texaco Station in the United States; National Bike Trail;
  gateway to Bluebonnet Trails.

This old house with a rounded bulge on the outside was built
in three stages. The first, in 1870, was by Herman Knittel, Confederate soldier and Texas senator who was the little town's first postmaster and merchant. Today's inn kitchen and utility area were his
post office and mercantile store.

Next, the front wing was added later as the family's residence.
Herman Knittel, Jr., added the dining room, the upstairs bedrooms,
and the first indoor plumbing in Burton. "But what this house is
really known for," Donna says, "is the third stage, the circular staircase." That accounts for the bulge, but that's not all. It was transported from Germany and took several years to get here. "It finally
arrived by oxcart—but the wrong stair risers had been shipped. It
had to be put in backwards!" We went to take a look, and I found it

imposing all the same. "I tell people the house looks like a Mississippi steamboat," Donna says. Painted cream and white? "No, that's chickpea," she says with a laugh.

Donna and Doug are another couple involved with their community. They are consultants advising on downtown revitalization, museum projects, and economic development in the area. Doug, an architect, was a Main Street Project Director in nearby Brenham for many years, and now he also builds high-performance automobiles. Donna is working on a cookbook as well. "I trade recipes with my guests, and we've started a recipe club," she says as she serves a fulsome breakfast of strawberries with Devonshire cream, savory egg puff, Burton sausage or bacon, raspberry streusel muffins, and her special fruit drink.

The plate rack, high on the dining-room walls, holds a collection of plates from the 1800s, and the pair of portraits from the 1700s are Doug's ancestors from Back East who, Donna explains, were in the ship business, making their ships available to the rebels of 1776. The couple have a letter from George Washington; another ancestor, Samuel Huntington, signed the Declaration of Independence; I have to say I was impressed!

Two of the upstairs guest rooms open onto the wraparound porch, and the back room has its own back stairs. Bath fixtures are the original ones, and Donna stocks all baths with Woods of Windsor soaps and bubble bath. "In these old-fashioned tubs a bubble bath is a must," she says. I was surprised to hear that the Blue Room in the back is "the quietest." In this village of 311 people, what could be noisy? Donna laughs. "On Saturday nights everybody congregates out front; all the locals come down to gossip in front of the post office and the bank."

If you'd rather have dinner than gossip, the cafe on the corner has been listed as number eight in the top-ten Texas cafes.

A local amateur historian, Donna researched nearby archives when guests who had been married in the house long ago returned to celebrate their fiftieth wedding anniversary. "I found out what they served back then and served all those things—and used their color scheme, which I learned from their relatives. It was great!"

How to get there: From Highway 290 take the Burton exit 12 miles west of Brenham. Go to Main Street; the inn is on the corner of Main and Washington opposite the post office.

Long Point Inn
Burton, Texas
77835

Innkeepers: Jeannine and Bill Neinast
Address/Telephone: Route 1, Box 86-A; (409) 289–3171
Rooms: 3; 2 with private bath.
Rates: $75 to $85, double; $25 extra person over 6; EPB. American Express accepted with 5 percent surcharge. Deposit required to hold reservation.
Open: All year.
Facilities and activities: Hide-a-beds, cribs, playpen, high chair, and booster chair; fishing in five ponds stocked with catfish and bass; 175 acres of cattle ranchland; swimming; hiking. Nearby: restaurants, Miniature Horse Farm at Monastery of St. Clare, Star of the Republic Museum at Washington-on-the-Brazos State Park.

"We're so pleased. We never expected to be so busy and to have so many happy guests," says Jeannine. The Neinasts opened their lovely chalet-style home to guests because they wanted to share the wonderful lifestyle they have created for themselves out on the land.

"Come and feed the cows, fish the ponds, traipse the woods, listen to the quiet," they say enticingly. They especially welcome families with children. "After all," Bill says with a laugh, "we have nine grandchildren."

And when you return from the cows, the ponds, and the

woods, you'll find yourself in the lap of luxury in the form of a large story-and-a-half house that is completely and wholeheartedly turned over to guests. There's a piano in the parlor—may guests play it? But of course. "In fact, we would love it if they would come and play. But so far nobody has," mourns Jeannine.

She compensates by lavishing on her guests such marvelous breakfasts as eggs Newport (with sour cream and bacon) or a casserole of cottage cheese, spiced ham, Monterey Jack cheese, mushrooms, and chili peppers, all with biscuits and homemade wild plum jam. The fruit compote is always a hit with children, "and of course we have cereal for the youngsters who want it," Bill says.

Exciting for city kids is a hike on the land and a chance to spot the deer, raccoons, possums, fox, and armadillos that live at Long Point Inn; rabbits, too, both jack and cottontail. Birds are there aplenty: bluebirds and jays, hawks and crows, robins and hummingbirds. "Kids especially like it when I take them down to feed the cattle," Bill says. "They're so gentle, they come and stick their heads in the truck for ranch cubes—that's like candy to them, and they'll take it from your hand." (They don't bite, he adds reassuringly. "They don't have the right teeth for it even if they wanted to which they don't.")

Other country doings include swimming in an old-fashioned swimming hole beneath a waterfall and fishing with a string and pole (or bring your own more sophisticated equipment) in the farm ponds. Outings include a visit to the miniature horses raised nearby. "The little folks, often that's the high point of their trip, especially if they get to see a little foal."

Pie, cookies, coffee, and always Texas's great Blue Bell Ice Cream are served in the evening. The Neinasts believe in Texas hospitality with a captial H. Long Point Inn is an ideal hideaway from the hectic pace of city living—and, for youngsters, a wonderful introduction to the joys of the countryside.

How to get there: From U.S. Highway 290 take FM (Farm Road) 2679 to FM 390. Turn right, and Long Point Inn will be on the left on a hill not far from the intersection.

"Our House"
Calvert, Texas
77837

Innkeepers: Brenda and Don Shafer
Address/Telephone: 406 East Texas Street; (409) 364–2909
Rooms: 5 share 2 baths. No smoking inn.
Rates: $65, double, EPB. No credit cards.
Open: All year.
Facilities and activities: Dinners in the Shafers' Posh Restaurant, only one in
     town (open Thursday to Sunday); block-square yard; bicycles. Nearby:
     National Historic District named for a descendant of Lord Baltimore,
     remains of world's largest cotton gin; Virginia Park with large gazebo
     and shady playground.

Quite a surprise is this spectacular old house in this very small
town (population 1,715). Built by P. C. Gibson in 1904–6, the
house was occupied by family descendants until Brenda and Don
were lucky enough to come looking at "just the right moment,"
says Brenda. "We were led to it."

The Shafers were fairly recent graduates of nearby Texas A&M
University and were expecting their first child when they went on
their hunt back in 1986. Now daughter Lorelei and son Hunter
keep the inn full of toys and fun.

"One of our attractions is our kids," Don says with a laugh.
"Return guests come back and say: We're going off walking. Can
Lorelei come with us? Soon they're off, talking and walking." Other

attractions are bound to be the magnificent house with its unusual staircase—which, Don likes to think, was once the hiding place of the Gibson family gold.

Don has other fanciful ideas, and one of the most fun is the "treasure hunt" he sends inn guests on. "They don't collect anything tangible," he says. But it sure is fun to track down the answers to his questions. "Myra Bell Shirley came to Calvert as a young girl with her family. By what name do we know her?" he asks. Or, "What, in our nation's history, do three Calvert men have in common?"

No, I'm not going to tell you the answers; you'll have to go see for yourself. Clue: Don is a great booster of Calvert. "I believe in ten years Calvert will be different. It has history and more beautiful Victorian homes than East Texas," he says.

Don is the breakfast cook, especially on weekends, as well as turning out fabulous chicken enchiladas smothered in sour cream in the restaurant. And, "My lasagna I'll put up to anybody's," he boasts. Brenda can boast about her pies, especially the strawberry one that won first prize in the McLennan County Fair.

Breakfast is a three-course feast with fresh fruit, Belgian waffles, then a giant mushroom, ham, and cheese omelet; so come with a hearty appetite. It's served in the huge mansion's huge dining room. There are also a parlor, a library, and in the corner of the vast entry hall, a grand piano. Most of the furniture is antique, and again the Shafers feel they were lucky—they had access to a houseful of wonderful furniture from a home in Alabama. "Family friends called and said to come get it, otherwise it would all go to Goodwill," Brenda says. "You can imagine how thrilled we were."

After this bonanza there was nothing left but to open as an inn. "Especially since there wasn't one in town and the antiques dealers begged us to open one." Now Brenda delights in serving her guests from a copious collection of pink Depression glass.

How to get there: Highway 6 between Waco and Bryan/College Station goes right through Calvert. Turn east on Gregg Street, go 4 blocks to Elm, turn south 1 block to Texas. Inn is on the corner of Elm and Texas; use circular entrance on Elm.

Landmark Inn
Castroville, Texas
78009

Innkeeper: Superintendent Leah Huth
Address/Telephone: 402 Florence Street; (210) 538–2133
Rooms: 8; 4 with private bath; no air conditioning (fans only). No smoking inn.
Rates: $35, single; $5, extra adult; $2 children 6 to 12; under 6 free, EP. No credit cards.
Open: All year.
Facilities and activities: Nearby: restaurants, fishing, historic town to explore, antiques shows twice a year, St. Louis Day Celebration in August, Old Fashioned Christmas first weekend in December; Heritage Dance Celebration first Saturday in April; Living History Exhibit first Saturday in June.

Landmark Inn is a Texas State Historical Park, and as such it's administered by the Parks and Wildlife Department. The whitewashed building has provided shelter for weary travelers for more than a century, and it may be the last bargain east of the Pecos.

The inn is on one of Texas's prettiest rivers, the Medina. The old gristmill over the underground millrace (both were built in 1854) is the place to catch lots of perch, catfish, and carp if you're an angler. The park is open all year, and the mill structures and several pieces of milling equipment can be seen along the trail that leads to the lower terraces of the river.

In keeping with the tradition of old inns, there are no telephones or televisions. Rooms are furnished with authentic period pieces, giving the nicest feeling of early Texas and pioneer days while being perfectly comfortable.

If you're lucky, you might get the room Robert E. Lee slept in, or the up- or downstairs room of the tiny bathhouse. Before the Civil War it was the only place to bathe between San Antonio and Eagle Pass. It gave up that valuable function when the lead lining the upstairs (which served as a cistern) was melted down for the Confederates.

Each room has an Alsatian motto on the wall: *"Qui tient à sa tranquillité sait respecter celles d'autres* . . . he who values his own tranquillity knows how to respect that of others."* One ell of the inn lobby is a museum, with artifacts and exhibits telling the story not only of the inn but of the town as well. Castroville, which calls itself the "Little Alsace of Texas," was founded in 1844 by Henri Castro, a French Jew of Portuguese descent, who brought 2,134 Alsatians. The ensuing mixture of French, German, Spanish, and English cultures has never obscured the ambience brought by those first homesick settlers. You'll find great bakeries, sausage houses, and restaurants in this "Little Alsace."

Inn grounds are quiet and serene. There are shady oaks and soft green lawns broken only by stepping-stones, which lead to the original kitchen (now an ice and telephone facility) and the gristmill. The park is open daily all year.

A wonderfully old and oddly shaped pecan tree stands near the river. One of the Famous Trees of Texas, it marks the approximate location of Castro's encampment back in 1844. Legend has it that Geronimo was chained to the tree overnight on the way from Mexico to imprisonment in San Antonio—while his captors spent the night comfortably in the inn.

A lot goes on at Landmark Inn. To preserve the ethnic dancing of the area, Alsatian, German, Belgian, and Spanish dancers perform in authentic costume during Heritage Dance Celebration. The Living History Exhibit lauds the Texas Rangers and demonstrates the lost arts of soap making and blacksmithing.

How to get there: Just after you cross the Medina River traveling west on Highway 90, turn left on the first street, which will be Florence. The inn is on the right.

The Browning Plantation
Chappell Hill, Texas
77426

Innkeepers: Mildred and Dick Ganchan
Address/Telephone: Route 1, Box 8; (409) 836–6144
Rooms: 6 in main house and Model Railroad Depot; 2 with private bath, 2 with TV. No smoking inn.
Rates: $85 to $110, double, EPB. No credit cards.
Open: All year.
Facilities and activities: Swimming pool, model train with 1½ miles of track, 220 acres of natural trails, fishing in lakes on property. Nearby: historic sites in Washington-on-the-Brazos and Independence; good restaurant in Brenham.

"There's no frownin' at the Brownin'" was the theme of the Browning float at a local county parade. The motto was a hit, as it very aptly describes the Browning atmosphere. This elegant antebellum mansion easily could be awed by its own splendor; but with Dick and Mildred as innkeepers, the spirit of fun rules instead.

"We have a good time," Dick says. "We feel that people are here to watch Mildred make her biscuits in the kitchen while they have their coffee. People don't want to hear how the house was put together or how old Browning died. Mildred and I tell them all *our* troubles, and we have a good laugh instead."

Still, the Ganchans have made an entertaining story of the resurrection of the old Browning plantation, which was truly a formidable undertaking. Mildred was looking for a cute little Victorian house to move to their property elsewhere when they made the mistake of stopping by to see a place that "needed a little attention." What they saw was a completely ruined mansion left over from cotton-and-slavery days.

Listed on the National Register of Historic Places, the inn once again has the fake wood graining that was the height of elegance back when the house was built in the 1850s. Daughter Meg Ganchan Rice spent ages practicing the technique as her contribution to the family restoration effort.

Upstairs guest rooms in the big house have 12-foot ceilings and massive windows and are furnished with nineteenth-century antiques, including plantation and tester beds.

Where to relax is a choice that can be difficult: the parlor, the library, or the south veranda, with its beautiful view over the vast acres of green farmland? Or for an even more breathtaking scene, climb three flights to the rooftop widow's walk that crowns the house.

And there is more. One son-in-law is such a train buff that he has built a model railroad on the property, and if he's in residence, you may be able to cajole him into a ride. "He has more rolling stock than the Santa Fe," Dick brags as he proudly shows off the new two-room "depot" he designed, a replica of a Santa Fe original. Guest rooms inside the depot have horizontal pine paneling and blue-striped ticking curtains and bedspreads.

You'll feel like Scarlett O'Hara and Rhett at breakfast around the huge dining room table, eating dishes like the inn's Eggs Sardou accompanied by a hot fruit compote. But first there's an Orange Julius eye-opener, and maybe there will also be hot biscuits. There's a social hour with snacks before dinner, too.

How to get there: From U.S. Highway 290 east of Brenham, take FM (Farm Road) 1155 south until you come to a short jog to the left. Immediately to your right you'll see a dirt road. Turn right onto it; continue south across the cattle guard and under the arch of trees until you reach the plantation house.

The Mulberry House
Chappell Hill, Texas
77426

Innkeepers: Katie and Myrv Cron
Address/Telephone: P.O. Box 5; (409) 830–1311
Rooms: 5, in main house and guest cottage; all with private bath and phone, 2 with TV. No smoking inn.
Rates: $75 to $110, double, EPB. No credit cards.
Open: All year.
Facilities and activities: Large back yard, croquet. Nearby: Brenham restaurants and shops; historic Chappell Hill with restaurants, Bluebonnet Festival in April, Fourth of July parade, Scarecrow Festival in October; Washington-on-the-Brazos (capital of the Republic of Texas), Star of the Republic Museum, miniature horses at Monastery of St. Clare 8 miles away.

Mulberry House was the home of prosperous cotton farmer John Sterling Smith and his wife, Marie, and their descendants from 1874 to 1983. Innkeepers Katie and Myrv bought the house as a country retreat from the hustle and bustle of Houston, an hour and a half away. First they built the "barn," a suite of two bedrooms, living room, and kitchen, and lived there three years while they restored the house. Now the barn serves as both lovely guest quarters and Myrv's woodworking shop.

Myrv is a consummate woodworking artist, and his shop occupies the first floor of the barn. Examples of his fine bird carvings decorate the inn. There are hooded merganser and bobwhite families, all perched on wonderful pieces of driftwood, all detailed down to the last feather.

I wondered how Katie and Myrv had gotten into innkeeping. "Myrv was always working in the yard or in his shop, and I was always in the house," says Katie with a laugh, "and one day I was in a gift shop (on nearby Brenham's square) and a young couple was looking for a place to stay. I said, 'Come home with me,' and they did, and we had a wonderful time!"

In Miss Marie's Room, named for the lady who lived there fifty years, you'll find two wonderful Jenny Lind beds that Katie hunted down expressly for that room. The huge armoire is a find, too, and the clutch of teddy bears sitting in a corner looked most pleased at their quarters. The inn is filled with unusual antique pieces—some from the Smith family, who lived in the house 110 years.

Katie makes delicious breakfasts in the large sunny kitchen: egg-and-cheese soufflé or ham and bacon-and-egg puff, with grits and cranberry-orange muffins. At 6:00 in the evening, before guests go out to dinner at one of Brenham's fine restaurants, there's an informal cocktail hour, with neighbors sometimes joining in. "We come and go," says Katie, "and expect our guests to make themselves at home."

"Lots of people bring their bicycles," says Myrv. "They ride from here to Washington-on-the-Brazos." A round trip of 32 miles is a good day's outing!

Chappell Hill was founded in 1847 and named for an early Texas hunter. Before the Civil War it was beginning to grow into a prominent educational and agricultural center. Today it's a charming small village—with several annual festivals to remind Texas it's still there.

How to get there: Turn north off U.S. Highway 290 onto FM (Farm Road) 1155 (Chappell Hill's Main Street) and drive to FM 2447 (Chestnut Street). Mulberry House is 0.2 mile east of the intersection.

Stagecoach Inn
Chappell Hill, Texas
77426

Innkeepers: Elizabeth and Harvin Moore
Address/Telephone: P.O. Box 339; (409) 836–9515
Rooms: 7; 2 in main building, 1 in Coach House with private bath, 2 in Weems Cottage, 2 in Lottie's. No smoking inn.
Rates: $90, double, EPB. No credit cards.
Open: All year.
Facilities and activities: Beautiful grounds and garden. Nearby: good restaurants in Chappell Hill, Chappell Hill; in the heart of early Texas history; Washington-on-the-Brazos; Star of the Republic Museum; St. Clare Monastery, which raises miniature horses.

"We want to excel in hospitality," says Elizabeth, who is carrying on the tradition of this historic inn. The Stagecoach Inn was built in 1850 and was once a major stop for the coaches it was named for. The gorgeous grounds, like a small estate, are on a corner surrounded by a white picket fence and are ablaze with color overflowing from beds and pots of flowers. All summer long flower pots are bursting with red, white, and pink geraniums; the flower beds are bordered in scarlet begonias; and the crepe myrtle trees shower blossoms all around. There are four separate terraces from which to drink in all this beauty. "People enjoy them so much. It gets more beautiful all the time," says this proud innkeeper-gardener.

"We start the bulbs in the middle of December, especially the bearded iris," Elizabeth says of the flowers that appear at each place on the breakfast table. If it's not iris time, perhaps a sprig of rosemary will be at your place, but it will always be something from this fabulous garden.

The inn fronts on the road, and both the Coach House and Weems Cottage are on the grounds in the rear, all part of the 3-acre historic site.

Breakfast can be short-order, like soft boiled or scrambled eggs, but I vote for cook Evelyn's "secret casserole," which is still a secret from me. "She loves to let you try to work it out," says Elizabeth, "but she's careful not to divulge it herself."

Evelyn might serve eggs Elizabeth or eggs Charlotte instead, along with apple strudel, whiskey coffee cake, homemade muffins, croissants, or zucchini bread, depending upon her mood. Oh, that Evelyn surely can cook! Add grape jelly, juice of your choice, and fresh fruit in season, and you have a feast.

Sometimes Elizabeth adds her touch with a mixed fruit and yogurt combination she calls *crème fraîche*.

Whether you stay in Weems Cottage, Lottie's, or the Coach House, you have the run of the place. Weems Cottage, with two rooms and a bath, was built in 1866, and the front and back porches are full of rocking chairs, just like in the good old days. Lottie's is a 133-year-old Greek Revival house across the road from the inn, and its five rooms include two living-room areas as well as the guest rooms, all furnished with authentic Texas heirlooms and antiques. The Coach House, newly remodeled into a one-bedroom suite, is way in the back under spreading old trees. "We're flexible," says Elizabeth. "We've slept an entire bridge club, an antiques group, a football weekend—as many as fifteen to twenty guests."

Whenever you spend the night, you can have a tour of the inn, which is listed on the National Register of Historic Places.

How to get there: Turn north off U.S. Highway 290 onto FM (Farm Road) 1155 (Chappell Hill's Main Street) and drive to FM 2447 (Chestnut Street). Stagecoach Inn is across the corner to the left, and Lottie's will be on your right.

Baron's Creek Inn
Fredericksburg, Texas
78624

Innkeepers: Kenneth and Brooke Schweers
Address/Telephone: 110 East Creek Street; (210) 997–9398 or (800) 800–4082
Rooms: 5 3-room suites; all with private bath, TV, refrigerator, microwave oven. No smoking inn.
Rates: $85 to $95, double; $15 extra person; continental breakfast.
Open: All year.
Facilities and activities: Nearby: restaurants, antiques shops, Admiral Nimitz Museum and Walk of the Pacific War, Pioneer Museum, historic "Sunday houses" and almost-monthly celebrations in historic Fredericksburg.

Baron's Creek Inn is half hidden by large old pecan trees, but I found it by its jaunty windmill, turning high above the leafy boughs. Named for the creek that flows through Fredericksburg, the inn was built in 1911, a date recorded permanently above the front door. As you enter the gate you can also see the name of the builder and first owner, Max Eckert, embossed in the concrete step.

There is a grape arbor between the house and the cottage at the rear. It's fun to stay in the cottage, which in Fredericksburg is called a "Sunday house." The historic town is known for these little houses; they were built by prosperous German immigrant farmers to use when the family came into town for the weekends. On Saturday night the family would polka and play; on Sunday it was off to church, and on Monday back to the farm.

The inn has been completely redone—new wood floors and the works. Revealed are the inn's high-ceilinged rooms with original beaded board and natural wood floors, beveled and etched glass, and solid wood doors. The upstairs suites have an eclectic combination of antique and rattan furniture. Bathrooms have brass fixtures and claw-foot tubs, and there are many authentic Texas antiques to admire. The stenciling on the walls is also new.

The continental breakfast of assorted muffins or pastries, occasionally sausage in a roll, and fresh fruit of the season is delivered to your suite—or served on the porch if you prefer. The other meals are up to you; that's what the refrigerators are for. And remember, Fredericksburg is famous for German sausages, cheese, and strudel, and most folks like to stock up on delectable fare in the town delicatessens. Restaurants serve delicious Wiener schnitzel, sauerkraut, and sauerbraten, too.

That windmill out front of the inn serves an important function even today. Water held in the upper portion of the cylindrical tank house provides a gravity-fed system that the inn uses to water the lawns. (The city water system serves the interior of the inn.) In the lower portion of the tank, Max Eckert stored his cured meat and practiced wine making—and though he is long gone, you can sample the grapes, still growing in the arbor, that he used for his personal wine.

There was another ingenious use of the building back then: Beneath ground level there's a concrete compartment that was used as a cistern. Water was channeled off the tin roof of the tank, filtered through charcoal, and pumped out for daily use. Clever, those Fredericksburg pioneers!

How to get there: Highway 290 goes through town, becoming Main Street. The inn is 1 block east and 2 blocks south of the courthouse on Main.

Country Cottage Inn
Fredericksburg, Texas
78624

Innkeeper: Jeffery Webb

Address/Telephone: 405 East Main Street; (210) 997–8549

Rooms: 7 suites; all with private bath, phone, TV, refrigerator, microwave oven, coffee maker. No smoking inn.

Rates: $75 to $105, per room, continental breakfast.

Open: All year.

Facilities and activities: Fully equipped kitchen available. Nearby: German restaurants, Admiral Nimitz Museum, Pioneer Museum, almost-monthly celebrations in historic Fredericksburg, antiques shops, small museums.

When this cottage was built in 1850, just four years after Fredericksburg was founded, it was the only two-story house in town. Cool stone walls are over 24 inches thick, and the hardware was forged in the owner's smithy. The walls are whitewashed; there are exposed hand-cut rafters. Most of the antique furniture was made in town in the mid-1800s.

One of the rooms is furnished with antiques from the birthplace of Admiral Chester W. Nimitz, hero of the Pacific Theater during World War II. He was born just 2 blocks away from the cottage. His grandfather's old Steamboat Hotel is now a first-class museum. Behind the museum there's a beautiful Japanese garden contributed by the people of Japan, and a block away you'll find the Walk of the Pacific War, lined with airplanes, tanks, landing craft, and other machines used in the Pacific during World War II. They're all there, out in the open, sunny hill country scenery, for kids and adults alike to touch and wonder at.

Country Cottage has other Nimitz mementos. The Pecan Room has a Nimitz night table, a chuck-wagon pie safe, an Amish quilt on the wall, and an eighteenth-century mantrap over the sofa; the coffee table is an 1825 wooden bellows from France. So many interesting details make it difficult to look at everything at once, so take your time!

The Oak Suite has its original fireplace, and guests are permitted to build a fire, but I love Jeffery's admonition: "Please build only small fires!"

The inn has two new suites, the Henke Suite in the original front room of the historic house (Henke was Admiral Nimitz's maternal grandfather). The Nimitz Suite is in a part of the house that was added back in 1873, and it's full of Nimitz family memorabilia.

The inn may be charmingly historic, but the bathrooms are beautifully modern—some of them have large whirlpool tubs. I was completely restored in one, after a wonderful day taking in all the small-town sights.

Breakfast is hot chocolate, coffee or tea, and sometimes sweet rolls from one of Fredericksburg's famous bakeries. Two of them, Dietz's and the Fredericksburg Bakery, have been in business since the town began, and I really recommend a sweet visit. But mostly innkeeper Jeffery Webb has fresh pastries and muffins of her own for you—she loves to bake.

The old inn building is beautifully restored and scrupulously clean, and the simple structure is enhanced by Laura Ashley fabrics and bed linens. Soft terry robes and ice water in each room made me feel like a fraudulent pioneer—it wasn't like this a little over a hundred years ago, when hostile Indians were near and the living was pretty tough!

How to get there: Highway 290 goes through town, becoming Main Street, and the inn is right there in the 400 block.

Das College Haus
Fredericksburg, Texas
78624

Innkeeper: BeBe Curry
Address/Telephone: 106 College Street; (210) 997–9047
Rooms: 3; all with private bath, phone, and TV. No smoking inn.
Rates: $65 to $78, double; $15 extra person; EPB. No credit cards.
Open: All year.
Facilities and activities: Nearby: Main Street, with German restaurants, Admiral Nimitz Museum, and other historic museums, and antiques shops, is 3 blocks away; public exercise track across the street.

"I've always wanted to earn a living in my own home," said BeBe when she first started out; "I love to stay home, I love people, I love entertaining." And she now reports that she has learned much as an innkeeper, all of it good. "I do all I can to make my guests comfortable and satisfied. This is a fun thing to do, and I have met many beautiful people."

The former Das Gast Haus is now Das College Haus, because BeBe decided that the name of her inn ought to reflect the street she lives on. She greets holidays with zest; the candy jar in each room will have Easter eggs or Valentine sweets to reflect the occasion. If there's no holiday? Well, I was more than happy with the chocolate bridge mix, chocoholic that I am.

Haunting farm auctions was a great hobby of BeBe and her late husband, and the inn boasts a wonderful assortment of old furniture from Indiana auctions. Das College Haus prides itself on this unusual mix of Indiana farm auction antiques with Victorian and country charm. It's an interesting change from the more usual German furniture of Fredericksburg—home of the first group of settlers brought to Texas by the Society for the Protection of German Immigrants in Texas. The kitchen has an old pie safe and a wood box, and the dining room of the seventy-five-year-old house still has its original country-scenes wallpaper. In corner cupboards on each side of the front window BeBe has installed the Rockwell and Hummel figures she has collected since 1972.

Upstairs, off the L-shaped porch, there's the Victorian Green Suite, which can sleep six; its sitting room contains a queen sofa bed. The Country Cream Room with a private bath is across the hall. Downstairs, the Mostly Mauve Suite (don't you love the name?) has a queen bed; the living room has a queen sleeper and a fireplace; and there's a private entrance.

BeBe's breakfasts, served in the dining room or the upstairs porch, are hearty bacon-and-egg affairs with homemade biscuits, jam, fruit, juice, and coffee and tea; or perhaps, for contrast, a delightful soufflé and muffins. BeBe eagerly invites guests to make themselves at home; and it's no sooner said than done, thanks to the enthusiasm of this hostess. Although she's not a native of Fredericksburg, BeBe, once she saw the town, was determined to live here. I suspect that her being a teacher of German may have had something to do with it!

In addition to all the new friends she has made since opening her inn, BeBe still says her best friend is her black poodle, Mollie, her "meeter-greeter," who by now is a pro as the official welcomer.

How to get there: Going west on East Main Street, turn right onto North Llano and go about 5 blocks to East College. Turn left and the inn will be to your right about a block up.

The Delforge Place
Fredericksburg, Texas
78624

Innkeepers: Betsy and George Delforge
Address/Telephone: 710 Ettie Street; (210) 997–6212
Rooms: 4; all with private bath, phone, and TV. No smoking inn.
Rates: $70 to $75, double, EPB.
Open: All year.
Facilities and activities: Lunch and dinner served by reservation, picnic baskets, patio with fountain, Ping-Pong, pool table, sandbox. Nearby: 7 blocks away is Fredericksburg's famous Main Street, with German restaurants, and *biergartens,* Admiral Nimitz Museum, other historic museums, and antiques shops; LBJ Ranch approximately 15 miles east.

"We get some of the most interesting people," Betsy says. "That's why we settled here; this is such a vibrant, international little town, what with the Nimitz Museum and the LBJ Ranch." The Delforge Place is interesting and international itself, what with the front Map Room and the Quebec Room sporting ancient maps and other mementos from Betsy's sea-captain ancestor, head of the first merchant fleet opening the Harbor of Yokahama to American sailing ships.

Guest room decor is ever changing, since Betsy lets her antique furniture and paintings go out on exhibit to museums on the East Coast. It follows that oriental pieces join with the American, European, and family heirlooms in furnishing the old house, once a one-room "Sunday house"—and you'll have to go to Fredericksburg to find out what a Sunday house is. This one was built in 1898 by German pioneer Ferdinand Koeppen on a tract of land set aside by the German Emigration Company as a communal garden. The house was moved to its present location in 1975 and during restoration was made considerably larger!

Guests relax in one of the two *versamel,* or "gathering rooms," with coffee and tea, quiet games, or books off the shelves (or television if they insist!). The Delforges stress that guests are welcome to come and go as they please: There's a lot to see and do in town.

And guests are sent off with a good start—one of Betsy's famous breakfasts. She has always featured her specialties of German Sour Cream Twists and San Saba French Toast (which is marinated in orange brandy and thick and crusty with orange peel and San Saba pecans. Delicious!). Now she's having fun varying them with no less than seven different breakfast menus. I hope you're lucky enough to catch her seven-course gourmet Fredericksburg Breakfast, a sampling of all the wonderful fruits, meats, breads, and pastries of the historical town.

"Food and fashion go together for me," Betsy says, and her past includes both food testing and fabric design. She grows her own herbs in hanging baskets over the flagstone patio. "When the apples come in the fall, we have sausage and apple crepes"—which sounds to me like a great reason for an autumn visit. Betsy's avocation now is the making of gift baskets she and George call Special Day Baskets. They're loaded with all the good things produced in Fredericksburg, and people order them from all over Texas and beyond.

The Upper Deck's named for Betsy's seafaring interests. It has its own outside staircase up to the deck, bright with nautical flags flying in the breeze. Skylights and an octagon window brighten the spacious guest room, which has such original touches as weathered wooden barrels set on end as nightstands and a globe of the world on a stand, for the sailors.

How to get there: From Main Street (U.S. Highway 290) turn south on South Adams to Walnut, then left on Walnut for 3 blocks to Ettie. The inn, at 710 Ettie, is the Victorian house on the corner to your left.

Magnolia House
Fredericksburg, Texas
78624

Innkeeper: Geri Lilley
Address/Telephone: 101 East Hackberry; (210) 997–0306
Rooms: 6; including 2 suites; 4 with private bath; all with TV.
Rates: $68 to $90, double, EPB.
Open: All year.
Facilities and activities: Porches, large patio with fountain and goldfish pond.
Nearby: restaurants, antiques shops, Admiral Nimitz Museum and Walk of the Pacific War, Pioneer Museum, and historic Sunday Houses.

Geri Lilley has a lot of ambition, the right sort: She has her guests' best interest at heart. "I want to be the very best inn in Texas!" she says. "Really," she adds earnestly, "That's my ambition. I want my guests to tell me a problem or about something missing so I can fix it right now. And I try to be very flexible. We've even served breakfast to two ladies at 7 a.m., even though we prefer 8:30, because they were judges at a local beauty show and had to be there early."

But it's not only Geri's gung-ho attitude that makes Magnolia House special: The inn itself is warm and bright and welcoming, with large, comfortable guest rooms, the kind of parlor (and dining room) you'd like to call your own, a game room for board games, and a large patio with a fountain and a goldfish pond. The house historically is the Stein House, and although the family took the original goldfish out when they left, years ago, the only surviving member of the family called Geri recently. "Would you like some of the descendants back in the pond?" the elderly lady asked. "So now," Geri crows, "I've got goldfish out there this big!"

Hospitality shows in the sumptuous breakfast Geri and her assistant, Yolanda Martinez, take such pride in. "We never serve the same breakfast twice," Geri says, "unless you stay more than five days. Then—well I guess we'll have to repeat—or get some new recipes!" We had fresh fruit salad with a secret "Magnolia" sauce, bran muffins, bacon and sausage, cheese quiche, and the lightest, fluffiest pecan waffles, topped with strawberries and whipped cream and/or maple syrup. I opted for the latter when Yolanda bragged that she concocts the maple syrup herself. Geri is a gourmet cook, and Yolanda is a willing disciple.

Although Geri has remodeled the historic house, she hasn't done away with an unusual and delightful pass-through she calls the "Mud Room." Overhanging a small washbasin is a genuine old hand pump. "All my guests have to try it," Geri says. I certainly did, and although it took some pressure, I finally got fresh spring water gurgling into the basin.

Built into the wall opposite this fun "toy" is the house's original icebox, now of course refrigerated. It opens on both sides of the wall, and guests can help themselves to the complimentary wine therein.

Both the Magnolia Suite and the Bluebonnet Suite have private entrances; the Magnolia has a huge living room with fireplaces; the Bluebonnet has a kitchen and a very comfy rocker, which, when it was reupholstered, revealed some buried treasure, an old shilling and sixpence, "so we know it's a genuine English antique," Geri says. All rooms are large and bright and delightfully decorated by Geri, who also paints. "I retired from the oil business in Houston because I had to have back surgery. That I'm now physically fit I attribute to my guests, to all the love and caring," she says, determined to return it full measure.

How to get there: From Main Street (Highway 290 east) turn north on Adams Street to Hackberry, which runs parallel to Main. The inn is on the southeast corner of Adams and Hackberry.

River View Inn and Farm
Fredericksburg, Texas
78624

Innkeeper: Helen K. Taylor
Address/Telephone: Highway 16 South; (210) 997–8555
Rooms: 5; 4 with private bath; 2 with phone, 1 with TV. Pets permitted.
Rates: $55 to $68, per room, EPB. Special rates in September, January, and
    February.
Open: All year.
Facilities and activities: Farm acres to wander over, river to fish in, cattle to
    visit, vegetable garden, books and games. Nearby: Lady Bird Johnson
    Municipal Park, with swimming pool, tennis, and 9-hole golf course is
    1.3 miles away; Fredericksburg has Admiral Nimitz Museum and Ger-
    man heritage museums.

Breezy is the word for River View Inn and Farm. It's set on a
hill in the hill country and has a breezeway that catches a round-
the-clock cool wind. I could just sit there for hours, taking in the
sweep of the green hills and listening to the lowing of the
longhorns that Helen's neighbors raise and that sometimes graze in
Helen's fields.

Helen herself raises native Texas herbs, and other native Texas
flora, and what a refreshing treat to have her show you her garden.
"You just ought to see!"—her enthusiasm is infectious. She also has
a vegetable garden close to the house, and young guests enjoy helping pick the crops, especially when they can take them home.

Helen's guests have the run of the house. The kitchen, the large and comfortably furnished living room with its big stone fireplace, the glass-enclosed sun porch, the breakfast room with its china cabinet full of heirloom china, the framed German mottoes, and the collection of framed bird pictures (mostly hummingbirds, which are Helen's favorite)—all conspire to make guests feel truly at home.

The front porch and the large upstairs area, in particular, are great for kids to read and play games in. "But we're never locked into the weather here," Helen reminds. "Not much rain, so everybody's usually out and doing, going to town or to the park."

The downstairs bedroom has a beautiful quilt draped over a handmade cedar chest. The furnishings are 1920s Queen Anne reproductions: dressing table, dresser, bureau, bed, and chair. The bathroom tub has a Jacuzzi, a nice luxury to find out in ranch country!

Helen's breakfast is hearty enough for a rancher, too. Fresh local German sausage, scrambled eggs with jalapeños (but not too hot, says Helen), cheese, biscuits, fresh peach and cherry cobbler, jellies and jams.

It's all topped off by the centerpiece, fresh fruit in season, which everybody proceeds to eat. "The kids run off to play, but the grownups always linger," says Helen, "having more coffee and munching on the centerpiece." I can taste why: The county is known for blackberries, nectarines, peaches, strawberries, mangoes, and melon—watermelon, honeydew, and Persian.

The Little House That Helen Built has an old-fashioned clawfoot tub in the bathroom and a newfangled microwave oven hiding in a closet with a small refrigerator and a coffeepot. There's a queen bed and a trundle for a child and a deck in back overlooking the Pedernales River. And now there's Little House II, with an antique Jenny Lind spool bed transformed into queen size, for comfort.

You'll find that if guests aren't munching fruit or sitting on the breezeway, they'll be on the porches, rocking or swinging on the dogwood glider and waiting for the cows to come home.

How to get there: Inn is 4.5 miles south of Fredericksburg on Highway 16; 1 mile south of Lady Bird Johnson Park. To the left you'll see a fence and a cattle guard. Drive over it and there you are.

The Badu House
Llano, Texas
78643

Innkeeper: June Holley
Address/Telephone: 601 Bessemer Street; (515) 247–4304
Rooms: 8, including 1 2-bedroom suite; all with private bath. Smoking permitted in Club lounge.
Rates: Weekdays: $45, double; Friday and Saturday, $65 to $75, double; $10 extra person; continental breakfast.
Open: All year.
Facilities and activities: Tuesday to Saturday, lunch 11:00 to 2:00, dinner 5:00 to 9:00. Nearby: hunting in the "deer capital of the world," fishing, the Llano Uplift for gem and rock collectors; Enchanted Rock and Vanishing Texas River Cruise.

The Badu House is an inn in a million: It began life as a small-town bank. Built in 1891 for the First National of Llano, this Italian Renaissance palace–inspired building housed the bank handsomely until it failed in 1898. Then the building was bought at auction by Professor N. J. Badu, a French mineralogist; Badu and his descendants used the imposing red-brick and checkerboard-gray-granite structure as home for over eighty years. Strong enough to have survived a 1900 tornado and a fire that destroyed the iron boomtown of North Llano, this building sure doesn't look like an inn, was my thought as I climbed the wide granite steps to the front door. But the stained glass windows of the doors, one emblazoned with the letter B, the other with an H, opened onto another world.

The doors opened onto a wide flight of polished wood steps leading to a landing furnished with an antique desk, a love seat and chairs, and a jewel-tone antique rug. I walked up a few more steps and around the corner to a sitting room with more Victorian settees and an antique sewing machine abandoned—a century ago?—in the midst of stitching.

Back downstairs, I found the Club, which is the bar and lounge where everyone gathers when not dining or sleeping. There I was welcomed heartily and invited to inspect the bar itself, a huge slab of llanite, the rare opaline stone discovered by Professor Badu and found nowhere else in the world.

The restaurant floors are the white marble of the bank. Solid brass hardware is decorated with an intricate flower motif echoed in the bright floral wallpaper. And I loved the three-part shutters that slide up and down to shade the large old-fashioned windows.

Innkeeper June, with her helper, Judy Miller, serves a simple coffee, juice, and homemade Danish breakfast with Judy's famous cinnamon rolls, but she really shines for lunch and dinner. While Judy loves to bake and be creative—"Everything she cooks and bakes is delicious; ask anybody in town," says a local admirer—Chef Jesse Martinez draws folks from far and near with his prime rib, quail, chicken Alfredo, and catfish however you like it: deep fried, grilled, or blackened. And Judy's baking her apple cobbler more often because, as June says, "Some of the guests griped when they didn't get it!"

How to get there: Llano is on Highway 16, northwest of Austin. Drive right through town and over the bridge, and the inn will be on the left at the corner of Highway 16 and Bessemer.

Forget-Me-Not River Inn
Martindale, Texas
78655

Innkeepers: Hermania and Edvin Rohlack
Address/Telephone: 310 Main (mailing address: Box 396); (512) 357–6835
Rooms: 7; 4 with private bath, 3-bedroom cottage with 1 bath. No alcoholic
    beverages permitted on premises; pets at discretion of innkeeper. No
    smoking inn.
Rates: $60 to $75, single or double; cottage, $100; EPB.
Open: All year.
Facilities and activities: On the San Marcos River with fishing, canoeing,
    swimming. Nearby: San Marcos with restaurants, antiques shops, his-
    toric buildings, Lyndon B. Johnson's alma mater, Southwest Texas
    State University; downtown Martindale with historic buildings; factory
    outlet mall shopping.

    Hermania joins the ranks of innkeepers who fell in love with a
house, and there was no turning back. "We were living in San Marcos (nearby larger town) in our 'forever' house after our years in
Alaska, and I drove up to Martindale to see a friend," she says.
"There was this decrepit house with a jungle around it. I didn't
even get out of the car," she adds, "because I loved it so much, and I
knew Ed would say *no!*" That's because she has cajoled an unwill-
ing Edvin into buying and restoring old run-down houses before.
    But you can see who won. More, wait until you see what Ed
has done with this "decrepit house." At first it was one-story, with a

high attic and dormers. Ed kept looking at that attic and saying, "I know there's room up there."

"He dragged in about four contractors who said it couldn't be done," Hermania says, "but he's a do-it-yourselfer." He lowered the high ceilings about 4 feet and built the most intriguing winding staircase—that was the first thing I wanted to know about. The resulting four guest rooms upstairs under the sloping roof are spacious, light, and delightfully furnished. There's a nook, as well, in the tower, called the Train Turret because youngest son, Korey, was into trains, and that's where he played. But when he couldn't see out of the windows—"No problem," Hermania says, "Ed just raised the floor!"

All five Rohlack offspring (grown now) have names that begin with a K, including Kiana, which is Eskimo for "thank you"—both Hermania and Ed taught in Alaska and have many fond memories. Breakfast would have stood even a traveler in the cold north in good stead. First course was, of all things, strawberry shortcake! It was refreshing, a light, fluffy biscuit with slivered berries covered with sour cream, just slightly sweetened. Next came corn bread, split and covered with sliced hard-boiled eggs in a creamy sauce and sprinkled with fresh green scallions and garnished prettily. Coffee, tea, and fresh orange juice, of course, and Ed started it off by saying grace.

The inn is furnished in a very comfortable and eclectic fashion. Most everything has a story because Ed says Hermania is quite a bargain hunter, haunting antiques shops, garage sales, and flea markets. The rose Irish Rose Room is named in memory of the year Kiana spent in Ireland and has a big old-fashioned claw-foot tub in a corner; the Russian Ivy Room is named for son Karleton's current studying of Russian, plus there's a touch of ivy on the towels.

As for the river just outside the back door, you can catch catfish and bass "and even turtles, even if you don't want them," Hermania warns.

How to get there: From I–35 take exit 205 and go east on Highway 80 for about 5 miles until you come to the blinking light. Turn right and go to the end of the street and turn left onto Main. The inn is just down the block on the right. You can't miss it if you turn into the drive lined with huge, round metal storage tanks, left over from the days when Martindale was big in the grain business.

The Castle Inn
Navasota, Texas
77868

Innkeepers: Helen and Tim Urquehart
Address/Telephone: 1403 East Washington Street; (409) 825–8051
Rooms: 4; all with private bath. Smoking permitted in hallway.
Rates: $74, single; $84, double; $20 extra person; continental breakfast and
evening wine and cheese. No credit cards.
Open: All year.
Facilities and activities: Dinners if house is booked by four couples who are
acquainted. Nearby: historic town with 14-foot statue of French
explorer La Salle, who came to an untimely end near here in 1687,
150 years before town was formed; museum, Navasota Nostalgia Days
festival in May, Main Street Project restoration.

This majestic Queen Anne house is well named The Castle. It
is so gorgeous it's hard to describe adequately. Local craftsmen built
the mansion in 1893 as a wedding present from a local businessman to his bride. Of now-extinct curly pine, decorated with ornamental brass and beveled glass, its sun porch enclosed by 100
beveled-glass panes, the house is outstanding. You know it the
minute you step into the elegant entry hall with parquet floor,
Tiffany light fixture, and the soaring 14-foot ceiling.

I love the turret on one corner, a tower that makes the house
stand out among the leafy trees outside and provides circular window seats inside on the almost-room-sized stair landings. There's

also a 20-foot stained glass window in the stairwell.

The inn is furnished with antiques collected for more than thirty years by Helen and Tim. The music room has a player piano, a hand-cranked Columbia Grafanola, and a carved wooden head of Tim in an aviator's helmet (Tim is a retired airline pilot). The collection is so extensive that private tours are often arranged just to show off this magnificent property. (Tours by reservation only.)

Breakfast can be served in your room or in the upstairs sitting room next to the upstairs porch. Delicious fresh-baked muffins, English muffins, and dry cereals, juice and coffee, and fresh fruit in season taste especially good in such baronial surroundings, and you can have it any time between 6:00 a.m. and the 11:00 a.m. check-out time. Evening wine and cheese, with individual loaves of hot bread, is often served on the upstairs balcony, the better to let you enjoy the evening breezes.

"A lot of times when people go out to dinner we don't know when they're coming home," says Helen, "so we leave a note telling them that their wine and cheese is waiting for them in the fridge." It's in the large upstairs hall and is also stocked with soft drinks, which are consumed "on the honor system."

Each bedroom has a fantastic antique bed, one more amazing than the next: first, a rosewood Louisiana plantation bed; then a tall half-tester; next, another half-tester, beautifully carved; and, finally, a 7 1/2-foot-tall black bed. Antique marble-topped dressers and tables blend perfectly to scale. Another thing to marvel at is Helen's doll collection.

Helen and Tim will provide dinner if four couples want it; it might consist of Cornish hens with wild rice, broccoli hollandaise, Mediterranean salad, and a peach cobbler a la mode. Delicious!

How to get there: The inn is 4 blocks west of the Highway 6 bypass on Highway 105, which becomes Washington, Navasota's main street.

Prince Solms Inn
New Braunfels, Texas
78130

Innkeepers: Ruth Wood; Pat and Bob Brent
Address/Telephone: 295 East San Antonio Street; (210) 625–9169
Rooms: 10; all with private bath.
Rates: $50 to $75, double, Sunday to Thursday; $60 to $110, double, Friday,
   Saturday, and holidays; $10 extra person; continental breakfast.
Open: All year.
Facilities and activities: Lunch and dinner in Wolfgang's Keller and Wolf-
   gang's Courtyard Café. Nearby: German restaurants, antiques shops,
   historic museums, Wurstfest in October, tubing and rafting on Comal
   River.

The Prince Solms Inn is a famous Texas landmark, having
been in continuous operation since immigrant German craftsmen
built the handsome building in 1898. Throughout its history families of its first patrons have kept returning to this elegant yet warm
and welcoming inn.

The beautifully restored building has front entry doors that are
10 feet high, with panes of exquisitely detailed etched glass. The inn
shines with antique fittings gathered from all over the world.
Bronzes are from Europe; solid brass doorknobs come from old
Lake Shore mansions in Chicago, doors and carriage lights from old
San Antonio homes. In fact staying here makes me feel as if I were
in a mansion back in the days of the Astor, Rockefeller, and Gould
railroad barons.

Guest rooms are furnished with beautiful (but sturdy) antiques, unusual light fixtures, and well-chosen, tasteful paintings and prints. Each room is named for the gloriously patterned wallpaper that decorates the walls.

New innkeepers Pat and Bob are joining with Ruth to keep up the tradition of hospitality of the inn. Fifth-generation Texans, they come from Beaumont, where they restored an 1890s home before they fell in love with New Braunfels and the Prince Solms.

Wolfgang's Keller, the inn restaurant, is in the cellar, but what a cellar! There are old brick walls and a fireplace—and with Wolfgang Amadeus Mozart's portrait setting the tone, the atmosphere is wonderfully old-world to match the mouth-watering continental cuisine.

I had Wolfgang's wonderful Wiener schnitzel and sampled the special linguine, in a rich cream sauce, so had to forgo the sinfully rich desserts until another time. Every Thursday is Italian Night, with pasta primavera, seafood marinara, veal saltimbocca, osso buco—magnifico! Mixed drinks, wine, and champagne are readily available from the bar.

Now the picturesque brick-paved courtyard in the rear has become Wolfgang's Courtyard Café, where guests can enjoy lunch and dinner in a delightful outdoor setting.

I enjoyed the complimentary breakfast of home-baked pastries, breads, and muffins wheeled into my room on a tea cart and beautifully served. Elegant as it is, the Prince Solms Inn provides the hill country friendliness that makes you feel truly at home.

How to get there: From I–35 take Exit 187 to Seguin Street, then turn right around the circle to San Antonio Street. The inn will be on your left.

The Inn at Salado
Salado, Texas
76571

1-800-724-0027

Innkeeper: Darlene Cosper

Address/Telephone: North Main Street at Pace Park Road (mailing address: P.O. Box 500); (817) 947–8200

Rooms: 9, including 3 suites, in main house and cottage; all with private bath. No smoking inn.

Rates: $65 to $85, double; $10 extra for use of sofa beds in suites; EPB.

Open: All year.

Facilities and activities: Meals for large groups by reservation, use of microwave and refrigerator in kitchen, playground and swings for children, two bicycles, a driving-tour tape of historic Salado. Nearby: restaurants, antiques shops, and boutiques; historic home tours; Central Texas Museum; Pace Park and Salado Creek; golf, tennis, and swimming privileges at Salado Country Club.

Stagecoaches used to rumble down the Old Chisholm Trail to ford Salado Creek and stop at the old Stagecoach Inn in Salado. That inn is now a restaurant and motel, but you can get the flavor of those past days by staying at The Inn at Salado, in the center of this historic Central Texas town. This very small town's past glories include the buried hope that it would be the capital of Texas.

The town was settled predominantly by people of Scottish descent, and every November there's a "Gathering of the Clans," with Highland games and other amusements. I loved visiting the museum to see the many colorful tartan banners hanging there.

The Inn at Salado stands 300 feet in front of a house built in 1855. The inn is newer—it was built in 1873. Darlene became the innkeeper when her mother-in-law, Kay Kelley, who manages nearby Rose Mansion, asked her to—it was as simple as that! "We work well together," Darlene says. "We're both people persons."

The Reverend Baines Room is in honor of LBJ's great-grandfather. Its antique bed came from the Governor Hogg estate; he was an early governor of Texas. The General Custer Suite is named after the general because he camped out on the banks of Salado Creek. Whomever they're named after, the rooms are large and comfortable. A favorite is the L. Tenney Room, bright and cheerful with lots of windows and well-stocked bookshelves. The two-bedroom cottage on the property once belonged to Mary Hardin Baylor College located in nearby Belton.

"People like to read," Darlene says. "We want them to make themselves at home, to use the common room, to feel free to go to the fridge with their cold drinks and wine. This is dry country, so our guests have to bring whatever they want to drink." Guests also make themselves very much at home with the fine assortment of games provided. And if a group of sixteen to eighteen people want to rent out the entire inn, they can have complete privacy.

Pace Park has a pavilion with picnic tables and grills for cookouts. A favorite pastime, when the creek is running, is to roll up your cuffs and go wading. The water is cool and clear and oh! so refreshing.

How to get there: Take the Salado exit from I–35 and drive right into town—that's Main Street. The inn is next to Pace Park and a stone's throw from Salado Creek.

817- 947- 5554 Creek
947- 9683
2 MILES from Downtown

The Rose Mansion
Salado, Texas
76571

Innkeeper: Kay Kelley

Address/Telephone: 1 Rose Way; (817) 947-~~5999~~ *8200*

Rooms: 7 in main house, cottages, and log cabin; wheelchair accessible. No smoking inn.

Rates: $70 to $95, double; $10 less during week; EPB.

Open: All year.

Facilities and activities: Porches with rockers, hammocks on 2.5-acre lot, bicycles, volleyball, horseshoes, croquet, barbecue pit, picnic tables. Nearby: restaurants, antiques shops, and boutiques; historic home tours; Central Texas Museum; Pace Park and Salado Creek; golf, tennis, and swimming privileges at Salado Country Club.

Kay is so happy with her work that she has encouraged daughter-in-law, Darlene Cosper, to take over management of The Rose Mansion's sister inn, The Inn at Salado. It's a treat to see these busy innkeepers keeping everybody happy.

"We just run back and forth like crazy," Kay says. She prepares the inn breakfast in her home down the street and takes a basket to either one of the inns. "Our guests get to meet both the innkeepers—but maybe not together," she comments as she visits with her guests in the evening, those that want to sit around and talk. She's not surprised to find that most of them are looking to get away from television, telephone, kids, and traffic. She herself is a "refugee" from New York, and she's delighted to be relaxed in Salado.

When she goes traveling, she likes to be waited on and pampered, so she turns around and pampers her guests. But on the other hand, "I let guests alone and give them their privacy, if that's what they want."

The Rose Mansion was built in 1870 by Major A. J. Rose, who had made a fortune in the California gold rush of '49. His wife, Sallie, a cousin of Stephen F. Austin, taught elocution at Salado College (which is no more). The major's rifle and desk are in the entry together with an interesting collection of old walking sticks.

The entire inn is done in white and shades of blue, from the blue checked wallpaper in the comfortable kitchen–sitting room, where everyone seems to gather, to the blue velvet chaise and wing chair in the Honeymoon Suite. The Quilter's Room is not the only one with a quilt—there are fine examples of this art in many of the guest rooms. Wide windows, with original glass, brighten the entire inn.

The Summer Kitchen and the Jersey Lily are two small cottages. The Jersey Lily looks just like Judge Roy Bean's office "west of the Pecos," and that's how the little house got its name.

The little log cabin, also in back of the property, is a perfect retreat for even more peace and quiet. There's a bedroom downstairs and a loft with an antique rope bed. The old cabin was discovered not ten miles from Salado. "It was taken apart, the pieces were numbered, and it was put back together here, plus a bathroom and a porch," Kay marvels.

Breakfasts are famous for a special quiche, as well as certain oat bran muffins. "They don't taste healthy but they are," Kay confesses. She will make dinner reservations for guests at the Tyler House or the famous Stagecoach Inn.

How to get there: From I–35 take Salado exit 285 going south or exit 283 going north, and go down the town's one Main Street to Royal Street. Turn east and go up the hill. A water tower will be on your left, the inn on the right, just past the Victorian Oaks sign on the right. The inn is behind a white picket fence, and there is a sign.

Bullis House Inn
San Antonio, Texas
78208

Innkeepers: Anna and Steve Cross
Address/Telephone: 621 Pierce (mailing address: P.O. Box 8059); (210) 223–9426
Rooms: 10; 1 with private bath, 9 share 2 baths, 2 with phone, all with TV. Smoking permitted except in dining room.
Rates: $41 to $59, double; extra adult with continental breakfast $10, without $6; child with continental breakfast $6, without $2.
Open: All year.
Facilities and activities: Full breakfast, lunch, and high tea by reservation; hostel on premises (inn is affiliated with American Youth Hostels); swimming pool, badminton, volleyball, Ping-Pong, board games. Nearby: Paseo del Rio (River Walk), with many restaurants; the Alamo, La Villita boutiques, Institute of Texas Cultures, Hertzberg Circus Museum, Brackenridge Park and Zoo, Spanish Missions, Sea World and Fiesta Texas amusement parks.

Bullis House Inn and San Antonio International Hostel make for an unusual experience, because the combination offers the best of two worlds. While staying in the historic home of Civil War General John Bullis, you get to mix with travelers from all over the world: More than 90 percent of the guests staying at the hostel at the rear of the inn are international visitors, and the inn's four parlors are open to all guests. In interacting with hostel guests from France, England, Australia, Germany, and Japan, I felt as though I were smack in the middle of an international voyage.

The innkeepers believe that inn guests tend to be warm, open people and that the lost art of conversation revives at an inn. "Guests can read or watch television in the parlors, but since the inn guests have TV in their rooms, mostly they come down to visit with the international hostel guests," said Nathan, one of three managers who help out when the Crosses are absent. "And the kids can keep busy with our new swimming pool, or play volleyball, Ping-Pong, badminton, board games . . . there's a lot for them to do here, plus we're within five minutes of downtown with the River Walk and the Alamo."

The Bullis House, a large white neoclassical mansion, was built by the general when he came to town from New York in 1865. But he didn't settle down. He fought hostile Indians in Texas and saw action in the Spanish-American War. The colorful general, called "Thunderbolt" by the Indians and "Friend of the Frontier" by the settlers, earned formal thanks from the Texas Legislature.

Large white columns support the front portico. Inside, parquet floors, marble fireplaces, and chandeliers attest to early Texas elegance. Guest rooms are large and high-ceilinged, and most have fireplaces—there are ten fireplaces in all! The rooms have been totally redecorated, with massive oak and cherry beds in king, queen, and full sizes. Especially fine for families is the trundle bed in each guest room; each room can accommodate four persons, and the large "family room" can sleep six.

Breakfast is fancier now, with homemade crepes or sweetheart waffles in addition to cold cereal and hot apple, cinnamon, or orange muffins, orange juice, coffee, tea, and hot chocolate. San Antonio abounds in fine restaurants, and the Crosses have many recommendations. Mexican ones in the Mercado (market) are special regional favorites. San Antonio, a warm and happy combination of Anglo and Hispanic cultures, always has some kind of parade or festival going on—I've never been in a city that parties so much. There are no strangers here!

How to get there: Take the New Braunfels–Fort Sam Houston exit off I–35 or the Grayson Street exit off Highway 281. The inn is on the corner of Grayson and Pierce, adjacent to Fort Sam Houston.

Norton-Brackenridge House
San Antonio, Texas
78204

Innkeeper: Carolyn Cole; Nancy Cole (no relation), manager
Address/Telephone: 230 Madison; (210) 271–3442 or (800) 221–1412
Rooms: 5, including 2 suites; all with private bath, 4 with kitchenette.
Rates: $75 to $95, per room, EPB.
Open: All year.
Facilities and activities: Nearby: the Alamo; the River Walk (Paseo del Rio) downtown, lined with restaurants, bars, and boutiques; the Mercado (market), Brackenridge Zoo, horticultural garden, SeaWorld and Fiesta Texas amusement parks, several fine Spanish missions.

Carolyn Cole has furnished her inn with such treasured pieces of her past as her grandmother's rocking chair and her very own small one from her childhood. The room she calls the Bridal Suite, because she likes to put honeymooners in it, has a white iron bed covered with a family quilt; her grandmother's chest; and "palms, because they're a Victorian-looking plant." There's lovely white wicker furniture in the sitting area.

The downstairs bathroom has a stained glass window, and Carolyn leaves magazines and catalogues "and razors and little bars of glycerine soap with the inn logo" for her guests' convenience. Other nice touches are roses from the rose garden in the rear.

Now a seasoned innkeeper, Carolyn likes to do things up right. "My idea is to do the simple, since I'm the cook, with casseroles instead of omelets-to-order for my holiday breakfasts, but to do the simple well!" she says enthusiastically. Breakfast, served either in the dining room or on the veranda, is a delicious one of honeypuff pancakes, quiche, or a blintz soufflé with apricot preserves, along with fresh fruit in season. Out of season, she prepares delicious fruit compotes with assorted dried fruits and almonds.

Like most innkeepers, Carolyn finds that the majority of her guests like to mingle, getting acquainted. "But you can take your breakfast back to your room if you prefer," she says.

The Norton-Brackenridge House was built in 1906. The handsome two-story home, with white Corinthian columns and spanking white porch railings, began life on another street. Somewhere along the way it was remodeled into four apartments. It was moved to its present location in San Antonio's historic King William district in 1985.

Carolyn has been busy repainting, covering the old beige walls with color. The Red Room is as bright as a hot red pepper; the Peach Room is a warm terra-cotta; the Blue Room is a cool Federal blue; and the Aqua Room "is now undoubtedly my favorite," Carolyn says.

How to get there: Take I–35 south to the Alamo exit and go left past Pioneer Flour Mills to Beauregard. Take a left, then a right on Madison, and the inn will be the fourth house on the right.

Terrell Castle
San Antonio, Texas
78208

Innkeepers: Nancy Haley and Katherine Poulis
Address/Telephone: 950 East Grayson Street; (210) 271–9145 or (800) 356–1605
Rooms: 8, including 4 suites; all with private bath and TV. Pets permitted.
Rates: $70 to $85, single; $85 to $100, double; $100 to $115, triple; cribs free; assorted rates when rooms are booked as suites; EPB.
Open: All year.
Facilities and activities: Fenced dog runs in the rear. Nearby: the Paseo del Rio (River Walk) downtown, lined with restaurants, bars, and boutiques; the Alamo; several fine missions; zoo, horticultural garden, SeaWorld and Fiesta Texas amusement parks.

Katherine Poulis and her daughter Nancy Haley have combined considerable talent in creating Terrell Castle. Different wings of the four-story stone mansion have been restored, from a start of three guest rooms to the present eight; the newest is the Ballroom Suite on the third floor.

The magnificent entrance hall has a red brick fireplace and built-in seats in a "coffin" niche; also restored are the parlor, library, music room, dining room, breakfast room, and enclosed porch.

The home was built in 1894 by Edwin Terrell, a San Antonio lawyer and statesman who served under President Benjamin Harrison as ambassador plenipotentiary to Belgium in the early 1890s.

He fancied a castle like those he saw in Europe, and as soon as he returned home he commissioned a local architect to build one.

Well, while the Terrell Castle doesn't particularly remind me of a European castle, it certainly does impress me as a very stately mansion. The front staircase is extraordinary. Antique furniture and lace curtains set off the fine parquet floors and curved windows in the parlor. The dining room has a huge fireplace and a wood-paneled ceiling, the first like it I've seen.

Rooms used to be named for their colors, but Katherine and Nancy have now gone genealogical. There are the Giles Suite and the Terrell Suite; also the Colonial Room; the Victorian Room; the Tower Suite; the Oval Room (with curved windows); and the Americana Room, with the best view in the house—its windows face all four directions and offer a grand fourth-floor view of San Antonio—as well as the new Ballroom Suite, in what once was the ballroom of the mansion. "We've given it an oriental flair," says Nancy, "while retaining the Victorian character of the house." Interesting . . . each room is more lovely than the last, so I leave it to you to make a choice.

All the fireplaces in the house are functional, including one with a green tiled mantel in the meeting room on the third floor.

Breakfast is "anytime guests wake up," Nancy says. It's a feast of bacon or sausage, eggs however you want them including a wonderful Mexican omelet, crisp hash browns or creamy grits, homemade goodies like popovers and sticky buns, as well as muffins, raisin bread, biscuits, preserves, dry cereal, juice, coffee, tea, and milk. "Most of our guests don't eat lunch after that," Nancy had told me earlier, and now she reports, "and we *still* don't know of anyone who has eaten lunch the same day! We've always served everything under the sun, and we still do!"

There's a television in the large library/office, and guests can watch whenever they want. "The whole house is open to you," say Katherine and Nancy.

How to get there: Grayson Street is between Broadway and New Braunfels Street, adjacent to Fort Sam Houston.

Aquarena Springs Inn
San Marcos, Texas
78666

Innkeeper: Pam Humphreys
Address/Telephone: One Aquarena Springs Drive (mailing address: P.O. Box 2330); (512) 396–8901
Rooms: 24; all with private bath, phone, and TV.
Rates: $65, per room; $10 extra person over 4; $7.50 rollaway or baby bed; continental breakfast and half-price tickets to park attractions.
Open: All year.
Facilities and activities: Inn is on a family amusement park at the site of prehistoric Indian remains, with Olympic swimming pool; lunch and dinner in park restaurant; lake with glass-bottom boats where children can inspect marine life; high sky ride to educational aviary and cliffside gardens; Texana Village, where Bertha the Bicycling Parrot performs; and a submarine theater where entertainment includes Ralph the Diving Pig and his famous Swine Dive.

This classic Texas getaway is all spruced up with new carpets, furniture, drapes, and fresh paint—although it's so special that everyone already loved it the way it was. Aquarena Springs Inn is built on the site of the oldest permanent Indian encampment in North America. I'll bet that's a surprise; it sure was for me! Archaeologists have found the remains of Clovis Man, the hunter-gatherer who lived on the San Marcos River over 12,000 years ago.

Another surprise—you can see where Clovis Man lived if you peer down from your glass-bottom boat on Spring Lake. I also saw some of the 100 varieties of aquatic life swimming or growing down below.

Over 150 million gallons of Texas's purest water filters through honeycomb limestone to make Spring Lake, and on the lake's shore is perched the prettiest white-and-aqua Mediterranean-style villa, Aquarena Springs Inn. It's been there since 1929, and nineteen of its rooms overlook the lake. Ducks and swans sail along, waiting to be fed bread crumbs—generations of inn guests have spoiled them rotten.

The back hall of the inn has huge glass windows so you can see the flora growing up the steep cliff immediately outside, so close you feel you can touch it, especially if you have one of the rooms in the rear. I also got a thrill from riding the Swiss sky ride and catching the Texas hill country view from the 300-foot-high Sky Spiral.

A generous continental breakfast is spread out in the lobby: croissants, rolls, bran and blueberry muffins, orange juice, and tea and coffee. Tea and coffee are served there in the afternoons, too, supplied by the friendly desk personnel, who will even make sure you get a special request like the nearest big city's Sunday paper.

"It can be quiet here even in a crowd," says innkeeper Pam. "The only noises we hear are ducks and trains—everybody mentions it. Even on the busiest days, it never seems crowded."

That's because there's plenty of room for everyone to spread out in this beautiful green parkland full of both fun and relaxing things to do. I munched on a plate of king-size nachos outdoors by the crystal-clear river at Peppers. Later, I sat on the inn veranda overlooking the lake and watched little children feeding the ducks. All I could hear was the laughter of the children and the quacking of ducks.

How to get there: From I–35 take exit 206 and go ¹/₂ mile west of Aquarena Springs Drive. There are signs—you can't miss it.

Crystal River Inn
San Marcos, Texas
78666

Innkeepers: Cathy and Mike Dillon
Address/Telephone: 326 West Hopkins Street; (512) 396–3739
Rooms: 12, including 3 suites, in 3 buildings; 10 with private bath, 3 with
    phone and TV. No smoking in rooms.
Rates: $40 to $60, weekdays; $60 to $90, weekends; EPB.
Open: All year.
Facilities and activities: Lunch and dinner by reservation only; "Mystery
    Weekends." Nearby: San Marcos River for water sports; Southwest
    State University, LBJ's alma mater; many special events in San Marcos.

Crystal River Inn rooms are named for Texas rivers because
"we are river rats," Cathy says. Both she and Mike are pleased to
show guests the ropes if they want to take on the nearby San Marcos River. Each guest room has its own watery personality. The Colorado Room reflects the iciness and blue color of the river, while
the Pedernales Room, in blue and warm peach, is folksy and friendly. The honeymoon suite is named for the beautiful Medina. The
house, designer decorated, is restfully clean and uncluttered, and
the rooms carry out this feeling.

"The peace, beauty, history, and happiness of this unique
chunk of Texas has been bottled up right here, just waiting to be
shared," Cathy says of her inn.

The veranda upstairs is the happy hour porch. "Usually our

guests come breezing in here from Houston or Dallas, and they're all tightly wound. We prop them up on the veranda or in the atrium-sunroom, with some wine in their hands, and in an hour the change is just amazing." The Dillons also pamper guests with bedside brandy and chocolates, although many of them linger in "the library," the lovely parlor with a cozy fireplace and walls lined with bookshelves.

Crystal River Inn is also known for its knockout weekend brunch. I feasted on fruit-filled cantaloupe ring, beer biscuits that Cathy calls "beerscuits," sausage, and the pièce de résistance, bananas Foster crepes topped with *crème fraîche* and toasted slivered almonds. Cathy invented the recipe, and when she made the crepes for a Chamber of Commerce fund-raiser, people were lined up and winding out the door, waiting for them.

Other great breakfasts are sour cream–apple walnut French toast, *huevos rancheros*—and I could go on and on with a whole assortment of homemade breads like zucchini-and-apple fritter bread. You can be sure of a gourmet feast to begin the day at the Crystal River Inn!

For the adventurous, Cathy has worked up some special weekends, like the Murder Mystery one; or she can suggest an exciting river trip, gourmet cooking lessons, and a romantic interlude complete with massage—and hot air ballooning. Just ask her for the schedule.

How to get there: Take exit 205 west off I–35. This is Highway 80, which becomes Hopkins in town. The inn will be on the right just before you come to Rural Route 12 to Wimberley.

Utopia on the River
Utopia, Texas
78884

Innkeepers: Polly and Aubrey Smith
Address/Telephone: Highway 187 (mailing address: P.O. Box 14); (210)
  966–2444
Rooms: 12; all with private bath and TV.
Rates: $59, single; $10 extra person; children under 6 free; EPB.
Open: All year.
Facilities and activities: Meals for large groups with planned menus; barbecue
  grills and picnic tables; refrigerator and microwave in some rooms, $5
  extra; gift shop, pool, Jacuzzi, sauna, volleyball, horseshoes, hiking
  trails, fishing, hunting, tubing on river. Nearby: stables with horses for
  hire and one restaurant in Utopia; Lost Maples State Park.

Early on Utopia had several other names, but then a town
postmaster happened to read Sir Thomas More's description of
Utopia. "This is it!" he cried. "Perfect climate, happy, healthy people—we live in Utopia!" and Utopia it became.

That postmaster was not far off base, and he would have felt
all the more vindicated if he could have seen today's Utopia on the
River, with its large, bright A-frame lobby and breakfast area. The
inn is run by Polly and Aubrey Smith—well, mostly Polly, since
Aubrey is sheriff of Uvalde County!

"I had managed property in San Antonio, so I knew what I
was getting into," Polly says. "But weekends Aubrey is in Utopia,

and sometimes he even helps cook." The inn is on 650 acres that have been in Polly's family for more than a hundred years, and rooms are named after pioneer settlers of the area. William Ware, an ancestor of Polly's, founded the town, and of course he has a plaque on the door of one room; another is named for Polly's grandmother. Rooms are large and airy, with touches such as quilt-pattern bedspreads and colorful duck appliqués, sewn by Polly, framed over the beds. The construction of stone with wood floors is typical of this hill country area, and the view from each room is a refreshing wilderness of mesquite and pecan trees.

The inn grounds are a veritable animal preserve. To begin with, it's a working ranch; you'll drive through a flock of sheep as you wind into the property. (Just honk your horn to get them off the road.) During nature hikes you can see the likes of such exotica as axis and fallow deer, audads, black buck antelope, and even a zebra. After that, the deer, turkeys, sheep, and goats may seem pretty tame by comparison! The place is great for the children. Bird-watchers, too. Special as well is the storytelling on the river every Saturday night March through October—and in front of a cozy fire November through February.

Breakfast can be fancy, with banana bran pancakes, or hearty, with scrambled eggs and biscuits as well as juice and coffee. Then you can wander down to see the falls on the cool, clean Sabinal River, go rock and driftwood hunting, or marvel at the old cypress tree. "We think it's from seven hundred fifty to eight hundred years old," Polly says. "Everyone wants to see it." The huge native pecan trees in front of the inn are something to see, too.

There is a collection of art and craft wares as well as T-shirts and other necessities in the loft above the dining room. Otherwise you'll feel far from the madding crowd. "We enjoy our guests," Aubrey says, "but we want to keep our tranquillity." Tranquillity and serenity are the words he uses to describe Utopia on the River.

How to get there: The inn is approximately 80 miles northwest of San Antonio. Take Highway 90 west to Sabinal, then Highway 187 north to 2 miles south of Utopia. The inn will be on your left, and there is a sign.

Casa de Leona
Uvalde, Texas
78802

Innkeepers: Carolyn and Ben Durr
Address/Telephone: 1149 Pearsall Road; (210) 278–8550
Rooms: 4, plus 1 cottage; 2 with private bath, cottage with private bath and kitchenette. No smoking inn.
Rates: $55, single; $15 extra person; EPB. No credit cards.
Open: All year.
Facilities and activities: Lunch and dinner by reservation, use of washer and dryer, sun deck, balcony, gazebo, seventeen acres of wilderness on Leona River with nature trails, fishing. Nearby: many eating places, Fort Inge Historical Site, John Nance Garner Museum, First State Bank's "Petit Louvre" Briscoe collection of art.

Mesquite and Spanish oak border the long drive into Casa de Leona, and catfish practically jump out of the river alongside the inn.

"A 35-pound catfish was caught in our river," Carolyn Durr says, "and recently a 10.3-pound bass. Wow!" The inn has two Spanish fountains, one in the garden by the side of the house and one inside the courtyard and frisky weimaraner Chockie, short for Chocolate, will greet you there, unless you don't care for dogs. Shannon, the German shepherd, has gone to live with a Texas Ranger. "She got so protective of us she wouldn't allow guests to get out of their cars or come out of their rooms," Carolyn says.

"That was obviously a little too much devotion."

While Ben administers the local hospital, Carolyn's interests are revealed by all the cookbooks in her kitchen and all the paintings hanging on the walls. One of the guest rooms, the Picasso Room, adjoins her bright studio, where china painting and jewelry making share time with painting on canvas. Business guests can use her typewriter and desk.

"I started painting in 1972, just to relax," Carolyn says. "Ben traveled, back then, and I needed to fill my time after I'd put the children to bed." She hasn't stopped; the whole inn is an art gallery, with her paintings for sale.

Each guest room is tastefully decorated, and there are some lovely antiques. "I love antiques and I would have more if they weren't so expensive," Carolyn says with a rueful laugh. Interesting decorative touches include needlepoint done by Carolyn and framed on the walls, onyx chess sets, and arrowheads found in the vicinity. In the Bethany Room, named for daughter Bethany, her tiny ruffled flower-girl dress (she was in a wedding when she was three) is framed. The Durrs are town boosters, and you'll find a packet of Uvalde "what to see" brochures, as well as a "good night Tiger" snack of Carolyn's making, in your room.

The Durrs enjoy relaxing and sipping thirst quenchers on the sun deck with guests. Some guests bring their own canoes for a float on the Leona River behind the inn, and there's fishing there, too.

"We had a guest from Houston who just threw in a line," Ben says. "He got a bass, a bream, some perch, and a carp. The carp are the biggest here, like Chinese carp." Now that Ben no longer travels, upon request the Durrs will guide inn guests across the nearby border for a shopping and dining excursion to Mexico.

Breakfast, for which there is a huge formal dining set—"we bartered two calves for it," Ben delights in telling—is what Carolyn calls Texican. Sundance eggs are scrambled and served in tortillas with refried beans, or there may be *chili rellenos*. Carolyn's homemade cinnamon rolls are a tasty ending to the meal, and there's always fresh fruit and juices.

How to get there: From Highway 90 in Uvalde take Highway 117 toward Batesville (post office on corner) for 1 mile to Highway 140, Pearsall Road. Turn left for 1 mile. Casa de Leona is on the right, and there is an inn sign at the driveway.

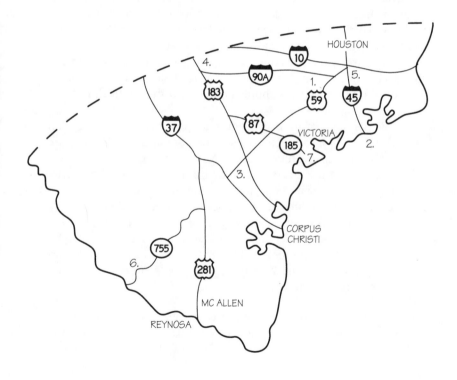

Gulf Coast/Border Texas

Numbers on map refer to towns numbered below.

The Farris 1912
Eagle Lake, Texas
77434

Innkeepers: Helyn and William Farris
Address/Telephone: 201 North McCarty Street; (409) 234–2546
Rooms: 24 in main house and courtyard guest house share 14 baths; wheelchair access to lower floors. Smoking permitted in guest house.
Rates: During hunting season (Nov./Dec./Jan.): $55 to $75, single and double, AP. Out of season: $48, single or double, continental breakfast.
Open: All year.
Facilities and activities: Meals for large groups only out of season, lunch served during Wildflower Festival (April), setups for drinks all year, two dog kennels, gift shop. Nearby: duck, deer, and goose hunting; golf course, and tennis courts; Wildflower Festival, entire month of April; National Wildlife Refuge.

The Farris 1912 is on the town corner where Eagle Lake began in 1857; before that, the site held a cowboy stage stop. Helyn and William Farris bought and renovated the hotel in 1974, and Victorian and turn-of-the-century antiques reflect the 1912 and earlier era that was Eagle Lake's Golden Age. The Bentley-Farris House in the courtyard, a 1920s vintage guest house, lets you park at your very door. Like the inn, the Bentley-Farris House is decorated with early twentieth-century antiques and memorabilia.

Today the Farris revels in the Hunting Age, and rooms are at a premium during the November-through-January hunting season. But the inn also caters to nostalgia buffs who like to see what hotel life was like in rural Texas in the good old days. Back then the Farris was called the Hotel Dallas, after the builder and first owner, and was hailed as the finest small hotel in the state. Well, the Depression took care of that, and the brick hotel on the square fell into terrible disrepair. But no longer: Now Helyn keeps the old hotel sparkling by day and glowing by night.

Room number 1 still has the original 1912 hotel furnishings— dark mission oak dresser, rocker, and even a hat rack. Every room has a washstand. The entire lobby is a gift, jewelry, and antiques shop; and many of the antiques throughout the hotel are for sale. Bedrooms upstairs open off a huge square mezzanine where the hunters can relax after a sumptuous meal, playing cards or dominoes in the cozy family atmosphere. During hunting season there's a 10:00 p.m. curfew there, because hunters rise early.

But the downstairs Drummers Room stays open all evening with a bar and game tables set up amid the stuffed game birds decorating the walls.

If you're not there for the hunting season, Helyn will send you down to the Sportman's Restaurant (the only one in town!), which has a good all-around menu.

In the hunting season, however, the inn's meals are really something to write home about. Helyn finally had to produce a cookbook: "After the many years of hunters trying to sneak recipes, I now have everything all spelled out!" The family-style buffet is a groaning board. Plates of Polynesian chicken, scalloped potatoes, and fresh green beans smothered in onions and tomatoes share space with both carrot and apple salads, and all is eaten by candlelight on a lace tablecloth. Out hunting all day or not, dinner means time to clean up and relax. And try to choose between Helyn's famous bread pudding and her chocolate mousse for dessert!

How to get there: Eagle Lake is one hour west of Houston via U.S. 59 and two and one-half hours east of San Antonio via I–10 or U.S. 90A. The Farris 1912 is two minutes from the town square.

The Gilded Thistle
Galveston, Texas
77550

Innkeepers: Helen and Pat Hanemann
Address/Telephone: 1805 Broadway; (409) 763–0194
Rooms: 3; 1 with private bath, all with TV. No smoking inn.
Rates: $115 to $135, per room, EPB and snack tray in evening.
Open: All year.
Facilities and activities: Nearby: historic Ashton Villa and the Bishop's Palace just down the street on Broadway; the historic Strand, with Galveston Art Center, Galveston County Historical Museum, Railroad Museum, and shops and restaurants, five minutes away; the Seawall and Gulf Coast beaches.

I asked innkeeper Helen Hanemann to explain the Gilded Thistle's name, because it seemed to me to be a contradiction. Helen, very much into the island's history, said that like native thistle, sturdy Texas pioneer stock sank deep and lasting roots into the sandy island soil, building a Galveston that flowered into a gilded age of culture and wealth.

Her home was part of those people and their times—in the late 1800s Galveston's Strand was known as "the Wall Street of the West"—and The Gilded Thistle is a lovely memorial to Galveston's past.

The beautiful antiques throughout the house make it an exceptionally elegant place to stay, but the atmosphere is so homey

288

that my awe melted away to pure admiration. Helen is on duty at all times, and I joined the other guests in her kitchen, watching her arrange the fresh flowers that fill the rooms.

It wasn't hard to get used to being served on fine china, with coffee or tea from a family silver service. Breakfast, Helen says, is "whenever you want," and I took mine on the L-shaped screened porch around the dining room, especially enjoying Helen's specialty, "nut chewies," and her crispy waffles. There's always a bowl filled with apples or other fruit on the sideboard.

Tea and coffee are available at all times, and I loved it when my morning began with orange juice and a pot of boiling water for coffee or tea at my bedroom door.

The evening snack tray could almost take the place of dinner; there are strawberries and grapes and other fruit in season, at least four kinds of cheese, and wine. "It's my gift to you for coming," Helen says. She loves company and is in her element when two of Galveston's big hotels send her their overflow. She'll even trade her bedroom with guests who prefer her twin beds to the guest rooms' doubles.

But I reveled in the master bedroom with its four-poster facing the bay window, a cozy setting for the antique sofa and chairs and the fireplace with mantel.

The Gilded Thistle has been gilded horticulturally: In recent years the inn's landscaping has won two prizes, the Springtime Broadway Beauty Contest and an award for a business in a historic building. But it's never easy; that's the reason for the Texas saying that if you don't like the weather, wait a minute, it'll change. "A few years ago we had that bitter winter," Helen says. "Now we've put in lawn sprinklers and wouldn't you know—too much rain."

I overheard a visitor asking Pat what was so lively about the Gilded Thistle. Pat's answer: "Our guests."

How to get there: Stay on Highway 45 South, which becomes Broadway as soon as you cross the causeway onto Galveston Island. The inn will be just beyond 18th Street, on your right.

Hazelwood House
Galveston, Texas
77550

Innkeeper: Pat Hazelwood
Address/Telephone: 1127 Church Street (mailing address: P.O. Box 1326);
(409) 762–1668
Rooms: 3; 1 with private bath, 1 with TV. No smoking inn.
Rates: $50 to $125, double; EPB. Weekly and monthly discount rates.
Open: All year.
Facilities and activities: Lunch, tea, and dinner by reservation; Jacuzzi, bicy-
cles. Nearby: swimming pool and tennis; sailboat cruises; 10 blocks to
Gulf of Mexico and the Strand, historic street of shops and restaurants;
Galveston attractions such as the Grand Opera House.

"Every inn is different," says Pat, a warm and down-to-earth
person who wishes she could house everyone in an inn. "I've never
had anybody here I didn't like, or who didn't like me. First they like
the house—and then they like the innkeeper!" she says with a
throaty chuckle.

An entrepreneurial type, Pat has remodeled ten houses in
Galveston's renowned East End Historical District. She also has
organized half a dozen tours to show off the charms of her beloved
area, among them a Gulf Coast train ride, romantic Dinner on a
Diner in a restored train dining car, and an evening at the Grand
Opera House.

Hazelwood House is a Victorian charmer hidden behind a tall

290

lattice fence, which in turn is hidden by masses of green foliage. The sign on the fence says BEWARE OF THE DOG, but Pat laughs: "There is no dog, just push open the gate and come on in." Steps lead up to the gingerbread porch and an interior filled with soft music, oriental rugs, and antiques. On a carved coffee table a tray of wine, cheese, and fruit is waiting, balm for the weary traveler.

Mornings at Hazelwood House begin with a coffee or tea tray placed quietly outside your door. Pat's breakfasts, served formally in the dining room or Texas style on the porch (it's up to you) are usually Belgian waffles with whipped cream and syrup sprinkled liberally with blueberries and strawberries, a colorful feast. There may be long-link sausage, hard-boiled eggs, and yogurt, too. New are Pat's delicious cherry pastry pizzas to start your day off sweet and lovely.

Rooms are imaginatively furnished with Pat's collection of antiques. The king-sized room has a wall of mirrors and a bed smothered in eyelet and ruffles. The tan marble bath has a Jacuzzi. "People really like that," Pat says in tones of surprise. It's no surprise to me—what a way to relax after a day of driving or sightseeing!

The double room with the carved French bed is decorated with Burmese tapestry. The bright private bath has stained glass doors and a "throne" commode with arms. The third guest room shares the Jacuzzi bath and adjoins the porch, where a hammock awaits the leisurely.

How to get there: Go south on I–45, which becomes Broadway as soon as you cross the causeway onto Galveston Island. Turn left at 10th Street and drive to Church Street. Turn left on Church (it's one-way), and the inn will be on your left at the corner of Church just before 12th Street.

Michael's
Galveston, Texas
77550

Innkeepers: Mikey and Allen Isbell
Address/Telephone: 1715 35th Street; (409) 763–3760 or (800) 776–8302
Rooms: 4 share 1 bath. No smoking inn.
Rates: $85, double, EPB.
Open: All year.
Facilities and activities: Bicycles, rose garden with fountain. Nearby: the
Strand with shops, galleries, and restaurants; historic Galveston attractions such as the Bishop's Palace, Ashton Villa, the Silk Stocking District, and the Railroad Museum; gambling cruise on the Gulf of Mexico; the Galveston Seawall and Gulf beaches.

Michael's is housed in an impressive red brick mansion built by Hans Guldmann, cotton exporter and vice-consul to Denmark, as a bulwark against the famous—or infamous—storms that blow in on Galveston from the Gulf of Mexico. The hurricane of 1915 destroyed much of the island but didn't touch the sturdy home, which was not yet inhabited. Even so, Guldmann was so impressed by the furor of the storm that he had the new house torn down and rebuilt atop a sloping terrace formed by storm-damaged bags of concrete. Mikey will take you down in the basement, an oddity on the sea-level island, and show you the wine cellar and the thick concrete walls.

Impressive is the Isbells' collection of Western art—Remington-inspired bronzes and paintings by Fort Worth artist Jack Bryant. Decoration was planned with an accent on light, enhancing the spaciousness of this house. The mix of family antiques and contemporary pieces together with original art is pleasing to the eye.

The rose garden, amid the broad green lawns surrounding the house, enables Mikey to fill the house with beautiful blooms and a wonderful scent. "It's great to sit out in the spring and fall, and someday we'll have a greenhouse," she says hopefully. The estate once had tennis courts, a grape arbor, and pergolas covered with roses, and Mrs. Guldmann's greenhouse, (now a garden room for winter plants and a party room other times of the year) and fish pond make a charming, nostalgic picture.

All of the rooms are extraordinarily large, from the entrance hall with its sweeping center staircase to the glassed-in sun room, bright with white wicker and green plants. Breakfast is served on Mikey's grandmother's huge dining-room table. "My mother made the chair seats," Mikey says, as I admire the rose and cream pattern hand worked in bargello needlepoint.

The full breakfast varies from Belgian waffles with berries to a delicious egg casserole with homemade bran muffins, and you may have it in the formal dining room or in the cheerful sun room. Mikey's renowned for her cheesecake, and the Isbells used to serve coffee and dessert at bedtime. "But we've found that most guests come in too late or too full," she says, "so we encourage them to feel free to help themselves to whatever's in the refrigerator—or have coffee with us."

Nanny's Room, with a bright blue iron bedstead, was once the room of the young Guldmann children's nurse and has a small antique student desk from now-defunct Terrell Military Institute. The Schoolroom, with a large green-tiled fireplace, recalls the children's classes with their tutor.

How to get there: Go south on I-45, which becomes Broadway as soon as you cross the causeway onto Galveston Island. Turn right at 35th Street, and the inn is on your right in the 1700 block.

The Victorian Inn
Galveston, Texas
77550

Innkeepers: Janice and Bob Hellbusch
Address/Telephone: 511 17th Street; (409) 762–3235
Rooms: 4, plus 1 suite; suite with private bath.
Rates: $75 to $125, double, continental breakfast.
Open: All year.
Facilities and activities: Nearby: the Strand historical district with shops, galleries, museums, and restaurants; the historic sailing ship *Elissa;* Railroad Museum, Seawall, and beach; restored 1894 opera house.

Isaac Heffron, who built the first sewer systems for both Houston and Galveston and the first phase of the famous seawall now protecting the island from hurricanes, built his family a beautiful red-brick residence with a wraparound veranda and a gorgeous circular porch upstairs off the master bedroom. That room is named Mauney's Room, and it was the one for me. Green and yellow, two of my favorite colors, decorate the big room, which is filled with brass, wicker, and antiques. It shares a bath with Isaac's Room, brown and turquoise with patterned cloth wallpaper. Both rooms have recently been redecorated, keeping the original color schemes.

There's not room here to describe all the beautiful things in this house. The entry hall is immense. There is a hand-carved wooden settee by the fireplace, and two more face each other at the end of the room, with a checkerboard set up for guests on the table between them. The parlor has a floor done in a hand-cut and -laid birds-eye maple design, a hand-carved mantel, and its original crystal chandelier.

But the best part of this elegant inn is the welcome innkeepers Janice and Bob offer to guests—I just know they love their job. Janice has added personal touches and uses her own special recipes for the hearty continental breakfast that she serves.

In addition to local history lessons, guests get homemade cookies and fresh flowers in their rooms, coffee and tea any time they want in the sunny yellow butler's pantry, and perhaps a glass of sherry. Breakfast is orange juice, coffee, tea, milk, fresh fruit in season, cold cereals or hot oatmeal (depending on the temperature outdoors), a variety of homemade breads, croissants, and granola.

I sat on the curved upstairs porch with a refreshing glass of iced tea in my hand and rocked; a fresh breeze swept off the Gulf. Ryan's Room has a balcony and Amy's Room has an open porch, so I wasn't the only one savoring the breeze. And of course, there's always the veranda that wraps around the house, with its view of shady green trees and other grand old houses. The third-floor suite may not have a porch, but it's a favorite hideaway for honeymooners.

The inn is a perfect setting for storybook events, and Janice loves to plan small business meetings, weddings, and retreats. Romantic, in keeping with the ambience of the inn, is a carriage ride through the historic East End District to view many other late nineteenth-century homes, neighbors of the 1899 Victorian Inn.

Galveston is synonymous with seafood; there are many wonderful restaurants where you can get your fill of shrimp, soft-shell crab, fresh flounder, and other fruits of the sea.

How to get there: South on I–45 into Galveston; the highway becomes Broadway. Turn left at 17th; the inn will be on your left when you reach the 500 block.

The Virginia Point Inn
Galveston, Texas
77550

Innkeeper: Eleanor Catlow
Address/Telephone: 2327 Avenue K; (409) 763–2450
Rooms: 5 share 3 baths. No smoking inn.
Rates: $65 to $135, per room, EPB and snack tray in evening.
Open: All year.
Facilities and activities: Private parties by reservation, bicycles. Nearby: historic Silk Stocking District; the Strand with shops, restaurants, museums, galleries; Railroad Museum, gambling cruise on the Gulf of Mexico, and Seawall with beaches.

The Virginia Point Inn towers above a garden so lovely that when owner Tom Catlow was alive, he was in demand as a landscape designer, although he was a retired chemical engineer. Standing foursquare with huge screened porches both upstairs and down, the inn is as large as the welcome extended by innkeeper Eleanor, who enthusiastically gives tours of the circa-1907 house.

The inn's name was inspired by a letter written in 1864 by Tom's great-grandfather, R. S. Guy. He was stationed in a Confederate Army fort on Virginia Point, a spit of land in Galveston Bay overlooking Galveston Island, and the letter makes fascinating reading.

The big bedrooms open off porches, and you can enter the shared bathrooms without leaving your bedroom. I was fascinated by all the built-in wall cupboards surrounding each room's quite-modern closet. Even more, I loved the thoughtfulness of terry wraps and sun hats in guest closets.

Early-morning coffee and juice are brought on trays complete with tiny vases of fresh flowers. The hearty breakfast that follows may be cold ham and cheese, cereal and hot breads, French toast or Eleanor's breakfast pie. New is her Mexican breakfast, a tribute to Texas's Hispanic heritage. The meal is served from 8:00 to 10:00 a.m. in the large formal dining room with long windows onto the veranda.

At 6:00 p.m. a wine-and-cheese tray appears in the parlor, where Eleanor often joins her guests, answering questions and giving advice about what to see and where to go in historic Galveston. And there are always chocolate chip cookies in the cookie jar, as well as the makings of tea and coffee, in the large square butler's pantry off the kitchen. "I toast the pecans; I think that adds a lot," said Eleanor as I shamelessly dug into the cookie jug for yet another treat. An old fridge is there for guests to store soda and beer in, too.

With 24-hour notice, Eleanor will prepare (Mondays only) either a low-fat, low cholesterol gourmet dinner, or, she chuckles, "a high-fat, high cholesterol gourmet dinner!"

What guests like most of all, says Eleanor, is to go sightseeing for a while, then "return and sit on a porch all afternoon and read." The inn's breezy screened verandas are so delightful they've been used as settings for fashion-magazine photographic shoots. One husband arranged a stay at the inn as a surprise for his wife; while they were ostensibly waiting to check into a motel, he drove her around the historic district. "Look at that!" exclaimed the wife, pointing to the inn. "Wouldn't you just give anything to get inside that house?" Eleanor chuckles as she recalls that the wife "literally couldn't get it together—her mouth was open in surprise the whole time he was signing them in."

How to get there: South on I–45, which becomes Broadway as soon as you cross the causeway onto Galveston Island. Turn right at 24th Street, and the inn is in 1 block on your left on the corner of 24th and Avenue K.

The White Horse Inn
Galveston, Texas
77550

Innkeepers: Robert T. Clark and Robin Gunter
Address/Telephone: 2217 Broadway; (409) 762–2632 or (800) 762–2632
Rooms: 6; all with private bath. No smoking inn.
Rates: $90 to $115, double; $10 extra person; EPB.
Open: All year.
Facilities and activities: Lunch and dinner by reservation. Nearby: historic
    Ashton Villa and the Bishop's Palace just down the street on Broad-
    way; the historic Strand, with Galveston Art Center, Galveston County
    Historical Museum, Railroad Museum, and shops and restaurants five
    minutes away; the Seawall and Gulf Coast beaches.

Innkeepers Robert and Robin call their inn a nineteenth-century experience, and indeed it is that. One of the last Victorian
mansions on Broadway remaining in private hands, it is a treasure,
a pleasure to look at even if you don't go inside—which would be a
pity! The house was built in 1884–85 by J. F. Smith, who had one
of the largest hardware businesses in Texas back then. "He's turning
out to be of great importance as far as Galveston and Texas history
is concerned," Robert says, "and that's one reason for the interest in
preserving the house." The other reason, obviously, is the beauty of
the house.

The outside has been painted in shades of light and dark beige.
"It's called Victorian Rose," Robert says with a laugh, "but I'd say

it's really just beige, and it makes the details show up." The interior colors were as carefully chosen: The wallpapers are hand-printed Bradbury papers, meticulous reproductions of period designs. The beautiful pine floors, refinished, shine, and it's hard to believe that the home was built for about $13,000. Of course, that was a lot of money back then. A curious note is that the front parlor's brass chandelier was gas powered until 1984.

Two guest rooms are in the main house; each has an antique half-tester bed and its own gallery. The large carriage house, in the rear facing the garden, has four guest rooms furnished with a nice collection of antiques and reproductions; I'm not knowledgeable enough to detect any difference! One room has twin/queen beds, another a four-poster so high that a small stool is needed to get you into bed.

The house was constructed of first-rate materials, especially fine woods. The two staircases are mahogany, the 12-foot-tall doors were painted to look like fancy burl woods, and elsewhere there is gleaming cypress and yellow pine.

Why would this Victorian mansion be named the White Horse Inn? I asked Robert, wondering how such a name could relate to Galveston's history. "That was the name of one of the very first inns in Galveston County," he said. "It was torn down in the 1930s."

Food is important at this inn, with delicious lunches and dinners by reservation. Chicken White Horse is breast of chicken in a mushroom sauce, accompanied by a pretty salad, crunchy broccoli, and a rice dish, all crowned with turtle cheesecake, a confection of chocolate, cheesecake, nuts, and caramel in a chocolate crust—sinful! Breakfast might be what the inn dubs Helen's Favorite, an egg-and-meat dish. And of course fresh fruit, coffee, tea, and juice.

How to get there: I-45, which dead-ends at the Gulf of Mexico, becomes Broadway as it enters the island and the city of Galveston. Just keep going down the oleander-planted esplanade until you come to 2217. There is a sign.

The Dial House
Goliad, Texas
77963

Innkeeper: Dolores Clarke
Address/Telephone: 306 West Oak Street (mailing address: P.O. Box 22);
    (512) 645–3366
Rooms: 5, including Bridal Suite; suite with private bath, all with phone and
    TV; wheelchair accessible. No smoking inn.
Rates: $45 to $55, single; $55 to $65, double; EPB and large evening snack.
Open: All year.
Facilities and activities: Breakfast for non-inn guests; lunch and dinner by
    reservation (minimum four persons). Nearby: Goliad State Park, with
    Spanish missions and the Presidio de La Bahia, a fort infamous in
    Texas history; County Courthouse with "Hanging Tree"; town and
    antiques shops.

The first thing you'll notice about the Dial House is its landscaping, which is lush and green and bountiful. Dolores is a passionate gardener, and you may have to hunt for her somewhere on
her grounds.

"Everything out here, including trees, has been planted by
these gnarled old hands," she says with great good humor. Dolores
is also passionate about the Dial House, which is a family home furnished with pieces that were in the house "before I was born."

Dolores grew up in the Great Depression. Her parents went
from one place to another, looking for work, and they would send
young Dolores to her Aunt Dial in Goliad.

"This was my refuge. I loved it here, and my aunt gave me the house before she died." Dolores's refuge was my delight; it is a real treat to stay here. Dolores does things like putting sheets with pink roses in the room that has pink roses all over the wallpaper. She laughs about what she calls the "vile green" wallpaper in the dining room, which she papered years ago when her aunt asked her to redo those walls.

"I don't know why I picked it—guess because I liked green. It's quite a conversation piece!"

So are the breakfast and the evening snack tray, both evidence of Dolores's supreme hospitality. The breakfasts always have two kinds of meat and several main choices, such as scrambled eggs, quiche, and sausage rolls. "In case people don't like one thing, they can have another," says Dolores. A delicious specialty is an asparagus-mushroom crepe covered with a rich cheese sauce. "Don't know whether this is better than my quiche," she says modestly, "but both get eaten all up."

There's always a big plate of fruit (I recommend particularly a bowl of Dolores's home-frozen peaches) and hot biscuits. "They're full when they leave my table," Dolores can well boast.

What Dolores calls her "evening snack tray" filled me up! There were finger sandwiches along with an old family recipe called "waxed pecan squares," old-time bread pudding with warm peach sauce, a banana cream cake with whipped cream and fresh bananas, and brownies besides. Dolores is an innkeeper who truly loves her calling and loves to see you eat.

She has two kinds of oatmeal cookies that "I keep ready to pull out at any time; German chocolate cake, cheesecake. . . ." I had to cry halt—at least until the next day.

I loved relaxing in Dolores's "plant room," which she built to house her plants and collection of the dolls she played with when she was a little girl, or on the wraparound porch, lolling on the filigree chairs or swinging on either of the 5-foot wide swings.

How to get there: From Highway 59 turn north at Mt. Auburn and go 4 blocks. The inn is on the corner of Mt. Auburn and Oak.

The Madison
Goliad, Texas
77963

Innkeepers: Joyce and Wallace Benson
Address/Telephone: 707 North Jefferson; (512) 645–8693
Rooms: 3; 1 with private bath, all with TV. Smoking permitted in kitchen, on breakfast porch, and on patio.
Rates: $45 to $60, double, EPB.
Open: All year.
Facilities and activities: Lunch and dinner by prior arrangement, stationary bicycle. Nearby: restaurants; Goliad State Park has Spanish missions and the Presidio de La Bahia; County Courthouse "Hanging Tree"; antiques shops; county fair and festivals.

The Madison is named for the Bensons' home town in Wisconsin, and guest rooms are named for three of that state's many lakes: The Wingra, The Mendota, and The Monoma. Each reflects Joyce's elegant designing taste combined with Wallace's artistic eye. The Wingra and The Mendota share a large whirlpool bath (or you can reserve it privately). The house is the old Linburg homestead, built in 1888 in the bungalow, or craftsman, style of that time. Sitting in either one of the two parlors, with their plum-colored swags over crisp white lace curtains, it's hard to believe Wallace when he says, "This was a horror story at one time!" But you begin to when he mentions how the beautiful old oak floors were painted over, and in brown, and when he describes the condition of the walls.

Now the decorator floral wallpapers and coordinated borders, beautiful light fixtures, and attractive furniture make the old house picture perfect. Many pieces are old family furniture; the comfortable sofa and matching chair were Joyce's mother's; a wonderful pre–Civil War buffet in the dining room comes from Wallace's family. "I never would have believed I'd put three buffets in a dining room," Joyce says. But all three fit in perfectly and hold the lovely linens she serves with.

Joyce was a home economist and bridal designer; Wallace a former art teacher and audio/visual consultant in the Wisconsin school system, and the inn reflects their many talents. You'll find cheese and fruit in your room, wine and ice water, and there are tea-time and bedtime snacks. "I play it by ear," Joyce says, "depending on what I feel guests want." This guest (myself) thoroughly enjoyed tangy lemon squares and homemade *kolaches* with coffee in the evening. As for special occasions, Joyce rose to the occasion even with a pair of newlyweds who decided to arrive early. "I had to quick bake a wedding cake!" she says. You'll also get a small cake if it's your birthday or anniversary.

Joyce prides herself on her six- or seven-course breakfast, and you'll do well if you can stay the course. At any one time you might have fresh fruit and juice, homemade breads, *kolaches* and other sweet rolls, mushroom blintzes, beef tamales with enchilada sauce, roast beef hash, Swiss potatoes, a Madison specialty of eggs with cheese, and possibly tortellini with shrimp. "Mercy!" I cried, "This isn't breakfast—it's an all-you-can-eat brunch!"

The Bensons have taken to Goliad like ducks to water, or better, like native Texans. Being active on the Goliad County Historical Commission is only one of their activities.

If you like pets, be sure to walk back to the kitchen and get acquainted with Julie, the well-behaved German shepherd, as well as a pair of beautiful cockatiels, Sugar and Spice, and E.T. the bright, black-faced lovebird.

How to get there: Go north on Jefferson Street, which is also Highway 183/77A, to the north edge of town. The inn is on the west side of the highway just past North Street. There is a sign in the front yard and guest parking in the rear.

St. James Inn
Gonzales, Texas
78629

Innkeepers: Ann and J. R. Covert
Address/Telephone: 723 St. James Street; (210) 672–7066
Rooms: 6 share 5¹/₂ baths. No smoking inn.
Rates: $65, per room, EPB.
Open: All year.
Facilities and activities: Picnic baskets and dinners by reservation, tandem bicycle. Nearby: historic walking tour, Gonzales and Old Jail museums, local dinner theater, Palmetto State Park, Independence Park with 9-hole golf course and swimming pool, fishing in Guadalupe River.

The St. James Inn occupies a home built in 1914 by a descendant of a family that was involved in Texas history right at the beginning. The first shot of the Texas Revolution was fired right here in Gonzales in October of 1835.

"Walter Kokernot, who built the house, was the grandson of a merchant seaman who came over from Holland and was the captain of three ships of the Texas Navy," J. R. says. "For that, he was granted several leagues of land, which he turned into the Big Hill Ranch. His oldest son was a 'cattle gatherer.'" Cattle gatherer? J. R. laughs. "Well, he gathered what cattle he could find and made his fortune on the Chisholm Trail, which today goes right by here with the name of Highway 183."

Well, however he came by his fortune, he surely built a beautiful mansion. The house must be about 12,000 to 14,000 square feet—the Coverts aren't sure how large it is if you count the basement and the attic. Downstairs ceilings are 12 feet high, upstairs 10. The home is absolutely breathtakingly large, and the guest rooms and baths (and bathtubs!) are about the most spacious I have seen anywhere.

All the rooms are charming as well as huge: the Sunny Meadow Room, the Bluebonnet Room, the Cactus Flower Room, Josephine's Room—it's hard to make a choice. The Children's Playroom on the third floor has all sorts of nooks and crannies under the eaves. A wonderful collection of antique children's toys is in one ell, and Ann's basket collection is under the eaves outside the door. And there are other collections, all interesting, all over the inn, which also has nine fireplaces. "Guests may burn imitation logs," J. R. says, "but not real fires!"

The Coverts are fugitives from Houston; J. R. is an architect and Ann was executive director of the Republican Party of Harris County. "But I'm among Democrats here, "she says with a laugh. "We just got tired of the Houston rat race—we'd been working on an escape plan for seven years."

"We found this place quite by accident," J. R. says. "I said, 'Here we are, this is what we're looking for, what can you say?' Ann said, 'Let's take it!'"

Breakfast might be pecan pancakes topped with Ann's special bananas Foster sauce. She also fixes "Treasure Basket" picnics filled with "little surprises"; "I find out something about our guests and put in little mementos. One guest crocheted, another went fishing, we're in a pecan-growing area . . . it's fun."

You can enter the inn either from the formal front porch or by the side door. Either way, you'll be floored by all the room there is to make yourself comfortable in.

How to get there: Highway 183 becomes St. Joseph in town, and St. James runs parallel to it 1 block west. The huge house is on a huge southwest corner lot at St. James and St. Andrew.

Durham House
Houston, Texas
77008

Innkeeper: Marguerite Swanson
Address/Telephone: 921 Heights Boulevard; (713) 868-4654
Rooms: 5; 4 with private bath. No smoking inn.
Rates: $50 to $60, single; $60 to $75, double; EPB.
Open: All year.
Facilities and activities: Mystery dinners, large screened back porch, gazebo, garden, radios with cassette tapes of old-fashioned radio shows. Nearby: Houston Heights area of historical interest.

The lovely rose-carpeted living/dining area of the Durham House lends itself to comfortable chatting as well as to the many weddings and mystery evenings Marguerite delights in hosting. Each Durham House mystery is original, written for an inn setting. You don't have to spend the night in order to attend a mystery dinner—but it's certainly more fun if you can retire after the mystery has been solved to the Rose Room, with its 1860 walnut Victorian bed; or the Turret Room, with an entire Eastlake bedroom suite; or the Carriage House Suite, furnished entirely in American oak.

Durham House is a well-restored Queen Anne Victorian listed on the National Register of Historic Places. "I grew up in a Victorian house, in the Monte Vista section of San Antonio," Marguerite says. "And my husband did the same, only in an aunt's house in California. We're very different," she says with a laugh. "That's the only thing we have in common!" A prize possession is a photograph of J. R. Durham and his German wife taken in Galveston in 1897. Caught in the 1900 storm that all but drowned the island, the Durhams lost everything in the famous flood. They moved to Houston and built on the Heights, the highest part of town.

The Carriage House has a private entrance off the garden and its own little refrigerator, in case you want to cool a few snacks. Each bathroom in the inn has a basket with fancy French milled soap, shampoo, and the like, and each guest room has terry robes to lounge in. If you get lonesome for your pet, Sherman the basset hound is available on request.

Delicious items on the Durham House breakfast menu are apple or peach upside-down French toast or mushroom-scrambled egg casserole and homemade banana-wheat bread with strawberry butter or pumpkin-streusel muffins. "And the newest favorites," says Marguerite, "are banana–chocolate chip muffins." You also might have lemon ginger, or ginger pear, orange pecan, or fresh apple muffins. Marguerite says the best "commercial" for her muffins is that businesswomen staying at the inn want her to bake extra for them to take to their presentations. It tickles her that when they're asked, "Where did you get them?" they say "oh, it's something I just make!"

Health conscious, Marguerite tries to stay away from fried foods. "I try not to give people eggs every day; I watch their cholesterol. And I've never subscribed to the edict that bed and breakfast means breakfast at a certain time." If you must leave extra early for the airport or another commitment, Marguerite will pack you a little take-along breakfast.

The dining-room breakfront contains Marguerite's fine cut glass collection: "I especially like things Victorian." That's hardly a surprise to me!

How to get there: From I–10 (Katy Freeway) take the Studemont exit and go west along the feeder road to Heights Boulevard. Turn right and the inn will be on your left about 5 blocks along.

La Colombe d'Or
Houston, Texas
77006

Innkeeper: Steve Zimmerman
Address/Telephone: 3410 Montrose Boulevard; (713) 524–7999
Rooms: 6 suites; all with private bath; wheelchair accessible.
Rates: $195 to $575, per suite, continental breakfast.
Open: All year.
Facilities and activities: Restaurant, bar. Nearby: within five minutes, Houston
   central business district, Houston Museum of Fine Arts, Rice Universi-
   ty, and Menil Art Foundation; the Astrodome.

It's no surprise to find this exquisite inn so close to two art collections: The inn is patterned after one of the same name in St. Paul
de Vence, France, where many famous French painters traded their
work for lodging. Houston's La Colombe d'Or (the "golden dove") is
hung with fine art, too, and each suite has a name I certainly recog-
nized.

I stayed in the Van Gogh Suite, named for one of my favorite
Impressionist painters. Others are named for Degas, Cézanne,
Monet, and Renoir; the largest suite, up at the top, is called simply
The Penthouse. The suites are decorated with fine art, although
there are no original works of their namesakes.

But I didn't miss them, so swathed in beauty and luxury was I
in this prince of an inn. On my coffee table I found fruit, Perrier
water, and wine glasses waiting to be filled from my complimentary

bottle of the inn's own imported French wine.

Owner Steve Zimmerman has succeeded in bringing to the La Colombe d'Or the casual elegance of the French Riviera. European and American antiques, as well as his own collection of prominent artists' works, are set in the luxurious house that was once the home of Exxon founder Walter Fondren and his family.

The twenty-one-room mansion, built in 1923, is divided into suites. Each consists of a huge bedroom with a sitting area and a glass-enclosed dining room where Queen Anne furniture, china plates, linen napkins, and cutlery are in readiness for breakfast. As soon as I rang in the morning, a waiter arrived with a tea cart from which he served a very French-style plate of sliced kiwi fruit, raspberries, and strawberries; orange juice; coffee; and croissants with butter and jam. I ate this artistic offering surrounded by the green leafy boughs waving outside my glass room.

You may have luncheon or dinner served in your room, too, but I feasted downstairs on meunière of shrimp and lobster, cream of potato and leek soup, the inn's Caesar salad, and capon Daniel; and as if that weren't enough, I ended with crème brulée!

If you long to visit France, you may decide you don't have to once you've visited La Colombe d'Or. The inn is a member of *Relais et Châteaux,* a French organization that guarantees excellence, and I absolutely soaked up the hospitality, tranquillity, and luxury.

How to get there: 3410 Montrose is between Westheimer and Alabama, both Houston thoroughfares.

Sara's Bed & Breakfast Inn
Houston, Texas
77008

Innkeepers: Donna and Tillman Arledge
Address/Telephone: 941 Heights Boulevard; (713) 868–1130 or (800) 593–1130
Rooms: 10, plus 1 suite; suite with private bath. No smoking inn.
Rates: $50 to $120, per room, continental breakfast.
Open: All year.
Facilities and activities: Deck, sun balcony and widow's walk, television room, games. Nearby: Houston Heights area of historical interest; Farmers' Market; museums.

Sara's is named for the Arledges' young daughter, who loves having an inn so much that she's become a parent's dream. "Whatever I ask, she'll do," Donna says. "She loves the idea, she loves the place, she loves to help!"

This pretty-as-a-picture Victorian is easy to love. But it wasn't always so. "To give you an idea," Donna says, "the house had no front door, no back door, and all the wood had been pulled out." It was Tillman who fell in love with the house, and every day he would say to Donna, "Just look what we could do with it."

Donna gave in. "I finally said anybody who would want something that bad ought to have it."

It's hard to believe that Sara's began life in 1910 as a small one-story Victorian cottage. The downstairs parlor is "ready to encourage guests to relax and feel right at home," Donna says, while bright bedrooms are furnished with antiques and collectibles. A circular stairway leads up to the third floor widow's walk and a great view of the Houston skyline. Sunrise cheers early risers from the front balcony, and the large covered deck out back is a favorite lounging spot any time.

Rooms have books and luggage racks. Downstairs bedrooms have washbasins. The garden sitting area on the second floor is furnished with white wicker, and the four windows of the cupola shower the entire house with light. The Heights neighborhood has a small-town feeling, great to walk around (or jog) in, in spite of the big city less than 4 miles away.

Each charming room is named after a Texas town, with decor to suit that mood. The Galveston Room has nautical beds, the Tyler Room is white wicker, the San Antonio Room is Spanish. One guest surprised his wife by telling her they were going to Austin (Texas's capital city) for the weekend, and she was certainly surprised by the Austin Room at Sara's! (She loved it!)

I was intrigued by the plate collection on the dining room walls. "That's my grandmother's collection," Donna said. "We keep adding to it."

Breakfast of hot bread or muffins, fresh fruit cup, juice, and coffee is a friendly gathering in the dining room, with the plate collection for an icebreaker if need be. But many guests are repeaters, which makes them old friends.

How to get there: From I-10 East, take Shepherd Drive and turn right to 11th, then right on Heights Boulevard for 1½ blocks. Inn will be on the right. From I-10 West, take Studemont exit. Make a U-turn just before Studemont and turn right at Heights Boulevard. (This is necessary because of interminable road construction.) Sara's will be on the left in about 6 blocks.

La Borde House
Rio Grande City, Texas
78582

Innkeepers: Crisanto Salinas and Armandina Garza
Address/Telephone: 601 East Main Street; (210) 487–5101
Rooms: 21; all with private bath.
Rates: $59, double, historical rooms; $40, double, modern rooms; EP.
Open: All year.
Facilities and activities: Restaurant open for lunch and dinner Monday to
    Thursday, 11:00 A.M. to 2:00 P.M.; Friday, Saturday, and Sunday,
    11:00 A.M. to 9:00 P.M. Nearby: hunting, fishing, bird watching, Inter-
    national Bridge to Mexico, historic Fort Ringgold.

La Borde House is elegant, no doubt about it. Even though it
was built on the Texas–Mexico border in 1899, it was designed by
French architects in Paris (France, not Paris, Texas!). Leather merchant François La Borde had his inn designed at Paris's Beaux Arts
school as a combined home, storehouse, and inn. Its early guests
were often cattle barons who sold their herds on nearby Rio Grande
River docks or military officers en route to California. La Borde
brought to life his vision of European grandeur—and I reveled in
the reconstruction of that vision. Actually the ambience is New
Orleans Creole, and I felt as Scarlett O'Hara must have felt when
Rhett took her there to wallow in luxury.

Restoration in 1982 was faithful to the original as documented
by old records and photographs. The inn was originally built by

both European and Rio Grande artisans, and replacement brick actually was found from the same brickyard in Camargo, Mexico, that was used before.

I was entranced by opulence such as collector-quality oriental rugs and English Axminster carpets, and early ledgers also record such purchases. Each posh bedroom is named for a local history event, with antique furniture and wallpapers; and many of the papers and fabrics are duplicates of those used in the 1981 restoration of the Texas Governor's Mansion in Austin.

"It tells the whole history of the border, it's that simple," say the innkeepers. "It's dedicated to the proud past of all South Texas, and we really get a joy out of the smiles we see on people's faces as they reminisce about old times here in the valley." Old times include such mementos as Fort Ringgold, one of Texas's best-preserved old military posts, named for the first army officer killed in the battle that began the Mexican War. Interesting, too, is Lee House, once occupied by Robert E. Lee when he commanded here before the Civil War.

The restaurant is the place for great border cuisine. The Mexican plate of tacos, enchiladas, tamales, beans, and rice has a special flavor, just right for lunch.

For dinner I tried the chicken cilantro, which is sautéed in butter, seasoned with that savory south-of-the-border herb, and served on a rice bed. It was delicious. I topped it off with fried ice cream, a neat treat of frozen cream dipped in batter and deep fried in a hurry! For seafood lovers there are usually three selections, but the two favorite are the shrimp and the catfish.

How to get there: From Highway 281 take Highway 83 west, which becomes Main Street in town. The inn is on the corner of Main and Garza.

Hotel Lafitte
Seadrift, Texas
77983

Innkeepers: Frances and Weyman Harding
Address/Telephone: 302 Bay Avenue (mailing address: P.O. Box 489); (512) 785–2319
Rooms: 8, plus 2 suites; suites with private bath and TV.
Rates: $55 to $95, double; $5 less for single; EPB.
Open: All year.
Facilities and activities: Downstairs and upstairs verandas right on San Antonio Bay. Nearby: fishing, swimming, walking on the Seawall; Matagorda Island, Aransas Wildlife Refuge.

This long white wooden building is a treasure tucked away almost where Highway 185 ends at the Gulf of Mexico. It fronts right on the water, and you may just want to sit out on the veranda and rock, lazing the day away. The Hotel Lafitte is tailor-made for a perfect getaway.

"I grew up here," says Frances, "and Weyman, he's from Victoria" (just down the road a piece). "I love old things and I wanted this building. We got married here right after we bought it, and it took us three and a half years to restore the old place. It was built in 1909 as a railroad hotel—they called this type of hotel a railroad hotel because one always sprung up at the end of a line, and the Frisco Railroad ended right out on the docks." Frances learned from an unusual guest that in an infamous storm of 1919 the seas surged right through the second-floor windows. "The gentleman came for his ninety-second birthday. He remember the hotel from way back, and he went up to the third floor like he was a teenager!"

Hospitality begins in the parlor, where a wooden holder displays three kegs of wine for guests to help themselves. Rosé, chablis, what is your pleasure? Other pleasures of the parlor are rose-colored wing chairs flanking an organ, a soft flowered sofa, and old-fashioned lace curtains. There's a fireplace, and the walls as well as the floors are planks of wood.

The public rooms are backwards, says Frances: The parlor is the most informal, while the large lobby is formal. It boasts a player piano, a birthday gift to Frances from Weyman.

The guest rooms are airy and roomy, and those facing the front have a gorgeous ocean view. Rooms are all large and decorated becomingly, reflecting the inn's turn-of-the-century mood. Number 5 has a flapper dress of the 1920s hanging on the armoire. Room number 6 not only contains the original hotel furniture, but there's an antique wedding dress hanging up, a gift from a friend whose grandmother wore the gown.

The two large suites are on the third floor, and the Honeymoon Suite has a rose satin bedspread, an inlaid-wood card-table set, a Jacuzzi, and not one but two chaise longues. Hedonistic luxury!

Breakfast might be a ham-and-egg casserole or a quiche along with bran muffins, fruit, and juice. For lunch and dinner the Hardings will be delighted to direct you to the family restaurant, Barkett's, where seafood specialties abound. After all, here you are on the famous Texas Gulf Coast.

How to get there: From I-10 take Highway 77 south to Victoria and Highway 185 south to Seadrift, a small town approximately 35 miles southeast of Victoria. Bay Avenue is, of course, on the bay.

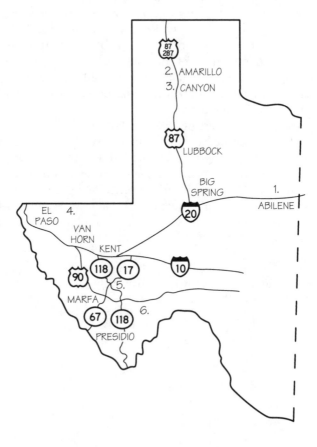

West Texas

Numbers on map refer to towns numbered below.

Bolin's Prairie House
Abilene, Texas
79601

Innkeepers: Ginny and Sam Bolin
Address/Telephone: 508 Mulberry; (915) 675–5855
Rooms: 4 share 2 baths. No smoking inn.
Rates: $40 to $50, double; $15 extra person; EPB.
Open: All year.
Facilities and activities: Nearby: restaurants, fine arts museum, Grace Cultural Museum, zoo, three universities, historic Buffalo Gap Historic Village.

This large and airy prairie house was once a Victorian mansion, home of an Abilene pioneer whose name was Colonel Christmas Comfort. "He never was a colonel," Ginny says. "That was just his name." Not only names, but styles change, too, and new owners in 1920 decided they preferred a simpler style. They remodeled the story-and-a-half house into a full two-story, smoothing the lines along the way.

"So it's considerably plainer than Victorian," Ginny says. "It was copied from that house across the street, whose owner back then studied with Frank Lloyd Wright in Chicago and came home and remodeled it. Guess it was just the latest thing."

Ginny, who likes to crochet, do needlework, sew, and garden, and Sam, who's a building contractor and knows how to do things right, spent months fixing up the old house, something Sam always wanted to do. As for Ginny, she was ready to retire from bookkeeping. She finds that the house is kind of restful and peaceful. "People come here; nobody calls them and bothers them."

The inn's color scheme is mainly red, white, and blue—pale, royal, and navy blue. The living room has an old wood-burning stove and pale-blue woodwork and shutters behind airy white lace curtains. Fabric is striped navy and white ticking. Large Raggedy Ann and Raggedy Andy dolls sit contentedly in an old rocker, and I relaxed just looking at them.

Around the dining-room walls, plate racks display Ginny's assortment of Depression glass and other collectibles. "I've been collecting it for twenty years, from England, California . . . so long as it's blue, I like it," she says. The old kitchen cupboard in a corner of the dining room—you know, the old kind with a flour sifter inside the door—was Sam's grandmother's. "I can remember my grandmother making bread in one of those big old wooden bowls," Ginny says. The Bolins grew up in a small town nearby and enjoy being closer to home after living in more distant parts, although Ginny says, "We always enjoy wherever we are."

The crystal, too, that Ginny likes to use, belonged to Sam's grandmother. And upstairs in the corner of the staircase is Sam's collection of old tools in an Amish trunk. Guest rooms are spacious and light corner rooms with lots of windows and distinctive color schemes. Love is decorated in blue and beige and has comfortable wing chairs; Joy is furnished with Mamma Bolin's old bedroom set, and Ginny has used a riot of pink roses, quilted roses, striped roses (wallpaper), and rose-covered pillows in rose-colored rocking chairs. Peace, green and cream, is full of green plants, and Patience has ornate twin beds and blue wing chairs.

Breakfast is plentiful: Ginny is another innkeeper who likes to say, "They don't go away hungry." Dutch Babies (oven-baked pancakes), grits, sausage, hash browns, baked egg dishes, homemade bread, and oatmeal with apples and cinnamon if you don't want eggs.

How to get there: From I–20 take Business Loop 20 to Grape Street; go north 6 blocks to North 5th then east 1 block to the corner of Mulberry and North 5th streets.

Galbraith House
Amarillo, Texas
79102

Innkeeper: Misty Evans
Address/Telephone: 1710 South Polk Street; (806) 374–0237
Rooms: 5; all with private bath. Pets in garage. No smoking inn.
Rates: $60 to $70, double, EPB.
Open: All year.
Facilities and activities: Luncheons, teas, and dinners by reservation, television, children's playroom, patio, use of office for business. Nearby: Amarillo College, Plemons-Eakle Historic District, Amarillo Art Center, Palo Duro Canyon, *Texas* (musical drama).

Galbraith House was built in 1912 by a lumberman, and you should see the woodwork in this 4,000-square-foot mansion; the construction cost the princely sum, back then, of $25,000. Oh, the beautiful hand-rubbed mahogany, walnut, and oak!

"People go around with their mouths hanging open at the woodwork," Misty says; also at the rich Bukhara oriental rugs and antiques and collectibles that fill the mansion. The home, while managed by Misty, is owned by absentee landlords Mary Jane Johnson, an opera singer, and her husband and manager, David, who is also a consultant to a local grocery chain. With two young children, they wanted to move into a neighborhood with more young families but didn't want to part with this lovely old home. So they've turned it into an inn, one in which they'd choose to stay themselves.

Misty is a registered dietitian. Breakfast? "I do a really good breakfast," she says, and I doubt she could find any dissenters. Egg casseroles, omelets—"and though I try to give guests light and heathful food that remains flavorful, the men like my southern-style biscuits and gravy . . . it just depends upon who my guests are that morning." With only three or four guests, she'll cook to order, happy as a lark in the large sunny kitchen of the big house. When guests come in there's soda and chips; in fact, "they're welcome to what's in the refrigerator! Carrot sticks, microwave popcorn—they can do their own thing; they have free use of the kitchen, the entire house, so long as they don't swing from the chandeliers!" she adds with a laugh.

"We're not strict or rigid on check-in or -out." That, says Misty firmly, is one of the advantages of an inn. I like her philosophy: "We're flexible; we cater to our guests. We're in the hospitality business, and the people who are the nicest get the nicest guests and the best business."

All the guest rooms are spacious and comfortable. The Christmas Room is the most popular; a king bed, a pair of lounge chairs, a large dressing table, and family photographs make it very homey. Guests have full use of the home's other rooms: living room, dining room, library, solarium, three balconies, even a butler's pantry—there's a lot of room to make yourself comfortable in.

An unusual feature of the home is the Gentlemen's Smoking Porch, a tiny outside balcony off the upstairs hall, where even back in 1912 smokers were sent outdoors. Handmade quilts by local artisans are on all the beds and many of the walls, as well as works of art by local artists.

How to get there: Take the Washington Street exit off I–40; go to 17th Street, turn east, and go 2 blocks to Polk. Turn right and the inn will be on the right at 1710.

Hudspeth House
Canyon, Texas
79015

Innkeepers: Sally and Dave Haynie
Address/Telephone: 1905 4th Avenue; (806) 655–9800 or 655–4111
Rooms: 8; 6 with private bath. No smoking inn.
Rates: $50; $110 for entire 2-bedroom loft; EPB.
Open: All year.
Facilities and activities: Health and fitness spa, sun deck, gazebo. Nearby: Palo
    Duro Canyon, second-largest canyon in United States; *Texas* (musical
    drama), Panhandle–Plains Historical Museum.

This huge old house has toys in the entry—you'll be greeted by
antique dolls waiting for you in a cradle and a dolly buggy. And
each large guest room has more wonderful memorabilia to offer,
thanks to the friendly citizens of this Panhandle town. Take the collection of 1912 and 1913 college yearbooks in the parlor, the ones
from when West Texas State was West Texas Normal.

"An elderly lady came by the other day and brought them to
us," Dave Haynie says; and it seems like that's not unusual here. An
elderly lady from Amarillo brought the Haynies the antique bridal
gown that's in the Roy Room on the third floor. "She said, 'I have
nobody to leave it to; no one will see it unless you display it,'" Dave
reports. "We're always getting things like that. Another lady told us
her daughter was in a wedding here—she was a flower girl—and
she gave us this picture. . . ." Which is why the Hudspeth House is

so popular as the place to find out about times gone by in the territory: The Haynies offer afternoon tours of the house by reservation.

Mary Elizabeth Hudspeth came to Canyon in 1910 as a member of the faculty of the new West Texas Normal College. (A more renowned faculty member was Georgia O'Keeffe.) At first Miss Hudspeth boarded with the family that owned the house; then she acquired it for herself, taking pride in the stained glass, the fancy chandeliers, and the four fireplaces that make the house a showcase.

All the rooms are large—they just don't build the way they used to, do they? The fancy parlor with both piano and organ, the huge dining room with a table that seats fourteen under maroon velvet swags draped beneath the ceiling—it's the grandeur of the past that's fun to experience. Sally and Dave have decorated with verve and zest for the period. In the Edgar Luscombe Suite there's an old Singer sewing machine and a dressmaker's dummy garbed in an appropriate outfit. Ready for bedtime reading on the counterpane in the Otto Stark Suite is an original edition of *Gone with the Wind*. In Henry's Room in the loft there's a teddy bear on a rockinghorse; Mollie's Rose Room has a wonderful assortment of collectibles, what my Aunt Lillian used to call "bezzagobbles."

Breakfast is set in splendor in the dining room and might be "brunch eggs Benedict." Sally has been in food service for a long time, and Dave taught school for more than seventeen years before he went into sales. Now they're busy with both their inn and local affairs. "It's just a lot of fun," they say. "You get to meet all the nice people, and you get to meet them like kinfolks."

In addition to the more usual inn stay, you can book one of four health and fitness programs the Haynies offer in their spa, where a doctor, nurse, cosmetologist, fashion consultant, masseur, and professional CPR-certified instructors are on staff. "Learn to love, laugh, and live longer" is the Haynie motto.

How to get there: From either I–27 Business or I–27 Bypass, take exit 106 (4th Avenue) west to 1904. The inn will be on your right.

Sunset Heights Inn
El Paso, Texas
79902

Innkeepers: Richard Barnett and Roni Martinez
Address/Telephone: 717 West Yandell; (919) 544–1743 or (800) 767–8513
Rooms: 6; all with private bath and TV, 3 with telephone jack. No smoking inn.
Rates: $70 to $165, double, EPB.
Open: All year.
Facilities and activities: Dinner for minimum of six people; pool and Jacuzzi. Nearby: many museums and historic fort, old Spanish missions, Tigua Indian Reservation, zoo, scenic drive, Ciudad Juárez in Mexico just across the Rio Grande.

Built in 1905 up in the high and mighty area of El Paso over-looking downtown, this inn on the National Register of Historic Homes is a three-story corner house of dark-yellow brick surrounded by an iron fence. Tall palm trees wave over it, and the large grounds of almost an acre are graced by roses blooming much of the year. "Twenty-nine bushes," Richard says, while he confesses that he doesn't take care of it all by himself.

Food, gourmet food, is his specialty, and you won't be able to predict what he'll feed you for breakfast because he doesn't know himself. "I don't decide what to serve until I look at my guests the evening before," he says, which brought forth a contented groan from an earlier guest, who was recovering from the morning-before feast in a corner of the beautifully decorated parlor.

The five- to seven-course meal is more like a lunch or dinner buffet to me than a breakfast. It began with prunes in cream and went on to quiche served with kiwi and purple grapes; then came Cordon Bleu chicken on rice with tomato and avocado, and eggs Benedict with papaya and star fruit, followed by angel food cake with blueberry yogurt. This took me through the day until the champagne and late-night snacks.

Richard, late of the military, raised three daughters by himself and learned to cook in self-defense. "We entertained a lot and couldn't afford a cook, so we all learned to cook. When the girls were small, sometimes we had sit-down dinners for thirty." But he prefers buffet because "people circulate better." Now at Sunset he has a helper in daughter Kim, responsible for many of the gourmet meals they serve.

Roni, who is a practicing physician, displays a second talent in the decorating of the inn. She did most of the pleasing color selections, while much of the furnishings are antiques from Richard's family. The parlor has a Victrola dating from 1919, and it still plays. Although the old table radio is a replica, the kerosene lamp is one Richard studied by when he was a boy on a farm in Oklahoma. "We didn't have electricity," he says. "That old lamp got me through school." But what I loved looking at was the wonderful Coromandel screen behind the old sewing machine in the parlor. Richard tells the story of how he was able to get it out of China—back when we weren't speaking to China—by shipping it through Panama.

The inn is a decorator's dream, with beautifully coordinated fabrics and wall coverings, mirrored doors, and sybaritic bathrooms. The Oriental Room has another Coromandel screen as well as a brass bed. The bathroom, with brass fixtures and a huge bathtub, is on what was once a porch. But not to worry: All the windows are now one-way mirrors.

How to get there: From I–10 West take Porfiro Diaz exit and turn right for 2 blocks to Yandell. Turn right for 6 blocks (count the ones on the right, not the left) to Randolph, and the inn will be on the far corner to the left.

Hotel Limpia
Fort Davis, Texas
79734

Innkeeper: Lanna and Joe Duncan
Address/Telephone: P.O. Box 822; (915) 426–3237 or (800) 662–5517
Rooms: 20 in hotel and annex, all with private bath. Pets welcome.
Rates: $48 to $85, double, EP.
Open: All year.
Facilities and activities: Restaurant; Fort Davis National Historic Site; McDonald Observatory; Overland Trail Museum; Neill Doll Museum; Davis Mountains State Park with hiking trails; Big Bend National Park.

The Duncans like to welcome guests to their mile-high turn-of-the-century hotel in the Davis Mountains of West Texas. "Come on out to God's country," they say happily. Joe's father, J. C. Duncan, Jr., was responsible for the restoration of the old hotel, and Lanna says, "As you can imagine, we are pleased to be the new innkeepers."

So if you're looking for a real-life Old West experience, you'll surely like it here. The Limpia is a real old-timey Western hotel, the kind of place that makes you expect to see a prospector or two, complete with panning equipment.

The first deed to the land the hotel stands on was to one Pedro Guano in 1855, for having served "faithfully and honorably in the Army of the Republic of Texas." Constructed of pink limestone quarried from nearby Sleeping Mountain, the hotel sits solid and sturdy on the town square, along with the town's one bank and post office. It was built in 1912 to accommodate a sudden surge of tourists coming to take advantage of Fort Davis's healthful climate. The reason they didn't come earlier is the same reason the town is named Fort Davis: Indians. The fort was established in 1854 to protect settlers and the Butterfield Overland Mail from the Apaches and Comanches. They were vanquished about 1886, but it took a while for local merchants to capitalize on the peace and safety.

The Limpia was considered quite elegant in the Fort Davis of 1912, with its pressed-metal ceilings and solid oak furniture, and it was illuminated by gaslight. Today it still has pressed-tin ceilings and oak furniture, but the gas has of course been replaced by electricity and such newfangled notions as private bathrooms and air conditioning. But guest rooms still have transoms over the doors, and the long oak counter that serves as the front desk is decorated with the stained glass panels and ornate doors from the nearby Duncan ranch, built in 1894. There are two parlors, one with a fireplace for those chilly mountain evenings. Afternoons, I loved to sit on the old-fashioned glassed-in veranda, where I could rock under trailing wisps of potted fern and enjoy the bright geraniums, while watching the sun set over the Davis Mountains.

For dinner the dining room specializes in regional Texas fare as well as Italian dishes, fresh vegetables, and homemade pies. The Limpia West is the hotel annex, containing eight guest rooms, the dining room, and the country store. (The hotel offers additional accommodation in a two-bedroom cottage on four acres on the edge of the mountain.)

Just around the corner on the side street, the sign hanging in front of the old-fashioned drugstore boasts THE BEST COKES IN TEXAS. Inside the large, square store, folks sip through straws at the round iron and marble tables, while old-timers rally round the pool table at the rear. Fort Davis is really rustic, and that's what makes for a different experience in this crowded and hectic world.

How to get there: Highway 118 goes right into town, and the hotel is on the town square across from the bank and the post office.

Indian Lodge
Fort Davis, Texas
78734

Innkeeper: Michael Crevier
Address/Telephone: Box 786; (915) 426–3254
Rooms: 39; all with private bath, phone, and TV.
Rates: $40 to $50, single; $45 to $50, double; children under 6 free, 6 to 12 $2, over 12 $5; EP. No credit cards.
Open: All year except two weeks in January.
Facilities and activities: Full-service restaurant, heated swimming pool, board games in lobby or to take to rooms. Nearby: Fort Davis, an old western town; Fort Davis National Historic Site, with museum, barracks, and "soldiers" in Civil War uniforms; McDonald Observatory; nature and hiking trails in Davis Mountains State Park.

Indian Lodge is unique in several ways, all delightful. To begin with, it's set in a state park in the midst of the beautiful Davis Mountains and consequently is managed by the Texas Parks and Wildlife Department. Secondly, it was built by the Civilian Conservation Corps (C.C.C.) in the 1930s. Finally, it was built Indian pueblo–style, and it was built to last—the lodge's adobe walls are more than 18 inches thick. Still in use are many of the massive cedar beds, chests, dressers, and chairs the C.C.C. crew built.

In 1967 a complete renovation added twenty-four rooms, a heated swimming pool, and a restaurant. The restaurant serves a wide variety of food—seafood, steak, Mexican food, hamburgers, sandwiches as well as celebrating special "evenings at the lodge" with Oktoberfest, Halloween, Valentine's Day, Mardi Gras, and St. Patrick's Day theme buffets. At Christmas the inn puts on a traditional Spanish Posada. That's a good thing, because the lodge is in an isolated, if beautiful, spot! "We fix box lunches for our guests who want to be out in the park all day," innkeeper Michael says. Which is what most people want to do.

This part of trans-Pecos country (west of the Pecos River) is greener than I expected. It seems that the mountains surrounding the lodge catch moisture-filled winds, causing more rain to fall. Added bonuses are the cool nights even in the middle of summer.

"Indian Lodge is so popular, you'll need to make reservations well in advance," says Michael. "Not only is the lodge a fine place in which to stay, the surroundings are heaven for nature and wildlife buffs as well as for bona fide geologists, botanists, and other nature experts." The historical rooms, newly redecorated, all face east, so everybody gets a gorgeous view of sunrise over the mountains.

The lodge lobby is huge, with massive cedar furniture around fireplaces at each end of the room. I joined most of the guests, however, outside on the verandas, drinking in the great view of the landscape, with its prickly pear, yucca, and other desert plants marching up to the mountains.

Although delighted guests agree that the lodge is a perfect place to rest, relax, go hiking, and then "sleep a lot," be sure to save time for the many sights offered in the surrounding areas. McDonald Observatory is operated by the University of Texas, and there are public information lectures and displays. (Visitors' viewing through the telescope, however, is limited to the last Wednesday night of each month.)

Fort Davis National Site has a sound re-creation of an 1870s military retreat parade, with a present-day volunteer in period costume at attention. He sits silently on his horse while the recording of bugles sounding the retreat mingles with the sounds of shouted orders and the jingle of horses' harnesses. It's vivid and haunting.

How to get there: The lodge is in the Davis Mountains, 4 miles northwest of Fort Davis via Highway 118. Take 118 west 3 miles to the Park Road 3 entrance and follow the park road to the lodge.

The Gage Hotel
Marathon, Texas
79842

Innkeepers: Laurie and Bill Stevens
Address/Telephone: P.O. Box 46; (915) 386–4205
Rooms: 37; 17, 8 with private bath, in hotel; 20, all with private bath, in new addition next door.
Rates: $38 to $52, double, in hotel; $75 to $85, double, in new addition; EP.
Open: All year.
Facilities and activities: Restaurant serves three meals a day seven days a week; bar serves beer and wine only; swimming pool. Nearby: guided tours through Big Bend National Park, Rio Grande River canyons, horseback trips into mountains of Texas and Mexico, deer and antelope hunting; county park, The Post, on site of 1880–93 Fort Pena Colorado.

The Gage Hotel was built in 1927 by prosperous banker-rancher Alfred Gage, who really lived in San Antonio. He wanted comfortable accommodations when he visited his West Texas holdings, so he built this two-story yellow-brick house to serve as his headquarters.

The hotel was a true oasis then, more so even than now. Marathon (named by an obscure sea captain who claimed the land reminded him of Greece) and Alpine are the only towns in Brewster County, although it's the largest county in Texas.

I'm sure I wasn't the first visitor to be pleasantly surprised by the sight of this tidy, compact building with its arched doorway and its porch full of rocking chairs, just waiting by the road for a weary traveler.

The rooms in the hotel, named for such Brewster County sites as Persimmon Gap, are comfortable but Spartan, definitely more in the masculine mode, with ranch-style decor, pine floors, and Mexican colonial furniture mixing with English antiques. I was particularly interested in the lobby's original front desk and key box and the antique Chuso (a kind of primitive roulette) game in the bar. The new addition is as authentic a copy of an old adobe building as you can get, with walls 4 to 7 feet thick, built, says Bill, "of 900,000 real adobe bricks." He's proud, too, of the five Mexican gates into the new compound. "They're 125 to 200 years old," he says.

Bill Stevens shows off the hotel artifacts with enthusiasm. "I like meeting people," he says, "particularly people on vacation, who are having fun. It's a lot more fun working with people who are having fun," he says with a laugh.

The restaurant has some interesting specialties on the menu. I liked the breakfast egg enchiladas—eggs scrambled with green onion, rolled up, and liberally covered with ranchero sauce—and the dinner enchiladas pesto, "a cross-culture dish you won't get anywhere except at the Gage," says Laurie. If you feel that two cultures in one dish is almost too much of a good thing, the menu also has standard West Texas fare.

I really fell for the alligator pear pie, an amazing concoction of avocado, cream cheese, lemon, and sugar, but it's seasonal out here in Marathon, where avocados don't grow on trees. Always deliciously available are the buttermilk and chocolate chess pies. Grown here are the herbs that flavor the food and garnish the plates. And the flowers in the lobby.

"Marathon is in a little pocket, good for gardens," the Stevenses say. "We're cool at four thousand feet, and we have that good wall of mountains to keep out the storms." An interesting note: The Post county park has a spring that was a major gathering place for Comanche Indians. Now the spring has been dammed and is a pleasant pond.

How to get there: Highway 90, straight through town, goes right by the Gage. I certainly recommend a stop!

Indexes

Alphabetical Index to Inns

Inns with Restaurants

Inns Serving Meals by Reservation Only

Inns with Kitchen Facilities or Privileges

Inns near Water

Inns with, or with Access to, Swimming Pools, Hot Tubs, or Spas

Inns with, or with Access to, Golf or Tennis Facilities

Inns with Downhill or Cross-Country Skiing Nearby

Inns Where Pets Are Accepted with or without Restrictions

Inns That Especially Welcome Children

Inns That Permit Smoking with or without Restrictions

Inns That Do Not Accept Credit Cards

Inns with Wheelchair Access

About the Author

Eleanor S. Morris is a freelance travel writer living in Austin, Texas—a "refugee," she says, from the big cities of Houston and Dallas. A member of the American Society of Journalists and Authors and the Society of American Travel Writers, she has been published widely in national newspapers and magazines, and she has stayed at country inns in such diverse places as Australia, Portugal, Canada, Mexico, and Japan.

Eleanor says a country inn is a place where you are never a stranger, no matter how far you are from home. When not traveling, she is at home in Austin with her husband and working on a novel.